15

W9-BCF-035

LT- N

BLEEDING OUT

Book design by Sunset Design
Cover design by Nightwood and Sunset Design

Printed in the United States by McNaughton & Gunn

10 9 8 7 6 5 4 3 2 1

Library of Congress Cataloging-in-Publication Data

Clare, Baxter, 1959-
    Bleeding out : a mystery / by Baxter Clare.
        p. cm.
    ISBN 1–56341–119–9 (alk. paper) —
    ISBN 1–56341–118–0 (pbk. : alk.paper)
    1. Los Angeles (Calif.)—Fiction. 2. Women—Crimes
against—Fiction. 3. Policewomen—Fiction. 4. Lesbians—
Fiction. I. Title.

PS3553.L2487 B58 2000
813'.6—dc21
                                        00–024291

BLEEDING OUT

A Mystery

BY BAXTER CLARE

Firebrand Books
Ithaca, New York

1

One of Crocetti's techs was working the corpse while Noah and Briggs scavenged the area around the body. The streetlight was shot out so they searched by flashlight and neon glare. So far they had two shell casings from a .22 and a bloodied tooth.

"You know, I've almost got enough teeth to make a necklace." Johnnie Briggs made an imaginary half-circle under his collarbone. "Or maybe I should mount 'em and turn 'em into earrings. Sell 'em to all the tourists who want a genuine souvenir from L.A."

"You'd get richer doing that than this," rejoined his partner, digging another slug out of the window sash. The owner of the liquor store paced outside, scowling at the body and muttering darkly in Korean.

The tech laughed up at him, removing the dead man's clothes. "Welcome to the American Dream, my friend."

The Korean man said something else in his language and spat into the gutter.

Holding a driver's license under a Budweiser sign glowing behind iron bars, Lieutenant L.A. Franco read the victim's pedigree to the prowling detectives. "Charles Mackay. 5319 West 53rd. DOB 11/19/79."

The tech turned the body, and a small round hole at the base of Mackay's head leaked blood. So did another hole just under his left shoulder blade. As he watched this, the store owner explained that he'd heard Mackay being shot, saw him get hit, but that from his cash register he couldn't see the shooter. The lieutenant stretched a long, trousered leg over the body and walked behind the counter. She looked out the window and clearly saw Noah talking to the slight man. But Frank was almost 5'10". She bent her knees a few inches and her vision was obstructed by a promo sign for Miller Genuine Draft. Their old jingle ran through her head as she recognized that the owner wasn't lying.

He stood outside, glancing nervously through the window, trying to see what Frank was up to. She smiled to herself and peeked at the cluttered shelf under the cash register. There it was. A long-barreled .357. She knew he wouldn't have a permit for it, but that wasn't her quarrel tonight.

He was obviously relieved when she walked out the door. The tech was loading the young black male onto a metal gurney and Johnnie was talking to a skinny woman he'd ferreted out of the adjoining alleyway.

If anyone can find a pross, it'll be Johnnie, Frank thought, though in all fairness, hookers on Florence Avenue were as common as cracks in the sidewalk. Frank eased under the police tape toward Johnnie and the girl. If she wasn't so strung out she'd almost be pretty. Frank folded her arms and leaned back against the crumbling brick wall of the alley, gleaming loafers casually crossed at the ankle.

The pross eyed Frank nervously and asked Johnnie, "Who dat bitch?"

"That bitch is my boss," he confided. "And she doesn't like being dragged out of bed at 3:00 A.M. Makes her kinda grumpy."

Frank let her eyes drift over the skinny young woman. She was bare bones, literally and figuratively, dressed only in a skimpy skirt and blouse against the chill night. It wouldn't be long before she was being wheeled off on a metal gurney, too. Frank ended her perusal at the woman's face, holding the hooker's jumpy eyes with an iron gaze. The girl shivered, wrapping herself even tighter.

"So whatcha doing here all alone in the middle of the night, Angela? This ain't no good place to be hangin'," Johnnie warned, his voice oozing concern. "You lookin' to score maybe? Huh?"

The prostitute's eyes danced back and forth between the big white dude, hunched over her, smiling, and his creepy boss. Angela squirmed under Frank's pitiless scrutiny, her nerves on fire, her muscles twitching. She giggled tensely.

"Yeah, okay. That what I be doin'," she admitted to Johnnie, nodding her head vigorously.

"Yeah, I don't blame you," Johnnie sympathized. "I'd be out lookin' too if I had to. Now tell me what you saw here, Angela."

"I din't see nothin'," she insisted.

"For real? See, that don't make much sense to me, 'cause if I wanted to be scoring I wouldn't be hidin' in a goddamn alley. I'd be out cruisin', hustlin'. You know what I mean?"

She nodded her whole torso up and down, hugging herself.

"And that little guy over there? He says you're hangin' around the store all the time. Now the way I see it you'd be out cruisin'" near the store, waiting for guys to walk in an' maybe lay a little green on you 'fore they drop it in the store. Am I right?"

"Yeah, you right," she agreed, then realizing her mistake she started shaking her head back and forth. "But I din't see nothin'."

Shoving off the wall, Frank spoke almost absently. "I don't have time for this. Bring her in for loitering with intent."

As Frank moved out of the alley the crackhead shouted, "Hey, you can't do that! I ain't done nothin' wrong."

Frank spun quickly and took two strides toward Angela, who involuntarily stepped backward.

"Whoa," Johnnie said as he placed himself between the two women. "I'll get her, Frank," he said over his shoulder, then to Angela he whispered, "See? Now I gotta take you in. It'll be hours before you can score."

Frank stayed where she was, glaring at Angela, who wailed, "I don't want no trouble."

Johnnie draped his beefy wrists on her shoulders and drawled, "I know, darlin'. Just tell me what you saw and then I can let you go."

"Fo' real? You gonna lemme go?"

"For real."

"On'y thing I seen was a tall dude come outta nowhere, come 'roun' the corner. I sees him liftin' his arm at Smack-Mac and I run down here."

Angela swallowed hard as Frank turned away. Johnnie took out his notepad and started writing. Angela Barry was suddenly very cooperative. Frank had that effect on people.

Two hours later Frank watched the dawn sky transform itself from gray murk to a pale, delicate blue. Johnnie was driving back to the station house. Noah leaned over the front seat and said to Frank, "You know, if there really was such a charge as 'loitering with intent,' we'd have to run Johnnie up on it."

"Yeah," Briggs agreed. "Loitering with intent to get laid."

"Nah. Loitering with intent to work." Noah guffawed at his own joke, and Johnnie said, "Yeah, yeah. I can do more work in one day than you can in a month."

"That's true," Noah conceded, "you can. But you never do."

The RTO interrupted the boys' banter. She was radioing a patrol car about a possible 187 on 8th and 52nd.

"That'd be Ike and Diego's," Noah said merrily. "Geez Louise. Not even seven o'clock and we've already got a doubleheader."

Frank didn't share Noah's enthusiasm. "Let's go look," she said tiredly.

Spying the Winchell's Donuts on the corner Johnnie said, "I gotta get some coffee first."

They followed the dispatcher's address to Crenshaw High School and found two squad cars working the area. One of the patrolmen was stretching tape around the scene, while another stared uselessly at the body. Two other cops were talking to a clump of onlookers.

The detectives carried their coffee to the edge of the tape.

"Haystack!" Johnnie greeted the old cop pulling the tape, then motioned to the cop hovering over the body.

"What's with the zombie?" he asked, shoving the last bite of a Bavarian Creme into his mouth.

Tying off the final knot, Officer Heisdaeck straightened and pushed his hands into the small of his back. He ambled over to Johnnie.

"Well, if it ain't the Happy Clapper," he grinned, euphemistically referring to the detective's legendary propensity for women as well as his frequent, nonchalant bouts with various STDs. Glancing over at the rookie, he explained, "Second day on the job."

Johnnie grinned happily. He loved rookies.

Frank looked toward the body. "What do you know about her?"

"See that lady over there? The one in the brown dress?" Heisdaeck squinted dramatically and pointed to a bent, gray-haired woman who was talking to a female officer. "She found it."

"*It?*" Noah frowned, shooting the officer daggers.

"She was walking down to Price's Market," Heisdaeck continued, tossing his head in the direction of the grocery store on Crenshaw—

Noah interrupted, "They don't open until seven."

Heisdaeck pasted Noah with an exasperated glare, as if he hadn't been working the nine-three since this putz was still a wad stuck up his daddy's Johnson. He sighed with infinite condescension and said, "You watch her walk, kid. If we let her go right now she *might* make it there by eight o'clock."

Noah rolled his eyes and went to talk to the old lady himself.

"Punk's got no idea what it's like to get old," he complained to Johnnie. Briggs was only a few years older than Noah, but he nodded sympathetically.

"So the old lady found her, then what?" Frank prompted.

"Then she goes across the street—she's been livin' here all her life, knows everyone in the 'hood—and knocks on the green house over there."

He indicated a fading bungalow across the street, framed in orange and red bougainvillea. It needed some paint, but like the little houses next to it, the bungalow was tidy and squarely framed by a trim green lawn.

"Her friend lives there." Heisdaeck was pointing to the crowd again. "The lady in the pink bathrobe. The old lady tells her there's a white girl laying out there and her friend invites her in for a cup of tea and calls the cops. I'll betcha the tea came first," Heisdaeck grumbled.

Frank ducked under the tape, leaving the two men bullshitting, or "networking" as Johnnie likened his endless hours of griping and bragging.

"What do you have?" she said, strolling up to the pale rookie who was struggling to keep his breakfast in his belly. Frank didn't expect to learn anything from her question. She'd asked it to get the rookie focused, moving around, looking for clues. Though she doubted she'd get any of those from him either. This already looked like a dump job.

"Ma'am?"

"I want you to go to that unmarked over there. Find the bag in the back seat and take it to that detective talking to Heisdaeck."

"Yes, ma'am."

Frank sipped from her styrofoam cup, kneeling before the body. Dump jobs were the worst. The killing was done one place, the body dumped in another. Then she saw the KTLA news van rolling down the street. She watched Johnnie offering the rookie a donut from the bag he held open under the kid's nose. The kid groaned and finally set his breakfast free. Johnnie neatly stepped aside, shooting Frank a thumbs-up. Frank nodded, pointing to the woman exiting the news van. Johnnie returned the nod and went to intercept her.

Frank cringed as she turned back to the Jane Doe and heard Johnnie holler, "Hey, good-lookin'! Out slumming this morning?"

Momentarily free of distractions, Frank scanned the body. The victim appeared to be in her midteens, probably Caucasian. Livid bruises covered almost her entire body. There was no obvious cause of death, but blood crusted around her rectal area suggested a possible internal trauma.

Two facts immediately bothered Frank: the lack of clothing and the dump site. That the girl was completely naked indicated somebody had taken the time to undress her, either before or after she was killed. Second, there were plenty of better spots to leave the body. Even in a panic their perp probably wasn't dumb enough to just open his car door as he was driving by the high school and push her out. That he chose to dump her in an area where she'd be quickly found, and where he could easily have been detected, indicated further deliberation on his part.

Within half an hour two more detectives from Frank's 93rd squad showed up, Ike Zabbo and Lou Diego. Wide and blocky, Ike looked like a gangster in his flashy three-piece suit, diamond pinkie rings glinting in the new sun. His partner was a thin, wiry Hispanic man everyone called Taquito. Frank briefed them on what Briggs and Noah had culled so far, which took all of five minutes.

The coroner's tech pulled up soon after. He was still in the area from the Mackay pickup, so the detectives were ready to bag the body in a few hours. That was the only good thing about this case so far. Instead of decreasing as the scene processing dragged on, the number of news vans ominously increased. Frank had called in the crime scene unit. Although they'd bitched her out, telling her it was obvious to a five-year old with a blindfold on that there wasn't any evidence at the scene, sixteen years with the LAPD had taught Frank to always plan ahead. She could already see *brass* written all over this case, and Frank was carefully covering her ass.

"Ready for the shit storm?"

Noah grinned at her, rubbing his hands together with glee.

Frank surveyed the fleet of news crews behind a second line of police tape, then scouted the crowd for any brass that might have shown up. Nine times out of ten they barged onto the scene fresh from a good night's sleep and power breakfasts, only to contradict everything she'd said.

"No Fubar yet," Noah said, almost reading her mind, also looking around for Captain Foubarelle. The SID techs had left already, disgusted with Frank, and as she headed toward the hungry cameras she told Noah to take the tape down after the news vans left.

Paul Massey from the *Times* was the first reporter in her face. He was tall, balding, openly queer. Over the last year she'd watched him thin and lose color. Makeup didn't conceal the bruises and blotches that erupted on his skin. Pain in the ass that he was, there was no pleasure in watching the man slowly die from AIDS.

"Do you know who the girl is?" he asked. "How old is she?"

"We don't know who the victim is. She appears to be in her midteens, but we won't know until we have a positive ID."

"What was the cause of death?"

That was Sally Eisley, from KTLA. Loud, obnoxious, in your face, absolutely without scruples. Absolutely knockdown gorgeous.

"We don't know yet. The—"

"Oh come on, Lieutenant! You must have some idea."

Lieutenant Franco twitched her lips in a semblance of a smile but her eyes remained cool, locked onto Sally's.

"I have plenty of ideas," she admitted, "but no facts. When I know the facts—"

"You'll know the facts," Sally finished in a frustrated singsong.

An Asian woman Frank didn't recognize said, "Lieutenant, you've been here for over three hours. Do you have any indication who might have done this?"

"We do not."

"She looked pretty battered. Do you think it was a hate crime? Racially motivated?" asked Tom Blake from the *L.A. Weekly.*

Frank slid around the battery comment. "At this time we have no motive."

"Doesn't it seem obvious that a white girl killed in a black neighborhood might involve a racial motivation?"

"That is not at all obvious." Frank didn't add that the girl was dumped there but not necessarily killed in the neighborhood.

"But it *could* be," Blake persisted.

Frank reiterated, "We have no reason to suspect that at this point."

They both knew it *could* be a race crime, but admission would come across as confirmation that it *was* a race crime. Frank wouldn't take the weak bait, and Blake shared Sally Eisley's frustration.

Above the din of questions Frank could hear a siren wailing toward them. That could only mean Foubarelle or some other brass-hat was on the way.

"Sorry. That's really all we have right now. We'll let you know as soon as we learn more."

Frank spun on her heel, motioning Johnnie and Noah toward the unmarked. Sally Eisley and her cameraman tried to block her path.

"How do you think she was killed, Lieutenant? Just between you and me?" Sally spoke in the confidential tone of a co-conspirator. She was new to the station, but aggressive and a real go-getter. Frank doubted she'd be on the morning crew for long. Frank offered another neutral comment and tried to move around Sally, but again the reporter dodged in front of her.

"Off the record, Lieutenant. I swear."

The tic of a smile Frank had given Sally earlier was a little wider this time and lasted a second longer. It almost reached her eyes.

"Promise?" Frank asked, and Sally agreed eagerly. The lieutenant lowered her head toward Sally and glanced around as she opened the car door. Then she bent closer to the perfectly coifed hair framing Sally Eisley's perfectly gorgeous little ear. Frank's lips moved against the starched blonde strands.

As Captains Foubarelle and Bedford stepped self-importantly from their car, Frank slipped into hers. Johnnie steered them quickly into the light traffic and Noah leaned over the seat.

"Hey. What'd you say to Sally?"

Frank was mulling over the peculiarities of the case and she answered laconically.

"Told her she'd stepped in dog shit."

Johnnie chuckled. Twice already, Frank had made his day.

2

The way he stormed into her office, Frank knew that if she had balls, Fubar would be busting them. Almost shouting, he demanded, "Why didn't you wait for us at the high school this morning?"

Frank sighed and tipped her chair back, steepling two fingers against her lips.

"What the hell was going on out there?"

The captain wasn't a bad guy, just incompetent, and Franco resented incompetency. In her line of work it could get people killed. She'd admit he'd only been captain for six months, but she was sure if his learning curve was graphed it would show up as a horizontal line.

In a monotone Frank explained, "We'd been on that case for hours. Before that we were at another scene for three hours. The good citizens of L.A. pay us for an eight-hour day, John. We were already into the seventh hour of our day, with no paper generated on either case. We could have wasted more time standing around like idiots for the cameras, or we could have come back here to do some work."

Foubarelle opened his mouth to interrupt, but Frank dropped her chair and leaned toward him.

"If you want to pay my guys overtime, I'll have them jumping around in monkey suits for you, but until then, we've got murders to solve. We don't get that 74 percent clearance rate by dicking around with Tom Brokaw all day."

Finished, Frank sat back.

The captain had read dozens of management books, replete with all the tricks about how to jockey oneself into a position of physical power, but even standing over Frank he felt smaller than her. Foubarelle hadn't come up through the ranks, and at times it cost him. In eleven short years he had jumped from patrol cop to patrol sergeant, served briefly as a vice detective before making vice lieutenant, then on to homicide captain. He was making strides in the political process but at the cost of respect among the people he supervised. They knew he fell asleep at night dreaming that CHIEF was stenciled on his office door. But Foubarelle wasn't out to bust chops, he was merely being politically expedient. When his chain was yanked, he turned around to yank Frank's.

Now he took a softer tack with his contumacious lieutenant. She was right that he enjoyed supervising a homicide squad with such a large percentage of cleared cases, large at least for the Figueroa district. He knew Frank was responsible for that number and he knew it made him look very good.

"I'm sorry," he offered, turning up his hands in conciliation. "I know you've got a lot of work to do. Tell me about this girl."

Frank ignored the patronization, wondering just how much she could trust Foubarelle with. He had a tendency to leak valuable details, but then she realized they didn't have any valuable details. Yet.

"White girl, midteens. Noah may have ID'd her on an MP bulletin. I asked Crocetti to do her ASAP."

She paused for a moment knowing the captain's next step would be a call to the coroner. He never actually went to the morgue but he was the first to redball the old coroner when a hot case was pending. That was good for Frank; Foubarelle's phone calls usually got the autopsy done faster while keeping the heat off Frank and her squad.

"Valley girl coming to score a little coke in the 'hood?" he asked.

"I don't think so."

The girl didn't have any of the earmarks of a kick down. Frank explained how the victim had been brutally assaulted, how some of her bruises looked older than others. She told Foubarelle what the coroner's tech had told her, that the cause of death was possibly due to internal trauma. There were no obvious external causes. Usually someone in a jammed-up drug deal was capped or stabbed and just left for dead.

"But she was dumped?"

"Yeah. Nothing at the scene. I called SID in just in case—you might get a call about that." Frank shrugged again, then added, "I'm going to work this with Noah."

Foubarelle nodded, pleased.

"Keep me posted on this, Frank. I want to know everything

you know, when you know it, okay?"

"Sure."

Foubarelle turned to go, saying, "And I want to see the protocol as soon as you have it." He knew it was important to leave with the upper hand.

"What an asshole," Frank thought, watching him leave with his imaginary dignity intact. She picked up a stack of messages and sifted through them, crumpling some and tossing them in the trash. She pulled the phone toward her but then sat back, rhythmically tapping the small slips of paper into a tidy pile.

Frank visualized the dead girl sprawled naked on the concrete. She'd been mauled, from her neck down to her knees. Some of the bruises looked older than others, indicating she'd been beaten over a period of time, not just in a sudden pique of anger. Frank remembered that her face was relatively unscathed.

And why was she dumped in plain view on a sidewalk in front of a school? Vacant lots, weedy road shoulders, empty buildings— those were common dump areas. Ike and Diego were working a possible connection to the school, either the girl's or the killer's.

She traded the messages in her hand for the MP bulletin. It looked like the same girl. Melissa Agoura. Sixteen years old. From Culver City. She'd disappeared from Kenneth Hahn State Recreation Area three days ago. The bruises could be consistent with those dates.

She'd *been* attractive, Frank thought, sailing the bulletin back onto her desk, then dialing the phone. Returning her calls and waiting for a correct ID was more productive right now than speculating.

Noah was bent over one of the two typewriters in the office that actually worked. Slipping into her jacket, Frank informed him, "Coroner called. Handley matched our girl to the bulletin. And Crotchety's ready to cut. Let's go." She slapped him on the back and started walking away.

"Aww, man, Leslie's got a game at 3:30. If I left now I could just make it," he pleaded.

"Come on. It's good for you. Builds character."

"I've *got* character," he argued, rising nonetheless. He grumbled all the way to the morgue, and she let him. Noah was off hours ago, adored his kids, and hated autopsies. She'd have watched the autopsy alone on a less sensitive case but she wanted him in on this one.

Awkward, skinny, all flapping hands and feet, Noah looked more like a scarecrow than a crack homicide detective. He was consistently the worst shot in the department and the best cop Frank had. What he lacked in physical presence he compensated for with instinct, intelligence, and compassion. He was rarely more than a step behind Frank and often one or two ahead. She'd felt a twinge of guilt reassigning this case to Noah, knowing it could be messy. It was already distracting Noah from the little family life he had, but selfishly, Frank was glad to be working with him. The least she could do was let him carp. Besides, that was another of Noah's specialties.

Noah grimaced when they entered the cool, tiled autopsy room and started breathing through his mouth. The girl's body was on a metal autopsy table. An assistant was measuring it. Frank didn't recognize the woman in scrubs standing next to Crocetti.

"All right, ladies and gentlemen—" he peered over his bifocals at Frank—" and I only use the term *ladies* because Dr. Lawless is present, let us begin."

Unlike many of his contemporaries, Crocetti didn't mind women in law enforcement. In fact, he rather liked it, but he expected them to act like women. Frank was more like one of the guys, and this irritated the old man. He was cranky by nature, hence the nickname Crotchety, but he was getting crankier the closer he got to retirement.

As he swabbed the body, the coroner made introductions.

"Dr. Gail Lawless, Detective Noah Jantzen," Noah extended his hand, "and Lieutenant Franco." Frank nodded curtly, not even looking at the woman she was being introduced to. Crocetti continued. "Dr. Lawless is my hapless though far more attractive replacement."

The old man swung his head from one woman to the next and remarked curiously, "They certainly grow you girls tall these days. It must have been all that Wonder Bread."

Frank glanced at the new ME. She was indeed tall, but flat and thin, like Modigliani's blue woman. Frank thought Bobby Taylor— one of her detectives who'd minored in art—would have been pleased with the analogy. Dr. Lawless had smiled wryly at Crocetti's comment, and Noah was grinning goofily. He had a thing for tall women. Frank could tell he was already smitten.

"Any idea what made the bruises?" Frank asked, all cool business and efficiency.

Bending intently over the body, Crocetti responded, "Hasn't anyone ever told you, Lieutenant, that patience is a virtue?"

He poked and prodded for a moment, made a few comments to his colleague, then straightened, frowning sourly.

"It looks like this poor girl was mistaken for a bowling pin. There are so many bruises here it's hard to tell where one ends and another begins. You know," he said toward the body, "I have a granddaughter this age."

A shake of his head chased the thought away, and he gruffly asked for details about the case. Noah told him what they had so far.

"Well," the old man sighed, "let's see what we can find here."

Crocetti lowered his bald head over the table, enunciating carefully for the microphone.

"Victim appears to be a healthy teenage Caucasian female. Brown hair, brown eyes, height—?"

"Sixty-four inches," Handley responded loudly. Crocetti repeated the height and when he asked for the weight Jack called out, "One hundred twenty-four pounds."

"You don't have to scream," complained the old man, then calmly continued.

"Victim has all her teeth, in good condition. No apparent scars, tattoos, or abnormalities. Right shoulder appears dislocated."

Crocetti measured a cut on the left side of her chin and noted the associated hematoma.

He carefully examined the rest of the bruises, asking Dr. Lawless for her opinion. She outlined specific ones with a gloved finger, noting, "The patterns appear more rounded than linear where the contusions don't overlap. The bruises are deep, but the absence of laceration suggests she was hit with something relatively flexible or soft. The varied discoloration suggests they were inflicted over time."

"Do they look like they could be older than three days?"

"It's possible, but these are certainly consistent with that time frame...don't you think?" she asked Crocetti.

He was beaming at his replacement. "I do indeed, my dear.

Now tell me what else you see."

"Well, there are slight adhesive traces on her wrists and ankles, along with a mild abrasion, and the skin's a little paler there, suggesting she was bound with some sort of tape."

"Was she gagged?" Frank thought aloud.

Lawless bent closer to Agoura's face.

"Probably," pointing to faint traces of adhesive around Agoura's mouth.

"This looks consistent with the other adhesives, and we'll see what we get back from the mouth swabs."

"Well done," Crocetti said, snapping his gloves off. Except for Noah, everyone waited patiently while Crocetti wrote down notes. Although he taped the autopsy proceedings he still insisted on hard copy. Frank appreciated his lack of faith in technology, even though it slowed the whole process. She looked around at four other steel gurneys, each being autopsied by one of Crocetti's staff. She knew there were plenty more bodies waiting in the cooler and was pleased the old man had gotten to Agoura as soon as he had.

"Were any of those blows enough to kill her?" Noah asked.

"I can't say for sure until I see inside," answered the coroner without looking up. "From the bloat on her abdomen it feels like we'll find a significant trauma of some sort."

That told them nothing, and Noah continued his restless pacing, biting on a thumbnail. Pulling on new gloves, Crocetti turned and said, "All right, Jack. Let's scrape the nails, and Dr. Lawless, if you would care to comb her hair out I will proceed with the rape test."

The three whitecoats went efficiently about their tasks, wresting clues from the hidden holds of the victim's body. Frank watched Crocetti apply toluidine solution to the oral, anal, and vaginal areas, while Noah continued his pacing.

"I wonder if they've put Les in the game yet," he said to Frank. "We've been working on her dribble. I hope she keeps her head up like I showed her."

He turned around when Crocetti murmured, "There we go."

The toluidine had showed up on the anal cavity, staining the entire area dark blue as it reacted to the polysaccharides on the abraded skin tissue. Frank found that curious. Whoever had this girl had plenty of time to rape her, in any way he wanted, yet curiously he'd only sodomized her.

With the external exam over, Crocetti was ready to cut the big coroner's *Y* that would show them the inside of Melissa Agoura. The two doctors and two detectives peered into the body and no one there needed a medical degree to realize blood had pooled in places where it should never be.

Crocetti's replacement said, "Wow," and as the old coroner cut away the chest plate he noted into the mike, "Massive hemorrhage is apparent."

The old man could probably do this with his eyes shut and one arm tied behind his back, yet he cautiously and daintily cut the thoracic organs from their moorings, another meticulous attention to detail that drove the detectives batty. After examining the right lung he put it in a weighing pan and instructed Dr. Lawless to explain what she saw. She rearranged the organ and studied it for a moment, then pointed at a tear.

"You can see where it's been punctured at the bottom here. The tissue is ripped, not cut, and the puncture doesn't extend more than," she quickly grabbed a ruler, "four centimeters."

"What made it?" Noah asked, but Crocetti shook his head at him. He didn't want to commit to that yet, and Noah returned to his frustrated pacing. Chin in hand, Frank continued her impassive observation. When he was satisfied the young woman on the table hadn't been asphyxiated, Crocetti turned his attention to the abdominal cavity. He poked and prodded, then straightened, arching the stiffness out of his back.

"What do you see, doctor?"

Dr. Lawless quietly poked and prodded too, finally saying, "There's considerable trauma to numerous organs, any of which could have been the cause of death."

Pointing with a scalpel tip she traced the path of the injuries, starting with the grossly ruptured rectum. Perforations in the bladder and intestine followed the trajectory of perforations in the liver, stomach, and pancreas.

"Good," Crocetti commented when she was done, then continued excising and measuring organs. Further inspection showed that the bruising continued well below the skin, involving numerous bones and organs as well. She'd been hit pretty hard, but the lack of lacerations suggested she may have had some type of padding between herself and the assailant's weapon. The doctors couldn't say what sort of weapon that might be.

With a flourish, as if he were asking her to dance, Crocetti asked his replacement if she'd like to finish the autopsy.

"Sure," she said easily, and proceeded to excise the neck organs. Without flinching, Frank could watch the torso being slit and eviscerated, or see the skull-saw spray hot bone before the brain was lifted out with a last, small gasp, but cutting into the neck still made Frank glance down at her feet. When Dr. Lawless moved onto the head area, Frank resumed her observation. Other than a mild concussion, the doctors found no further injury to Melissa Agoura.

"Jack, please finish."

Handley proceeded to replace the various body parts while the old man gave the detectives his back to write further notes. Noah rolled his eyes at Frank and tapped his watch. Arms folded patiently, Frank nodded. Finally the coroner gave them his full attention.

"Well, detectives, I think you pretty much have your answer. In my opinion this girl died of massive internal hemorrhage induced by multiple organ rupture, seemingly initiated by a pointed, long-handled instrument. The shape of the perforations seems consistent with the use of an irregularly-sided instrument, such as," he held up a small specimen bottle, "a tree branch. I believe the lab analysis will conclude that these fragments, found around various perforations, are wood. Dr. Lawless?"

"I'd say that's it in a nutshell."

"Oh, one more thing," Crocetti added playfully. "According to the path of insertion, the fellow you're looking for will probably be left-handed."

"Aww, man." Noah flapped his arms and shuffled in a tight circle. He complained to Frank, "For *this* I'm missing my kid's ball game?"

He'd really enjoyed the first few games. He was barely able to keep the football helmet above his eyes but he'd had fun anyway. His dad seemed to enjoy it, too, and he'd been struck with wonder: for the first time in his six years he was having fun with his father. It was an unusual feeling, but a good one, and the boy wanted it to always be like that.

Sometimes his father would yell when he dropped the ball or tripped over his own feet. Once, the Pop Warner coach had gently interceded, explaining to the angry man that six-year olds weren't very coordinated, that that would come with time.

"It better," his father had menaced.

By the next year, he made it clear that he thought the boy's coordination should have arrived. Shoves and smacks replaced the verbal threats. The other parents would look away. The coach refused to have the boy on his team if the father continued hitting him. So his father stopped. In public.

3

Franco spent most of her days and many of her nights in Figueroa, LAPD's roughest district. The 'hood had started as a peaceful community in which mainly black sharecroppers strived for their piece of the American Dream. As industry waned over the ensuing decades, crime and the inevitably profitable drug markets became the 'hood's economic mainstay. With more crackheads and gangbangers in Figueroa than any other division in the LAPD, the American Dream had twisted cruelly into a nightmare. Now the population was largely Hispanic, with blacks accounting for slightly less than 20 percent of the residents. Asians, many of them Korean, rounded out the demographics.

Taquerias crowded next to fried chicken stands, and Easter egg-colored stores advertised fish cleaned and fresh chitterlings. Old brick buildings, peeling paint and heavily graffitied, sported architectural flourishes that were too high off the ground to be ravaged by vandalism and testified to the more optimistic roots of South Central Los Angeles.

Frank had been assigned to Figueroa right out of the academy, probably with the assumption that she'd quit. But instead of leaving, Frank had embraced the 'hood, sharply aware no other division could challenge or test her as much. At thirty-nine, her mastery of the mean streets was no longer a question, either for herself, her colleagues, or the *veteranos* and OGs within the division. Except for the unending mysteries of who killed who and why, Figueroa offered few surprises.

After a grueling sixteen-hour day, Frank pulled gratefully into her driveway. Though she lived in an old suburb of South Pasadena, her house was not the typically modest Los Angeles bungalow. Its last owner had been an architect with more imagination than money and a penchant for split-level ranch houses. Consequently, the center of the house was dominated by a huge sunken living room with a beamed ceiling. It was surrounded by two tiers of polished wood leading up to a tiled corridor. On the north and south sides doors opened off the corridor into various rooms, but to the east behind the living room the floor widened to accommodate an open corner kitchen and a large dining table, which Frank used as her desk.

Loafers clicking noisily on the tiles, she walked to the bedroom, turning lights on along the way. She paused in front of an old mahogany dresser to dump her service revolver, badge, ID card, and beeper, then emptied her pockets of coins, latex gloves, her wallet, notepads, pens, scraps of paper, and an unused roll of film. Feeling ten pounds lighter, she changed out of her work clothes into ripped shorts and a holey T-shirt that Mrs. Fontina had laundered and folded as carefully as if they were part of Frank's trousseau.

In the den at the other end of the house an expensive stereo system nestled between walls of books. Frank checked the CDs in the turntable, then hit the play button. Van Halen pounded through the house. Frank padded into the adjacent room, a garage that years ago she'd converted into a gym. A Soloflex was bolted in the center of the room, a bench and racks of weights lined one wall, and a punching bag hung on the opposite side next to a treadmill. Frank set it for the highest angle, then started burning off the day while David Lee Roth begged a pretty woman to stop a while. But Frank didn't hear him; she was busy thinking about the Agoura case.

She and Noah had spent the evening first with the girl's parents, later with her boyfriend. They had quickly ruled out Fubar's idea about a drug buy gone bad; Agoura had no reason to be in the area, and no one could think of who she might know in the 'hood or at Crenshaw High. Although the Agouras lived only a dozen miles from the high school and had been in Culver City for eight years, they never had occasion to venture into even the fringe of South Central.

From all her family said, Melissa Agoura seemed like a pretty typical teenager. She was a sophomore at Culver City High, a B-C student, with no extracurricular involvements. She babysat for a couple of neighborhood kids, made enough money that way and from her allowance to go to the mall with her girlfriends and the movies with her boyfriend. He'd admitted they liked to drink and smoke dope, but adamantly insisted they never used anything harder.

He and Melissa had been going together for almost a year. On weekends, if the weather was good, they liked going to the beach, but a lot of times they just went over to the rec area and hung out in the sun or splashed around near the fish ponds. He acknowledged that he fooled around in the scrub with her and tried to get her to go on the pill, but she wouldn't do it. His grades were a little lower than Melissa's. He didn't like school, worked part-time at a mechanic's on Cienega, and said he wanted to drop out of school and work full-time.

Noah was going to run him through the files tomorrow, but it didn't seem likely at this point that he was involved with Agoura's death. There were the girlfriends to interview, too. Two of them had called her house when she failed to meet them at the park. They'd planned on watching some boys from their school play baseball, a common activity for them on weekends. Weekdays, the same two friends came over to do homework and watch *Oprah*. Agoura and her brother were always fighting over the TV. He was only thirteen. Her little sister was twelve and adored Melissa. Posters of Leo DiCaprio and Hanson hung in their shared bedroom between posters of *Titanic* and the Spice Girls.

Jaime Agoura managed a tire store in West Hollywood, and Virginia Agoura was a bank teller at the Wells Fargo on Sepulveda. The Agouras were struggling to get by and somehow managing. Their kids weren't exceptional, but they were good kids. And now this. Frank had seen the shock and disbelief a thousand times, the certainty that the cops standing in their doorway had to be mistaken, that it couldn't be *their* child.

By the time she slowed the treadmill, Frank's T-shirt was heavy with sweat. The machine always made her feel wobbly, so she dismounted carefully, letting the effect fade as she toweled off. She eyed the Soloflex and thought about skipping it. Instead she straddled the seat and briefly worked her torso. She'd do arms and legs tomorrow. Right now she was ready for a beer.

The beer and a warm shower made Frank sleepy, but she sat on the kitchen counter in her pajamas and chugged another bottle, flipping through the paper. After years of nightmares and insomnia, Frank had hit on a formula that usually guaranteed sleep: brutally long hours on the job, hard work in the gym, and a specific blood alcohol level. Though she was tired, she wasn't about to start tampering with the combination.

When Noah poked his head in Frank's office the next morning, he could tell his boss had already been there for a while. She looked up, saw him grinning at her, and sat back.

"What's up?" she yawned.

"Looks like you've been."

Frank's hair was dry where it touched her collar in a sharp line, but it was still damp where her sunglasses held it away from her face. She was wearing a V-neck sweater over a button-down shirt and her sleeves were shoved over her elbows. That usually happened after at least her third cup of coffee.

"How long you been here?"

Frank ignored the question, holding up the *L.A. Times* instead.

"See we made the third page of the Metro section?"

"Yeah. The eleven o'clock news, too. 'Racially motivated attack.' Jesus. Like we don't have enough trouble already. RHD on this yet?"

Frank shook her head and swung her polished loafers onto a corner of the desk. RHD was the LAPD Robbery-Homicide Division. They handled the more sensitive cases, the ones they thought the average homicide dick was too stupid to work properly. Frank hated it when they snagged her cases, and she was damned if she was going to let them have this one. Though she knew she'd be powerless to stop them if they wanted it.

"I'll work Fubar to stave them off, but I don't think it's a big deal yet. You going to run the boyfriend?"

"Yeah, first thing. Him and her savings account, make sure her money's where it should be."

"Good. We need to go to the school, talk to people there. I want to talk to people across the street, too, and get back to Culver City, talk to the girlfriends."

"Okay. I got a wit coming in at nine to sign a statement."

Frank nodded and bent back over the stack of reports on her desk. Everyone was in the cramped squad room by 6:20. The morning meetings always started late because one of the detectives, Jill Symmonds, was chronically late. It was a condition the squad had gotten used to.

After the briefing, Frank stayed to talk with Jill and her partner, Bobby Taylor. Bobby looked a lot like Johnnie, only black.

Both men were tall, big-chested and broad-shouldered. In college, Bobby played fullback and Johnnie had been a linebacker, but where Bobby had stayed rock-hard, Johnnie was running to fat.

Frank appraised Jill and asked, "Hey, Fire Truck, you going to make it a couple more weeks?"

She was seven months pregnant and her huge belly looked out of place on her slight frame. Jill nodded her bright auburn head. She was going out on maternity leave soon and Bobby would be partnerless. Frank talked about their caseload. She didn't want Jill to be the primary on any new cases. She'd pick up slack for Bobby unless Fubar drummed up another body. Not likely, though. The LAPD was notoriously short-handed, and the workload left by a vacancy was usually distributed among the remaining employees. At Figueroa the detectives were already handling more than twice, sometimes more than three times the average yearly caseload. The burnout rate among regular detectives was high enough; at Figueroa it was off the charts. Frank knew she had a pretty good squad and she was determined to hold it together, even if that meant shouldering much of the load herself.

Sitting at the desk next to Bobby's, a red-haired detective who could have passed for Jill's father chimed in, "Hey, Freek, who's gonna pick up slack for Nookey when *I* leave?"

Peter Gough was fifty-six years old and should have been long retired. Ironically, it was Peter who had given Frank her nickname during her first week on the job. Gough had been a sergeant in the Newton Division when Frank and her partner had responded to a B&E he'd called in. He took one look at Franco and asked her partner, "Where's your sidekick?"

Her partner, as disgusted with female patrol cops as Gough was, spat bitterly, "She's it. Meet *L.A.* Franco."

"L.A.?" Gough had puzzled. "What the hell sorta name is that?"

"She says it's Dutch or something and that I wouldn't remember even if she *did* tell me."

With a cold appraisal Gough had concluded, "L.A. *Freako's* more like it, you ask me."

Her partner had laughed, and the name stuck. During the disco era there was a popular song that referred to "le Freak" and her name metamorphosed into that. Later, when she was commanding her own squad and it became clear to her detectives that she wasn't just another stat-gathering bureaucrat, her name evolved again. Frank's reputation for independence, plus presumption about her sexual preferences, created a play on words meaning she was on her own frequency, tuned in to a different radio band. Since then she was La Freek or Lt. Freek.

Gough had been flirting with burnout even then, and now he was completely fried. He'd had it with police work, wanting only to tend to his garden and start a specialty nursery. Dan Nukisona was the partner Gough had worked with for the last six years. Nookey was only a little younger than Gough, but he wouldn't hear of retiring. Every time Gough said the "R word," Nookey hissed vehemently.

"Boy-red, you are irreplaceable," Bobby said.

"I'm thinking Jill's going to like being a mom so much, she might never come back. I'm going to throw Nookey and Bobby together and see what happens," Frank answered, unhinging her long legs from the corner of Jill's desk.

Jill rolled her eyes skeptically. Nookey pretended to inspect the report he had rolled in the typewriter.

"Yeah," he said. "You've got your Starsky and Hutch, Cagney and Lacey, now we'll have Nappie and Jappie."

"No, no, no," Johnnie said in his gravely voice. "You'll be the Spook and the Gook, like in that book that cop wrote. Goddamn, that was the funniest thing I ever read."

"That's the only thing you've ever read," Gough grumbled.

Amidst the chatter, Noah's witness had nervously entered the squad room. He was dressed down in huge pants and T-shirt, cap turned back, thick gold chains called Turkish ropes around his neck and wrists.

"Where Detective Jantzen at?"

"Over here," Noah called, waving the wit into a chair. The young man was hesitant about giving a statement and balked at signing it. It took Noah and Johnnie most of the morning to get his signature against the banger who'd smoked his brother. He was afraid he'd be retaliated against, and Noah had to admit he had every reason in the world to be afraid.

Gough's right, Frank thought, we need rain.

The day was mild and clear as she walked toward the Kenneth Hahn Recreation Area office, but the sky was smudged with smog.

The scrub surrounding the park was pale and dangerously dry from the summer's drought. Oil derricks pumped behind a fence, bobbing into dusty, raw dirt that contrasted starkly with the park's freshly cut and watered lawn.

Frank eyed the scenery, calculating its strategic cover. The section she was in now contained a shady fishing lake and a large lawn studded with saplings. On the western edge of the park, there was a smaller, more isolated lookout planted with trees from around the world, surrounded by vegetation and scrub. A chaparral-covered slope occupied the northern part of the park, with closed trails leading up into a tangle of dense brush and vegetation. She'd been here before and knew that a paved road in the chaparral led to a higher section containing another large, grassy area. Sections of Leiderman were open and grassy, affording little cover, but the huge chaparraled hill to the north and all the wild vegetation surrounding the park offered great hiding spots.

Frank introduced herself to a receptionist and was soon welcomed by an energetic woman in khaki and olive drab. Seated in her crowded office, Frank requested personnel records for all park employees as well as interviews with them. Gravity replaced the ranger's ebullience. She was very cooperative, inquiring if a park employee was their suspect.

"That's a possibility we can't overlook," Frank responded vaguely. "I have detectives waiting to talk to your staff and I'd like someone available to us while we're here, to show us around, help with identification, that sort of thing "

"I'd be glad to help," she offered. Frank nodded, standing.

The ranger escorted Frank and the detectives around the rec area until a cool dusk descended. Johnnie suggested they compare notes at the Alibi, and while they waited for their round, Noah flipped through the pages of his notebook. He wanted to reinterview one of the landscape staff, a short Hispanic man who'd been awfully uneasy with Noah's questioning. Johnnie had two visitors and an employee that he wanted to talk to again.

While Frank described her uneventful interviews, Bobby and Jill walked in. Frank called for another round and Jill slowly sipped a beer. Her colleagues had busted her chops the first time she'd ordered a drink while carrying the baby. She condescendingly pointed out that her mother had produced five fat and healthy babies while puffing Salems, sipping martinis, and swilling coffee. She doubted that nursing one or two beers a week would turn her kid into a dribbling turnip.

As the talk shifted from work to bullshit, Fire Truck said goodnight. Before her marriage to an emergency room doctor, the redheaded detective had been fast in bedding partners, hence her nickname. Now as she lumbered wearily toward the door, Johnnie commented, "Goddamn, that don't look like fun."

Bobby nodded, adding, "She's tired a lot."

"Hey, Frank, when are you gonna have a baby?" Johnnie teased.

"Hell, I've got all of you. What do I need another one for?"

The badinage continued around the table, through another succession of beers and old stories. At one point, after Johnnie and Bobby headed for the can, Frank stretched her long legs under the table. She whipped the sunglasses off her head and Noah watched as she ran her fingers through her hair. It was dark blonde, streaked with rich colors that could never come from a bottle. She wore it slightly layered on the sides, longer in back, and between haircuts it was kept out of her face by the Ray Bans propped on her head. It was getting long and starting to curl up where it met her shoulders.

"Hey," Noah warned, leaning on one elbow and grinning tipsily, "you better get a haircut before kids start mistaking you for Butch Barbie."

Mellowed by the beers, Frank was caught off guard and chuckled out loud.

During a game three weeks into his third Pop Warner season, the boy stood on the thirty-yard line, waiting for the ball. They were a touchdown behind with only a few minutes left to play. The quarterback tossed the ball toward him. It floated down perfectly into his hands and he heard his father scream, "You got it, son! You got it!" Then he felt the ball slip through his fingers and bounce off his knee. A boy from the other team landed on it. He heard groans on his side of the field, cheers on the other. The boy who'd recovered the ball ran happily to his coach.

He was afraid to look at the sidelines. He couldn't move. The coach trotted out and walked him off the field, saying, "Good try. You almost had it. You'll get it next time."

The coach left the boy, and he could feel his father's presence behind him, felt the hot stare burning into the back of his brain. His little heart was tripping all over itself; he had to go to the bathroom. He watched the last couple of plays but didn't see them. When the game ended, his father put a light hand on his son's shoulder and steered him toward the car.

That evening there were no hits in the belly or fists to the arms. There was something new. His father threw the ball at him four times and four times the boy caught it. He smiled slightly, hopefully. His father smiled back and threw the ball. Hard. The boy couldn't hang on to it. Sadly, the father shook his head and retrieved the ball. He put it in his son's hands then moved toward the closed door.

Standing in the center of his roomy bedroom, uncoiling from the blow he'd expected, the boy couldn't believe they were done.

His father said patiently, turning at the door, "You've got to learn how to hold on to the ball." Then he launched himself across the room and tackled the boy. One hundred ninety pounds met sixty-six against the wooden floor. The boy's vision grayed. When he could focus, he saw his father's face only inches away. His lips were parted, and he was staring at his son in a new way. The boy closed his eyes and lay quietly under his father. In a life already filled with more than its share of fear, the new look on his father's face was more terrifying than anything the boy had ever seen.

4

Frank and her detectives were back at the rec area at nine o'-clock the next morning. Her first interview was with a surly punk just out of high school. He worked the entrance gate part-time and saw a lot of the park's users. Frank knew right off that this skinny, wannabe surf Kahuna had probably never surfed anything harder than his own dick. That he was too lazy and too cowardly to mastermind an abduction, no less carry out a premeditated murder. Still, she questioned him patiently and thoroughly. She showed him six-packs—six photos in a plastic holder of known offenders in the Baldwin Hills/Culver City area. The punk said he didn't recognize anyone in particular, but his eyes lingered on a few. Frank noted which ones.

"Besides," he sniggered, "I don't spend much time looking at *men.*" He eyed her contemptuously up and down, then challenged, "*I'm* a man. I'm supposed to like chicks."

Frank ignored the insult, producing a business card.

"If you happen to see something unusual call this number."

She deftly tucked the card into his shirt pocket and turned away, catching something churlish about "dykes and the LAPD." It was far from the first or last time. Cop-bashing was popular recreation in the 'hood. Being female and not acting the part only exacerbated the censure, but Frank had learned even as a recruit not to hear it. Or at least not care about it.

By noon she was ready to leave the rec area and check out employees who'd been off for the last two days or on leave. Frank gravely thanked the rec area manager for her cooperation and apologized for taking her away from her work for two days.

The woman laughed and tossed the hair off her freckled face. "Are you kidding? It was a relief to get out of that office! I just wish it could have been for a more pleasant reason."

Driving out of the rec area Johnnie observed, "Nice dame."

"*Dame?*" Noah glanced in the rearview mirror. Johnnie's arms were stretched against the back seat and an unlit cigarette dangled from his mouth.

"What are you, Humphrey Bogart?"

"Did either of you get hits on the pictures?"

Johnnie pulled a list from his pocket.

"Yeah, we got a couple."

Frank compared his list to hers. One of the pictures showed up on both their lists.

"Daniel Nathan Sproul," she said. "Let's check him out."

Turned out that Daniel Nathan Sproul had three priors, two drug-related, one for lewd behavior. The computer spit out an address for him and at six o'clock that evening Frank and Noah were on his doorstep. He lived in an apartment in Baldwin Hills and he came to their knock sleepily, as if they'd woken him.

Frank held her badge up to him, asking if he was Daniel Nathan Sproul.

"What if I am?"

"If you are we have some questions for you."

"This isn't a good time," he answered dreamily. "Why don't you come back later?" He slumped against the doorframe, his eyes on the detectives but looking through them.

"What are you on?" Noah asked politely.

"What do you mean?"

"I mean what are you trippin' on?"

He smiled. "Ain't trippin'."

"Internal possession's a felony, Sproul. But to be honest, we're not narcs. We're homicide cops. I don't care if you're shootin'. I just want to ask you some questions."

Sproul smiled, as if a long lost buddy was waving at him from behind the homicide cops.

"Do you know what today is?" Frank asked.

"First day of the rest of my life?" Sproul guessed.

"The date," Frank said patiently. "What is today's date?"

Sproul giggled. "I don't know. You're cops. You should know stuff like that."

Noah reached behind for his cuffs.

"Take him in?"

"May as well put him in the cooler and see what we can get out of him in the morning."

Noah hooked him despite a feeble protest, checking out the track marks on his arms. They drove him downtown, right through the bright lights and glamour that people called L.A.

Sproul didn't look very good when he came out of the chilled holding cell almost a day later. He was only twenty-two but could have easily passed for being in his late thirties. His skin was tinted yellow and he needed a shave. The muscles in his arms held no tone. He was nearly as tall as Noah, though, and broader. Even in bad shape a young girl shouldn't be trouble for him.

In the tiny interview room Noah asked Sproul basic questions—name, age, occupation, education—that required simple, innocuous answers. The detectives already knew the information, but it gave them a chance to establish their suspect's verbal and physical style when he was relatively relaxed and calm. As they questioned him, any changes in this style could be indicators that he had tensed or was nervous about something.

"So how long you been chippin'?" Noah asked.

"I don't know," he responded tiredly, "two, three years."

"Kinda dangerous isn't it?"

The young man shrugged.

"What's it to you?"

Noah shrugged back.

"What do you know about this girl?" he asked, slapping a color picture of Melissa Agoura under Sproul's nose.

Sproul peered closer, then squirmed back against his chair.

"Who the fuck is she?" he asked, glancing up at the detectives.

"Melissa Agoura. Recognize her?"

Sproul eyed the ugly picture again.

"Uh-uh. What happened to her?"

"You tell us," Noah said.

"Fuck if I know."

Then they could see it dawning on him.

"You think *I* did this?"

"Did you?"

"Fuck no! I'm a junkie, not a murderer," he said sincerely.

"There's no law says you can't be both."

"Well I'm *not.*"

"Why don't you tell us about the 288 you got pulled on?"

"The what?"

"The little incident when you were arrested for accosting women on the street?"

"Aw, shit, that wasn't anything," Sproul said dismissively. "I was messed up. Just being stupid with my friends."

"Doesn't seem like you got a lot of respect for the ladies."

"I got plenty, I was just fooling around. Didn't mean nothin' by it."

"Maybe you didn't mean nothin' when you started batting her around—"

"—I never touched her! I don't even know who she is. I never seen her before now."

Noah changed tack.

"You know where the Kenneth Hahn Recreation Area is?"

Sproul was puzzled by the switch but answered affirmatively.

"You ever been there?"

"Yeah. Lots of times."

"What do you go there for?"

Sproul hesitated, obviously reluctant to answer. The detectives pushed and he copped to meeting his dealer there.

"Did you ever see her there?"

Noah slid a family photo of Agoura across the scarred table. Sproul looked at it carefully.

"No. She the one who got beat up?"

"What do you do when you're in the park waiting to score?"

"I don't know. Just hang out."

"You ever talk to anybody?"

"I don't know. It's not like I'm hanging around a lotta people when I'm trying to make a deal go down, you know?"

"Think. Who have you ever talked to?"

"I don't know."

They could see him thinking.

"Maybe I've said hi to the guy picking up trash. Or the girl at the entrance."

"What girl?"

"The one in the booth as you come in."

"You ever said hello to any other girls?"

"I can't remember. I don't think so, at least none I remember."

Noah asked Sproul where he was on October 19th and Sproul laughed.

"Like I know just off the top of my head."

"It was a Sunday. What do you normally do on Sundays?"

"That's the weekend. I don't know what I was doing. I coulda been doin' anything."

"Like what? What do you like to do when you're not working or chipping?"

Frank watched silently as Sproul groped for answers. Noah asked about other dates, then changed subjects and quizzed Sproul about his social life. Sproul was answering easily, willingly. He was leaning over the table, facing Noah with his hands open, holding his gaze easily. Frank didn't get any indication that Sproul was their man, but she let Noah play out the interview.

An hour later he stood and motioned Frank to follow him outside.

"I don't think this kid knows shit," he said.

"I don't either. Let's lose him."

They went back into the box.

"Mr. Sproul, do you have any vacation plans?"

"No."

"So if we came to find you at home in a day or two, or at work, you'd be there?"

"Well, yeah. I mean if I wasn't out, or..."

"Or what?" Frank asked.

"Or in jail."

"Why would you be in jail?"

"Felony possession," he reminded her patiently.

"We're going to let you go, Mr. Sproul. Don't leave town. Here's our number. If you have to leave you'd better call us first or you're going to be in a world of hurt."

Sproul couldn't believe he was being let go.

"What's the catch?"

"No catch. Let's just say you owe us one."

Sproul clearly wasn't happy about owing the LAPD a favor, but he was eager to get home.

"So I'm free to go?"

Frank nodded dispassionately. She was hungry and tired, and it seemed like all the cases lately were diggers, but knowing that the interviewee was always watching the interviewer, Frank betrayed no emotion. She opened the door, and Daniel Sproul scuttled out to find his next fix.

His worst fears erupted into life when his father put the car in park and quietly told him, "Get up to your room." With a certainty that made his sphincter spasm, he recognized the flat expression reflected in the rearview mirror. Not only had the boy's terror come to life, it had grown and taken wing and was flopping about in the evening's growing shadows.

At the front door he cast his mother a soundless plea. She deftly fielded her son's glance and shot back one of her own. It too was sickeningly familiar, silently reproaching. You've disappointed your father and now we'll both have to pay.

The boy used the banister to drag himself upstairs. The terror flapped all around him. He heard his mother ask with a practiced tone carefully blended of equal parts concern and empathy, "When would you like dinner, dear?"

In a gritty voice, his father answered, "When I'm through with the boy."

Perched heavily on the boy's thin shoulders, the terror settled into its nest.

5

On October 19th, when Melissa Agoura failed to meet her friends at Kenneth Hahn, they called her house to find out where she was. By 9:00 P.M., three hours after dark, Mrs. Agoura called the police. LAPD was swamped with missing person complaints. A perfunctory investigation was conducted two days later, but the disappearance of a sixteen-year-old girl in L.A. didn't generate much investigative work.

Two weeks into the case, Noah and Frank interviewed and reinterviewed people in and around the vicinity of the park. Joggers, picnickers, old men and kids fishing in the small ponds—none recognized Agoura or recalled anything odd around the time she disappeared.

Heading back to the station late one afternoon, Noah sighed, "You know what gets me more than anything?"

Frank felt the question was rhetorical and just glanced at her partner.

"Not the stupidity, not the senselessness, not the blood or gray matter, I mean that's just biology and death, they're inevitable. What gets me is the goddamned apathy. How many people have we shown her picture to?"

Frank shrugged.

"And how many have cared?"

"This is L.A., No. People see dead faces every day."

"I don't care if it's Buchenwald! This is their neighborhood, one of their own. She died in their own backyard and no one gives a shit. No one wants to get involved."

With half an ear Frank listened to Noah's tirade. Of all the cops she'd worked with, and after fourteen years on the force, Noah was still the most passionate. Peace officers, especially in a huge metropolis, had to develop some kind of emotional armor against the daily traumas they dealt with. Noah's armor was forged of dark humor and constant complaints that belied an unyielding optimism. Tirades were his way of blowing off steam. After seeing the worst people could do to each other, he still believed in and expected the best. He'd explained once that it was the only way he could continue to do his job and raise three kids. He had to keep believing, but it was an effort in the face of what he dealt with every day. When it got too much, he blew.

On the other hand, Frank was always prepared for the worst. Noah was frustrated they weren't getting anywhere on the case; Frank accepted it easily and just kept chipping away. They'd talked to three of Agoura's girlfriends again, the ones she was really tight with. One of the girls had been a little hinky, and when Frank pressed her she'd burst into tears. Seems she had a wicked crush on the boyfriend and had been trying to lure him from Melissa. But that was all she was guilty of. The girls basically reiterated what the family and boyfriend said.

They interviewed casual acquaintances, classmates, an ex-boyfriend. Same story. Agoura hadn't been in any trouble, she had her steady friends, steady boyfriend. They engaged in the usual teenage mischief and highjinks—nothing serious enough to get her killed. Agoura was a square peg who'd somehow ended up in a round hole. Most murders were not accidental, but Agoura's victimology was all wrong. She apparently had no connection to anyone from the area or that school. She wasn't dealing or using, she wasn't hooking, she wasn't a banger. As far as Frank and Noah could tell, she had no reason to be in the 'hood.

Back at the station, Noah dropped all his paperwork on his desk and headed home. Frank lingered in her office, scanning Crocetti's terse protocol again. Time of death was roughly 7:00 P.M. the night before she was found. The rape test located three light brown nonvictim pubic hairs. He confirmed there was no evidence of oral or vaginal rape, only anal. The multiple contusions and hematomas were seemingly made by a large, rounded instrument. Crocetti wouldn't commit to a specific weapon. The nature of her wounds was consistent with the time frame of her absence. Her right shoulder had been dislocated before she was killed. There was no evidence of postmortem injury.

The forensic tests had finally come back, and Frank studied them one more time. The fragments of wood that Crocetti had plucked from the ripped tissues was elderberry, *Sambucus glauca*. Frank's knowledge of botany didn't extend beyond long-stemmed roses, and she'd asked the lab tech if elderberry was common in the area.

"Commoner than crabs in a whorehouse," he'd responded. "It grows wild all over the place."

There were isolated fibers found on Agoura: red nylon combed from her hair; white nylon and an additional red one pulled out of several lacerations. Cotton fibers corresponded to the last outfit she was seen in. Four blue nylon fibers appeared to be from vehicle carpeting, and a handful of green/gold carpet fibers were also found on the body. The adhesive from her wrists turned out to be a common 3M brand of packing tape. Nail scrapings revealed nothing, and her tox test was clean. It wasn't much to go on.

Frank sighed, closing the binder. She didn't need it open anyway; she had already memorized the sparse information within. She shut her eyes for a moment and indulged her fatigue. She should be home sitting on her Soloflex, not here. But it was quiet in the squad room after hours, and Frank loved the silence. She'd never admit it, but there was no place in the world she felt as safe. She doodled on a yellow legal pad and her thoughts rode in the wake of the pen.

Another puzzle was that Agoura had evidently been held against her will and tortured for three days. Death on Frank's turf was usually sudden—drive-bys, stabbings, ODs. Kidnappings and torture weren't unheard of, but they were usually highly personalized. That Agoura's face was basically unmarked and her sexual organs were free of mutilation suggested that Agoura might have been a stranger to the perp. The anal assault seemed to be the focus of his anger. That was a curiously gender-neutral area of assault, adding to the impersonality of the attack. It also suggested that he may have done time.

On one side of the paper Frank wrote *Average or Above Average Intelligence*. Whoever had done this to Agoura certainly was reasonably smart. Not only had he abducted her with no witnesses, but he'd managed to keep her and batter her for three days without anyone seeming to know about it. Then he'd dumped the body on a city sidewalk and still hadn't been seen.

Frank leaned out of her chair and pulled a dusty notebook off the shelf on the wall. A few years ago she'd participated in a criminal profiling fellowship with the FBI. Part of the work included analyzing the behavior patterns and personalities of serial criminals.

Frank scrutinized her Quantico notes and, just for kicks, started profiling Agoura's perp. Hunched over her desk well into the night, her doodling evolved into an intricate list.

Friday evening at the Alibi was packed. Nancy Kreiger had given up clearing the empties from squad nine-three's table. Except for Jill, who'd gone home exhausted, and Bobby, who was on call and nursing a Coke, the squad was pounding back Buds and Murphy's Irish stouts. The talk had gone from shop to football. Nookey was collecting money for the weekend games.

Taquito, Ike, and Briggs were in a heated discussion about why the Raiders sucked wind. Bobby nodded quietly, backing Johnnie, and over the din of happy-hour voices and clanking glass, Frank was explaining to the rest of the squad why the Chiefs should walk away with the AFC title.

Because she was his boss, Gough had to treat Frank with some respect at work, but off the clock he refused to take her seriously, especially about football. Now he was jabbing a finger at her, saying there was no way the Chiefs could sustain their momentum against the Broncos. They waged battle through another pitcher of stout and in the end settled on a fifty dollar bet. Frank conservatively took the Chiefs by two, and to put his money where his mouth was, Boy-red opted for Denver with a ten-point spread. Nookey held the money. No one came to the Alibi on Friday without cash in their pockets.

"I hope Jeannie doesn't find out about this," Nookey gloomily warned his partner.

"She'll find out when I take her out to dinner on La Freek's Ben Franklin."

Frank's smile was thin and enigmatic. Noah winked at her and said near her ear, "You're Mona Lisa gone over to the other camp."

Her smile widened a bit. She and Noah had been friends for a long time. In the early years he'd had a gentle crush on her, part of the allure being the impossibility of attaining her. The affection that had remained between them was built on mutual trust and admiration.

Reaching for a pitcher, Nancy leaned her considerable breasts between the two detectives. Noah made a pained expression and Frank was suddenly fascinated by a scar on the tabletop.

"'Nother round?"

"I gotta get going," Noah said to her chest. Bobby echoed, "Me, too."

Frank inclined her head toward Ike and Johnnie. "How about another round for the drunks at the end of the table."

After paying the tab, Frank walked out with Bobby and Noah. The air felt cool and fresh. She said good night to her detectives, offering to drive Noah home. He wasn't much of a drinker but he kept up with everyone on Fridays.

"I'm fine," he said.

"Alright. Say hi to Tracey for me, and the kids."

"Tracey misses you. Says she never sees you any more."

The grimace that passed for Frank's smile quickly twisted her face.

"Tell her I miss her too."

"You going back to the office?"

Frank leaned against her open door, considering. The beer felt good inside her. She was ready to call it a week.

"Nope. I think I'll go home."

"Good girl. You've put in your obligatory twenty, thirty hours of OT. Get some rest."

"Yessir."

"Goddamnit, I love it when you get all military on me."

"I'm going to get military on your ass if you don't get out of here."

"See? Look! Goosebumps," Noah said pointing to his wrist.

Frank wagged her head as Noah folded his lanky frame into his old car. They pulled out of the lot and already she missed his camaraderie, feeling the loneliness of the weekend seeping in like the chill around the window frames. As she approached the freeway, Frank thought about going back to the office, but that would only be putting off the inevitable. Instead she cruised slowly home, resigning herself to the company of the radio and the cheery glow of brake lights and turn signals.

She stopped at the grocery store, buying a pork loin and a good Pinot Noir, then picked up a bouquet of flowers from the hippie girl on the corner.

"Hi-i," the girl drew out the greeting with a big, dopey smile.

"Hey," Frank said. "How's it going?"

"It's so-o slow tonight," the girl said uncomplainingly. "You're only my fourth customer. I was gonna close up but I knew you'd be here."

"Well, now you can go home, get warm."

"Yeah," the girl giggled, handing Frank her change. "See you next week."

Frank rolled away, marveling at the wonder of good drugs. The girl was either always high, or she was an old stoner and had smoked so much for so long she'd become permanently goofy. But rain or shine, dark or day, the girl was on her corner peddling her flowers. It occurred to Frank she didn't even know her name.

Frank pulled into the dark driveway and the sensor light came on. Inside, a lamp was already lit. Frank didn't notice it anymore unless the bulb blew. In the beginning her heart had lifted when she'd seen the warm light coming from the window, until she realized it was just the damn timer and there was really no one home waiting for her.

Frank poured a glass of the Pinot, then studded the roast with garlic gloves. She pinched some rosemary from a bush in the backyard and sprinkled it over the meat, along with a generous dusting of salt and pepper. Quartered potatoes got tossed in a bowl with lemon juice, olive oil, and bay leaves, then snuggled around the roast to cook in its drippings.

Sliding the baking dish into the oven, Frank turned her attention to trimming the flowers, carefully standing them in the same vase she always used. The glass one Mag had always insisted on. She wiped up the kitchen, put the flowers on the big glass table, then realized there was nothing else to do. She changed out of her work clothes and into shorts. The gym distracted her until her watch beeped that the roast was ready. C-SPAN and the newspaper were her dinner companions at the coffee table in the living room. Later, while she did the dishes and finished the wine, she was buzzed enough to hum along softly with Ella Fitzgerald.

A typical Friday night followed by a typical weekend. Barring a call-out, Saturday morning she'd sleep late—dawn being late for Frank—then work out for a couple of hours. Then she'd return to the office, dropping her dry cleaning off on the way. She'd catch up on paperwork until evening, then stop at the Alibi for a while. It was usually slow on the weekends, but she'd stay for a pint or two and let Nancy flirt with her. Then it was back home to the news, law enforcement journals, and more beer.

Sundays started the same, only she'd go to the Alibi before the office to watch whatever games were on. Johnnie was always there, and Gough and Ike showed up fairly regularly. Nookey and Diego usually made it to the afternoon game, and sometimes Bobby would stop in. By Sunday evening, Frank would be feeling good that it was all downhill to Monday. There was safety in this numbing ritual and Frank didn't deviate from it. Nor could she possibly know it was all about to change.

He showed the boy his first Playboy *when he was eight. The boy had been nervous, not sure how his father wanted him to react. His father had called him into the office. Patting the ripped loveseat, he made the boy sit next to him. His father opened the magazine on his lap, pointing at women's parts and calling them names the boy had never heard before, not even in science class. The boy had been too nervous and too young to be excited by the pictures. His father touched him, trying to encourage the anticipated response. When it wasn't forthcoming he became agitated, angry. Called the boy a homo.*

He knew what a homo was. A couple of the boys at school called him that. The father continued berating his son as he unzipped his fly, proving what happened to men when they saw naked women. The boy only shrank up tighter. The father's tone was too familiar, and when he asked, "Are you my bitch?" he lost the shred of hope he'd harbored, sinking instead to his knees, bending over like a dog. While he waited helplessly for it to end, he dreamed how someday he'd be a man and he'd be the one in back, grunting and pumping instead of crying on all fours.

6

Y ou know I hate these goddamned machines," Frank said to Noah, indicating the lone computer sitting on a rickety table. The squad had gotten its first computer six months ago, but it still wasn't connected to the other seventeen divisions within the LAPD. Figueroa detectives either had to bribe someone at Parker Center to check information for them or get in their cars and drive downtown to do it themselves.

"What takes you twenty minutes takes me twenty hours. I need you go to Parker and run Kenneth Hahn through the database. Pull up whatever arrests and major incidents happened there over the last six months."

"Shit, by the time I do that I could teach you how to do it."

Frank peered mystified at the keyboard and muttered, "It's good to be king."

Noah told her as he walked out of the squad room that seeing as they were about to enter the twenty-first century, she might want to try and get a handle on the twentieth.

Later that day he tossed the report on Frank's desk.

"How'd you get that already?"

"Called in a favor. Hey, I got the subpoena signed to pick up Luther Jackson. Johnnie and I are gonna go serve him. Then I'm gonna try and get to the last half of Leslie's game."

"Who's she playing?"

"St. Joseph's. Wanna come? They're really good."

Frank was already reading the list.

"Next time. Thanks for getting this."

"Sure. See ya tomorrow."

Noah paused at the doorway. Frank was engrossed in the printout as he said, "You know, the nine-three would crumble if you ever got a life, Frank."

She grunted without looking at him. He reminded her, uselessly, not to work too late. Fishing around in the top drawer, she pulled out a green highlighter and started marking all the rapes on the list. Agoura's perp had been into rape. He might have started with them and worked his way up to homicide. Tomorrow she would go to headquarters and review the rape cases one by one, in more detail. There might be a pattern among them that resembled Agoura's.

When she finished coloring the list, Frank shrugged into her wool blazer and headed for the Alibi. She caught the second half of Monday night football, but later, after she'd only been asleep for two hours, she was called out on a domestic with Gough and Nookey.

She arrived at the Dalido Arms apartments and Gough told her the story.

"Twenty-eight-year-old male Hispanic. Girlfriend stabbed him in the heart. Neighbors say they were fighting all night 'bout some other bitch he's bumping. Suspect denied the whole thing. Said she was cutting onions and he'd startled her. She'd turned with the knife in her hand and he'd run into it.

"Man," Gough said through the exhaustion born of a career in homicide and too little sleep, "if I had a dollar for every time someone ran into a knife in this town, I could have retired ten years ago."

Nookey shot his partner a look and hissed. They took the woman back to the station and tried working a confession out of her. The two older detectives were masters at coaxing confessions. Frank observed from behind the one-way mirror. She'd learned a lot from them over the years and still took pleasure in watching them work off each other. Seeing them interact she suddenly realized just how much Nookey was going to miss his partner. Frank uncomfortably pushed the feeling aside and concentrated on the detectives' dialogue.

By the time the rest of the squad rolled in at 6:00 A.M., Nookey had a signed confession and his suspect was sleeping downtown in a jail cell. Gough was typing the report as Frank interrupted him to ask why he'd called her out on that case—he and Nookey could have handled it in their sleep.

"We were asleep," Nookey said.

"Yeah. Just thought you'd like to see the masters at work," Gough responded, without looking up.

As squad supervisors, Frank or Foubarelle were on call for all homicides. If it was an uncomplicated case, like this one, the responding detectives usually handled it on their own. If they were green or new to the squad, Frank insisted on a supe rolling with them. But her squad was all seasoned veterans. Gough and Nookey had needed her tonight like a dog needs fleas. Boy-red had called her out just to tweak her.

"You did good," she said, and walked away. Gough rolled his eyes and Nookey chuckled. His partner was forever failing to get Frank's goat.

Briggs was dressed nicely for a morning in court, but Frank recognized the bloodshot eyes and slight tremor as he pulled his papers together.

On her way to her office she clapped him on the back.

"Rough night?"

"Aren't they all?" he asked seriously, and Frank had to agree. She remembered vague, uneasy dreams and was relieved she couldn't remember more.

After the morning briefing, Frank headed over to Parker Center with the NCIC printouts in her briefcase. The Agoura case was getting as cold as Melissa in her grave. The longer cases sat, the harder they were to solve. But Frank was a master at perseverance, and Agoura was quickly becoming a personal challenge. Frank hadn't actively worked a case in months. She loved pitting herself against the perps, though, and Agoura's was offering a nice edge. Frank was ready for it, wanted it.

She offered curt hellos to the faces that recognized her and quickly settled herself in front of an empty computer. Even though she knew how to use the basic functions, she hated the machines. She liked the old-fashioned method of digging through files, pulling folders, having pictures and statements and notes spill out with their dusty smells.

As she was writing down information from the computer screen the pager on her belt went off. The watch sergeant. She called in from an empty desk.

"I got good news and bad news for ya," he teased.

"What have you got, Artie?"

The sergeant happily reported. "Bad news is you got a double at a rock house on 70th and Denker."

Frank sighed. There weren't supposed to be so many homicides this time of year. The weather was bad, days were shorter, people more mellow. Didn't the perps know that?

"So what's the good news?"

"Looks like they already got the shooter."

"Alright. Thanks."

Frank hung up, stuffing papers back into the briefcase. She backed out of the computer, figuring Agoura was going to get a little colder.

Frank got home around eight o'clock, pumped and pressed, slammed a couple of beers, and fell asleep with an *FBI Law Enforcement Bulletin* on her chest. At some point she woke up enough to turn off the light and stretch deeper under the thin down comforter.

A while later her own cries jerked her out of sleep. Frank stumbled from the bed, tears blurring her vision. Still not sure where she was, she groped toward the bathroom. She slapped cold water on her face but couldn't look at herself. Clutching a towel, she breathed into it deeply, unable to wash away the dream or the pain it had summoned.

The water running in the sink didn't drown the shotgun still pounding in her head, and no matter how tightly she squeezed her eyes, Frank couldn't stop seeing Mag's bewildered face. She rinsed and rinsed under the running water, sure she was still covered in blood. She fought for reality, forcing herself to acknowledge the blue towels, her pink brush, the words on the tube of toothpaste.

"Clean teeth...healthy feeling gums...a great taste," Frank whispered. Finally she dared a glance in the mirror, certain there'd be blood all over her. Instead, she saw her own bewildered face. That broke the spell. With a strangled cry, Frank slammed a fist into the mirror. The glass exploded and Frank cursed, slugging with her other fist. Panting like she'd just sprinted a quarter mile, Frank stared at her bloodied knuckles, wincing at the glass splinters stuck under the skin. The pain was clear and clean, and it distracted Frank from her inner anguish. A fat silver shard was imbedded in the back of her gun hand. Frank yanked it loose. Mesmerized, she watched as her blood flowed against the white porcelain. After her heart slowed a little and her breathing evened out, she plucked out the most obvious shards, clamping her teeth down against the pain even as she relished it. Welcomed it.

"Let's get you a drink," she murmured, wrapping the towel

around her hand and talking herself into the kitchen.

"You're alright," she whispered steadily. "Everything's okay. Everything's alright."

She was reassuring herself like she'd done as a kid, when her mom was on a manic high and breaking dishes so they could go out and buy a new set, or when she was in bed for the tenth day in a row and Frank had eaten absolutely everything edible in the house. Carefully taking a glass out of the cupboard, she filled it with Scotch. She drained it. Bleeding, still shaking, she poured more.

The alarm startled Frank out of a deep sleep. She was stunned by the ache in her head. She threw a hand over the buzzer only to feel worse pain. Then she remembered the dream and its terror, smashing her fist in the mirror, and the blood, and trying to wash it away with Scotch as she'd roamed uneasily through the empty house.

Frank sat up woozily, reaching for the bedside lamp with her left hand. It was stiff and swollen too, but at least it wasn't throbbing like the right. The light stabbed through Frank's eyes and lodged in her brain. When she rolled out of bed her stomach rolled with her. Stepping gingerly into the bathroom, she searched for lurking shards she hadn't mopped up last night. She groped under the sink for a bottle of Pepto Bismol, chugged a quarter of it, and chased it with four aspirin. She dozed under the hot spray of the shower until the pharmaceutical cocktail took effect.

The fine cut of her suit couldn't mask the slump in Frank's shoulders as she mixed sugar in water over the kitchen sink. The drink would simultaneously fight her dehydration and fatigue. Although the coffee trickling through the percolator smelled noxious, the caffeine would help move the fog out of her brain. Frank had been through this before, she knew the drill.

Thirty minutes later she was at her desk, still exhausted, her hand on fire, but at least the worst of her physical pain had eased. The other, she couldn't do anything about. The phone rang in the squad room and she heard Noah answer it, then a second later he whistled. When he draped his lanky frame around her doorway, she squinted at him through the haze of her hangover.

"We got a 187 at Carver Junior High. Female Caucasian. Looks like a teenager. Naked and beat to shit."

Frank was up and swinging into her jacket before Noah had finished talking.

"Come on," she said to Gough as she breezed by him. He protested he wasn't on the clock yet, and Frank whirled on him with more than fury in her eyes. He grumbled but put down his paper and followed. As they clattered into the garage Frank pulled out her cell phone and dialed Foubarelle's home number, but before it rang, she disconnected and began calling her detectives in instead. The three of them piled into the same car and drove under the low dark clouds that hovered over the city.

"Maybe we're getting that damn El Niño after all," Gough grunted from the backseat.

"I could live without it," Noah replied, but Gough, the gardener, insisted the rain would be good.

"It'll fill up all the reservoirs so we won't have to do water rationing. God, I hate that."

As usual, Noah drove and Frank turned her attention to the city outside her window. She saw the broken houses, rubble-strewn lots, crippled cars, cryptic banger messages on anything that held still long enough. An old woman slowly pushed a grocery cart piled with cardboard and tattered plastic bags. She looked as gray as the sky, and an image of the light fading from Mag's eyes squeezed into Frank's head. She clenched her jaw tightly and forced her thoughts back to work.

If this was another job by the same perp, they were fucked. RHD would be all over it, especially with another white girl. Fubar and his brass monkeys would be jumping down their throats, and the media would go ape-shit. That was the down side. On the up side, if this job was related to Agoura, it might provide new material for them to work.

As if reading her mind, Noah started speculating on the similarities so far between this call and Agoura's. He was excited, but Frank was withdrawn and answered him with only a small dip of her head, hoping he'd have the good sense to leave her alone today.

They'd been through a lot of blood and a lot of beer together. Frank had been there at the hospital when his first child was born—she was Leslie's godmother. When Tracey was on the warpath, Noah spent a lot of nights in Frank's guest bed, and Frank had crashed on their couch a time or two. He knew why she put in the excruciating hours, pounded mercilessly on the weights, and why he poured her into a cab sometimes at the Alibi. He was also the closest Frank had to a friend. She knew that sooner or later he was going to ask her what was wrong.

He parked across from the school. As she fumbled for the door handle with her bandaged hand, Frank noticed his wondering glance. Ike and Bobby were already there, talking with a knot of uniformed police and onlookers. A gust of raw wind blew Frank's jacket open, and she buttoned it with her good hand. She didn't bother talking with the responding officers, letting Noah do it instead. She stood within earshot, dreading the telltale signs of another dump.

Frank peered under the white sheet covering the victim's body. No clothes, no ID. The girl was heavily bruised, sprawled akimbo on the broken concrete. Frank looked around. There was nothing for them to work with, but she had already requested crime scene techs. She checked behind her, relieved at least that there were no news vans. She knelt on one knee and gently lifted the cover sheet away.

Under it, a young girl was fixed forever in the transition from child to woman. Bruises painted her soft skin with all the colors of an impending storm—deep purple mixed to black, dark gray tinged with yellow, magenta fused to sallow green. The girl's hair spread out behind her, dull and knotted. Her eyes were half open and buried in dark pillows of flesh that puffed up from the twisted nose below. Clots of old blood clogged the nostrils.

Frank made a couple of notes on her pad, then continued her examination. The skin next to the girl's nose was split deep enough to reveal her right cheekbone. Other than a rawness which could have come from a gag, the bottom of her face was remarkably untouched. Her lips were full and parted softly. Frank knelt closer and lifted the upper lip with her pen. Her right front tooth was chipped.

Discoloration in a line around her throat indicated strangulation, but when Frank searched under the eyelids she couldn't see any signs of petechial hemorrhage. The left collarbone jutted abnormally under swollen, vividly hued skin. The welter of bruises continued almost unbroken to her knees, which were scraped as well. They had already scabbed, indicating the abrasions were made before she was dumped. Frank checked the exposed edges of the body for drag marks, but the bruising was too severe to reveal slight marks. Heavier scrapes might show up when the coroner's people rolled the body. Chafing around her ankles and wrists suggested she'd been bound.

Frank chewed on the inside of her lip. She'd seen a lot of battery in sixteen years, but this was right at the top of the list. Agoura's beatings had been severe, but if the perp who'd done this girl was the same guy, he was escalating his assaults to a new level.

Handley arrived, out of breath, coat flapping. His buttons would never again meet their respective holes on the far side of his protruding belly. He started his perusal of the body as Frank looked over at Noah. He was kneeling too, on the other side of the girl, and Frank heard him whisper something. He had lost his characteristic enthusiasm. When his eyes met Frank's they were sad.

"This guy's a fucking monster."

Frank quietly sucked in a deep breath and nodded impassively. Much as she hated to, it was time to call Foubarelle. At least the press hadn't gotten wind of it yet. That looked like the only break they were getting. When Jack rolled the dead girl, they saw unmistakable signs of anal assault and lots of dried blood. Frank's ardor for the chase was suddenly dampened. Whoever had done this was loose, was good, and probably would do this again. What she'd read from her Quantico notes the other night indicated she could well have a serial perp on her hands.

The realization only made the gray day darker. When Foubarelle arrived, Frank didn't mention anything about a serial perp. She listened to the SID techs scream at him for being called out on a case with no evidence. They hated Frank but she didn't care; they were the evidence experts, not her. A lot of cops liked to hot-dog a scene, but Frank wasn't about to lose a case because of an evidentiary oversight on her part. If there was nothing there, she wanted to hear it from SID.

On the other hand, she and her squad had the rare respect of the coroner's personnel. Detectives were always pushing their vics to the front of the coroner's to-do list, but Frank rarely allowed her cops to do that. The morgue had enough work to handle without every homicide detective in the LAPD trying to get their victims cut first. Frank saved her requests for true emergencies, like today. As Handley made an incision over the liver, ready to insert the thermometer that would help determine the time of death, Frank said quietly, "Jack, I know you've got at least a dozen bodies in line before this one, but it would really help if you could push this ahead."

She tipped her head toward Foubarelle. "And it'll save Crotchety from having to deal with him because I can guarantee that's his next stop."

Jack frowned, playing with the power he had on the street. He knew it ended with a sharp command from his boss once they got back to the morgue.

"I'll see what I can do," he said pompously.

"I'd appreciate it."

Frank turned to deal with Foubarelle just as the first news van showed up.

The next time his father took him into the office with a magazine tucked under his arm, the boy knew what to do. He responded to his father's touch, feigned interest in the pictures, kept shoving his hand against himself like his father was doing. Just as he was beginning to think it wouldn't happen this time, his father ordered him breathlessly to get down and accompanied him quickly onto the bright green rug. He tried to pretend it was grass and that he was outside playing. Soon his mother would call him in for dinner and his father wouldn't hurt him with anything more than a hearty slap on the shoulder.

After his father got off, he told the boy to leave. He walked painfully up the stairs and quietly closed his bedroom door behind him. Curling into a ball under the covers, he reasoned that at least this time it hadn't taken very long. He slipped into a nap, comforted by a familiar image of himself straddling the stuffed bear he kept under his pillow.

7

Squad 93 spent the day canvassing the area. A janitor had found the body on the sidewalk in front of the school. Dispatch received his call at 0613 hours. It had been cold last night. Not a lot of people had been out, and parked cars obscured the body from the street.

The victim was found on her back, but lividity indicated she'd been dead for at least ten hours. She'd been left on her stomach—whoever killed her hadn't moved her until her blood had settled anteriorly. She had to have been dumped sometime before dawn, which also explained why she hadn't been discovered earlier. Frank had SID print the cars on the school side of the street. Maybe their guy had bumped into one and steadied himself with a bare hand. She copied the license numbers and makes.

Flanking the school were a shoe repair shop and a taqueria. Two vacant buildings, a styling salon, a mom-and-pop burger stand, a Frostee Freeze, and an Assembly of God church were across the street. They were all covered with sprawling gang tags. A boarded and crumbling building in a large, weedy lot looked like a shooting gallery, and Frank had uniforms bagging matchbooks and cigarette packs, torn soda cans, used hypos, potato chip bags—all the trash in there. She wanted everything printed. A pile of old clothes and rags looked like a makeshift bed. If somebody'd been in here last night she wanted to know who.

The church had had a service the day before but it had finished by 8:00 P.M. and there wasn't another scheduled until noon today. No one opened when they knocked, no lights were on. They talked to people at the food joints, which all closed at 11:00 or midnight. The salon was open 9:00-6:00, shoe repair 8:00-5:00. No one was around at the time they believed the body was dumped.

The detectives spent the morning showing Polaroids of the girl's face to everyone at the school, but they didn't get one good hit. She was pretty battered, though, so chances were they wouldn't have gotten an ID anyway. Missing Persons records were no help this time. They broke for lunch around one o'clock, ordering gorditas and tacos at the taqueria next to the school. The school kids didn't like all the heat around; they ate across the street at the burger place. Frank was feeling human again. She munched on fried pork between two soft corn tortillas, wondering why these girls were being dumped in front of schools. If it was the same guy, she reminded herself. So far they had nothing but speculation to go on. Frank glanced at her watch. She was waiting for Crocetti's call. His prelim would tell them more about any similarities between this case and Agoura's.

She was anxious for the ID on the vic, too. Handley had rolled her fingers, promising to have Frank paged as soon as the prints were run. She was wadding up the paper her tacos came in when her pager went off. She nudged her jacket aside with an elbow and glanced at the number. It was the coroner's office. She returned the call.

"Hey, Lieutenant," Handley bragged, "I've got a name for your girl."

"Tell me."

"Jennifer Peterson. DOB: 1/5/82." Handley paused.

Frank asked, "Address?"

Handley gave it to her. She thanked him tersely and hung up. She called the operator and referenced the phone number. When Frank tried it, all she got was the answering machine. She identified herself and told the machine she had some information about Jennifer Peterson that she needed to discuss with her parents. No one picked up.

Frank grabbed Noah. "Let's go for a drive."

She filled him in as they drove west on Manchester Boulevard to Sepulveda. The address took them to a tired house in Culver City bordered by frayed banana trees and overgrown bougainvillea. It looked tropical despite the spitting sky and sixty-degree weather. When their knock went unanswered, they split up to talk to the neighbors. Two houses down, the harassed mother of three preschoolers told Noah that Jennifer Peterson babysat for her. Her mother's name wasn't Peterson, it was Wyche, Delia Wyche, and she was a nurse at Brotman Memorial. She wasn't sure where the husband worked, but he was home a lot. Jennifer called him the grease monkey and didn't care much for him.

Noah thanked the woman, then flagged Frank back to the car. At Brotman, a meticulously dressed man in personnel confirmed there was a Delia Wyche, R.N., on staff. Frank asked him to page Wyche's supervisor, and he balked that it wasn't his job. Noah grinned as Frank leaned within inches of the fey young man and asked, "Have you ever had a nine-millimeter revolver shoved up your ass?"

Maybe because he saw Noah grinning, maybe because he was suicidal, maybe because he was more ballsy than smart, he swallowed hard and retorted, "No, but I think I'd like it."

That was absolutely the wrong thing to say. Before the clerk could even flinch Frank had his perfect Windsor knot clenched in her bad hand and twisted tight under his Adam's apple. Noah's smile had faded, and suddenly the clerk didn't feel so brave.

He tried to squeak "police brutality," but Frank tightened her grip, her blazing eyes still only inches from his. Blood started oozing through her bandage.

"Okay, funny boy. Are you going to call Mrs. Wyche's supervisor or do I charge you with refusing to cooperate with a peace officer and obstructing justice?"

He weakly shook his head.

"You going to help me?"

He nodded.

"Good boy."

Frank let go and the man wheeled his chair farther from Frank's grasp. Noah pulled a quarter out of his pocket and tossed it into the clerk's lap.

"That's for later. After you call Mrs. Wyche's supervisor you can call LAPD and register a formal complaint about her. But you'll have to be patient. There's a lot of people in line ahead of you."

Frank turned her back and glanced at the fresh blood on her gauzed hand. Noah's gaze followed, and he asked what she'd done.

"Cut it," she said flatly and stepped out into the hallway. When Noah followed, he said softly, "You shouldn't have roughed him up like that."

Frank's head jerked toward Noah. Her eyes were bottomless blue chasms that a man could fall into and never be heard from again.

"Don't even start with me."

He flashed his palms in a peaceful gesture.

"Alright. I'm just saying if something's bugging you—"

"Nothing's bugging me."

"Alright. Okay."

Frank had unconsciously turned to face her partner in a fighter's stance, and Noah bowed his head, backing off. The LAPD's reputation for unnecessary aggression was well-founded, but Frank's presence was usually intimidating enough to get what she wanted out of a wit or a suspect. She rarely engaged someone physically, especially just a cluck-headed desk boy, and she was embarrassed that she'd lost her temper.

The nurse supervisor arrived, and Noah explained without detail about Delia Wyche's daughter. The supervisor went back down the hall to retrieve her employee as Frank asked the clerk for Mrs. Wyche's next of kin. She was promptly, silently handed a slip of paper with a name and number on it. The clerk eyed Frank warily, making sure he was well away from her reach. It occurred to her to apologize to the little bastard, but she didn't.

Frank glanced at the clock on the wall, wondering where the hell Wyche was. Noah'd been done with his shift hours ago. Frank felt a flicker of remorse for her behavior, but that reminded her of the dream and she quickly focused on the square yellow paper in her hand. She joined Noah, who was still waiting in the hallway. He was leaning against the wall, chewing on a nail. His suit was wrinkled and a tad short at the ankles and wrists.

"Anybody have a game today?"

"Naw. Just practice."

"You should call Tracey."

"She won't be home 'til later. I'll call after we do Wyche."

"You don't have to go the morgue. I'll take care of it."

Noah absently flapped one of his boney hands.

"It ain't no thing. Besides," he tried to joke, "the last thing I wanna do is leave you alone with a bereaved parent." Frank didn't smile. They were both relieved when the supervisor led Delia Wyche down the hallway. She took them to an office where they could talk, but before Frank had finished the introductions, Mrs. Wyche interrupted with the practiced snort of the chronically bitter.

"What's Jennie done now?"

Frank herded the heavy-hipped woman into a seat, explaining that they had a few questions. She wasn't avoiding telling the woman about her daughter, but it would be easier to get answers from her before she was too upset.

"Mrs. Wyche, is Jennifer Peterson your daughter?"

"'Fraid so. What did she do?" the woman repeated suspiciously.

Frank ignored her, asking when she'd last seen Jennifer.

"Oh, I don't know," she said offhandedly. "Maybe three, four days ago. Let's see, it must have been Sunday because she didn't come home for dinner. I remember because I went to a lot of trouble to make something she and Randy both like—Randy's my husband. He's not Jennie's father. I made pork chops. I try to make something they both like or else one of them bitches all through dinner and ruins everyone else's appetite. They never seem—"

Noah interrupted her.

"So you haven't seen Jennifer for three days?"

"That's right."

"And you weren't concerned about that?"

"Detective, you've got to understand, Jennie pulls stunts like this all the time. At first I was concerned, but when they started happening on a regular basis I just quit worrying. She always comes home sooner or later."

Not this time, Frank thought, and asked what it was that started happening on a regular basis.

Delia Wyche gathered her patience with a large sigh and explained, "When she started running off. The first time was three years ago, right after I remarried. She and Randy don't get along so good—she ran away to show me how unhappy she was. She did it a couple of times after that. I was worried in the beginning, but she's always just at a friend's house. I finally figured, let her knock herself out. I don't have time to chase her all over."

"Mrs. Wyche, can you tell us exactly when you last saw your daughter?"

"Well, yeah I can, but what's this all about? What sort of detectives are you anyway?"

Frank again ignored the questions and drilled the woman with a pitiless gaze.

"Mrs. Wyche, what was your daughter doing the last time you saw her?"

Mrs. Wyche wiggled uncomfortably in her chair. When she

answered, her voice was tinged with a whine.

"The last time I saw her was in the kitchen. I was doing the dishes—God forbid she or Randy should do them—and she came in to make herself a sandwich. She'd just gotten up, and she had her backpack with her. I asked her where she thought she was going, and she said to the park. Then I—"

"Which park?"

"The one off Jefferson, by all the oil derricks. It gives me the—"

"Do you mean the Culver City Park? With the ball fields?"

"I guess. It's the one off Duquesne, right off Jefferson," she said impatiently.

"Alright, then what?"

"I asked her about her homework, which she'd been putting off all weekend, and she asked what did I think she had in her pack? Then when I asked why she had to go to the park to study, she started bitching about the noise Randy was making in the garage."

"What was he doing?"

"Shoot, I don't know. He's got an old jeep he's always tinkering with. It hasn't run since I've known him, but you'd think with all the time he spends on that thing he had it in the Indy 500 every weekend."

She paused, searching for a glimpse of sympathy from either detective and finding none.

"You know I still don't know what you—"

"Just a few more questions, Mrs. Wyche. What happened next?"

"I don't know...nothing I think. I didn't want to listen to her and Randy going at it all day so I just let her go."

"How did she get there?"

"The bus. She takes it everywhere."

"Did she go to the park often?"

The woman nodded, then realized Noah had referred to her daughter in the past tense. When she asked again what her daughter had done, it was with a genuine note of concern in her voice. Frank had been standing near the door, letting Noah ask most of the questions. Now she crossed the small room and sat on the arm of the empty chair next to Delia Wyche.

"Mrs. Wyche," she said, as gently as one could say such a thing, "Jennifer is dead."

"No," she chuckled, "you've got somebody else's Jennifer. Mine couldn't possibly be dead."

She turned her head, smiling at Noah as if in confirmation of this very simple error, and when he didn't smile she looked back at Frank. The detectives could see comprehension slowly sinking in around the shock of the words. She shook her head.

"How do you know it's Jennie?" she whispered.

"Fingerprints. But we'd like you to come to the morgue with us to confirm that," Frank said, still gentle.

Her last sentence penetrated the shock, and Mrs. Wyche broke down in huge, gulping sobs. Noah offered the wad of tissues he always carried for such occasions, as Frank left the room to call Delia Wyche's husband.

Foubarelle finally caught up to Frank in her office the next day. She was knocking back a bottle of water and wiped her mouth on the back of her hand, characteristically unfeminine, characteristically Frank.

"I understand we have an ID on the girl at Carver."

Frank confirmed that, and Foubarelle complained that he always had to hear his information secondhand.

"We got with the mother at the morgue kind of late last night. I wanted to wait until she'd ID'd her but I didn't want to disturb you."

Foubarelle hated being bothered once he'd left the office. He didn't press the issue.

"So what have we got?"

Frank filled him in. When she was finished, he said, "Any word on the autopsy yet?"

"Crocetti's going to cut her. Hopefully first thing this morning."

"He said it looked similar to that girl we found at Crenshaw."

Frank almost snapped, *Great. Now Crocetti's a detective,* but she checked her temper. When she didn't respond, Foubarelle said impatiently, "Well? What do you think?"

Frank was debating how to tell him the truth without getting him too excited. She didn't want this case, or Agoura's, walking out the door to Robbery-Homicide. If Foubarelle was nervous about it he'd send it up in a blink. Both cases had drawn media attention, but fortunately the public didn't seem to notice. If Frank could keep a lid on them, she'd be alright. RHD only wanted high publicity, politically sensitive cases, and Foubarelle only wanted to ditch the ones he thought might make him look bad.

"I think it's possible."

"Shit." Foubarelle wiped his hand over his eyes. "Level with me, Frank. How big is this?"

Frank shrugged. Even Foubarelle had to see the deep-shit potential here. Despite her own qualms she assured him, "We can handle it."

"That doesn't tell me anything."

"Are you going to toss it to RHD?"

"If we're in over our heads, yes. If you think we can handle it, no."

Foubarelle crossed his arms and waited for her answer. He was putting the decision in Frank's hands. She really had to admire his spinelessness.

"It could be an impressive coup," she countered, throwing the ball back into his court.

"How confident are you?"

"We don't even know if this is the same perp yet. Assuming it is, he's got to slip sooner or later. All we need is some time."

"Give me an estimate."

"I can't," Frank sighed, "you know that. But we've got more on him than anyone else does."

"Oh really? Like what?"

Simply, with no trace of pretension, Frank said, "Me."

He became a fearsome football player. Even the kids on his own team were afraid of him. He didn't respect pain or fear and couldn't understand it in others. The coach frequently had to take him aside and point out that they just wanted players temporarily stopped, not maimed for life. He tried to control himself, but it felt so good to let go on the field. It was the only place he ever felt safe. He was in control out there: just him and the ball and bodies to block and slam into and hurt. He loved hurting the other players, and in a contact sport—if he was careful—he could get away with it. Yet, as satisfying as it was to see a kid writhing on the field with a torn kneecap or snapped ankle, there was still something missing.

8

Homicide victims are frequently killed by someone they know, so Frank and Noah wasted no time interviewing Randy Wyche. He had plausible excuses at the garage for the days around both Agoura's and his stepdaughter's disappearances, but because the police couldn't pinpoint the exact time of either girl's abduction, his alibi wasn't infallible. What they could more closely approximate was the time each girl died, and for those times, all Wyche had was his wife's backing. He readily admitted to not much caring for his stepdaughter, though he resented the fact that he was in any way a suspect in her death.

"We have to pursue all avenues," Frank explained patiently. "It's not uncommon for stepparents, especially in the heat of an argument, to kill their stepchildren. We see it a lot. It happens. Usually no one *means* for it to, but things just get out of hand..."

Frank trailed off and Noah asked, "Did you and Jennifer ever fight?"

"We had arguments, yeah, but nothing like this."

"Did you ever hit her?"

Wyche's head drooped toward the chipped linoleum, and Frank had to prod the answer.

"A couple times. She was so fresh, thought she knew everything."

"A teenager," Noah lied, "I've got one at home."

"Then you know how they are?" Wyche insisted.

"'Fraid so," he agreed, siding with the man. "Curfew's a big thing in our house. What about you? What did you and your stepdaughter argue over?"

"Everything. But the worst was when she'd just take off. It worried Dee sick. We got into a big fight about that one time. She called me a lazy fucker, said I couldn't tell her what to do, so I hauled off and smacked her. That shut her up."

"Where'd you hit her?"

"I slapped her face."

"What did she do after that?"

"I don't know. Ran up to her room crying, I guess. Her mother went after her."

"What did you do?" Frank pressed.

"Went out into the garage, I guess."

"What do you do in the garage?"

"I got a '56 Jeep I'm fixing up."

"How long you been working on it?"

"'Bout two or three years now. I don't get as much time out there as I'd like, especially with the weather we've been having lately."

Frank made a note to have Johnnie look at the car, to see if it had been worked on lately. She also wanted to check out the garage at Wyche's job. Whoever had killed Agoura, and now Peterson, had worked them over in a secluded place where they wouldn't be disturbed. Maybe one of the garages offered a spot like that.

"You said you'd hit her a couple of times," Frank said. "What were the other occasions?"

"Shit, I don't know, let me think. I know we had a big fight when she got arrested for shoplifting. We grounded her and she had a fit about that. Started mouthing off again."

"Where'd you hit her that time?"

"I don't know. It all happens so fast, you know. I didn't mean to hit her, but I got a temper you know, and I'm not just gonna take crap from some kid."

"How do you think you hit her?"

"I probably slapped her. I never like punched her out or anything. Not like the guy that did that to her," he said, indicating the photos arrayed before him.

"How do you know it was a man who did that to her?" Frank jumped on him.

"Why would a woman do it? I mean, whoever did this had to be pretty strong."

"You're pretty strong aren't you?"

"Yeah, but so are a lot of guys."

"Yeah, but a lot of guys don't have a bratty stepdaughter hanging around the house insulting them all day."

"Well, you're right, she could be a pain, but you don't kill someone for that."

"Isn't it true that you wished she'd go live with her father?"

"Yeah. I would've liked that a lot, but Dee would've hated it. It's her kid. She loved her."

"But you didn't."

"No," he shrugged, "I didn't."

"Man," Noah sighed, shaking his head, "it's hard enough having your own kids copping an attitude with you, but it must be really hard with a stepkid."

"It wasn't always so bad. We usually just ignored each other. Sometimes I'd even forget she was around."

Noah grinned sheepishly. Turning conspiratorially away from Frank he asked quietly, "Randy, you know I look at my girls and I think, man, they are lookers, but you know they're my *daughters*, but Jennifer, man, she was a pretty girl and she wasn't really your daughter. You know what I'm saying?"

Wyche shared the grin.

"Yeah, I hear you."

"Was she like into that at all with you? You know, you being the older man. Girls like that, huh?"

"Naw, nothing like that ever happened, but I'll tell you it was hard to not stare when she walked around in her nightie or in some of those shirts."

"So'd you ever get any? A little feel? Brush up against her in the hallway kinda thing?"

Wyche was motioning no, but he was blushing. Noah whispered lewdly, "But you *wanted* to, didn't you?"

"Crossed my mind a time or two," he agreed.

Noah was folded over the table toward Wyche, leering at him. "Did you get any?"

"Naw, man, nothing like that. She's my wife's daughter."

"Man, you didn't even try for a little? Who'd have known?"

Wyche was shaking his head. "Nah. It ain't right, you know? How'd you feel if some guy was poking *your* girl?"

"That'd be different," Noah conceded. "But she wasn't your girl."

Noah's line of attack was slipping away so Frank bluntly took over.

"Mr. Wyche, who's to say that nothing happened between you and Jennifer. You certainly wouldn't tell your wife about this and the only other person who'd know is dead. Why should we believe you didn't have a sexual relationship with Jennifer?"

Ticking off points on her fingers, Frank continued, "You've already told us you were attracted to her. You've already told us you hit her in anger. You've said you have a temper. You said you didn't like her—"

Now Noah interrupted. "Aw, man, I totally feel for you. It'd be so easy to lose your temper and what starts off as a slap turns into something else. And man, if I had a hunk of her in my hands...I don't know. I mean, one thing leads to another sometimes. I've been there."

Wyche adamantly protested to Frank, "Nothing like that happened. I know I lost my temper a couple times, but I never hurt Jennie. Not like that."

"Then how?" Frank asked.

"Like I told you."

"Tell us again," Noah soothed, and that's how it went for hours. Wyche's accounts never varied. The detectives didn't catch him in a lie or break his composure. He was earnest, insistent, and paced around the table during a five-minute break. It was Frank's observation, after thousands of interrogations, that guilty people tended to nod off. Sometimes they were so deeply asleep they'd fall out of the chair. Other times they'd curl up in the corner and be cutting Z's. But Wyche was worried, as well an innocent man should be with two homicide detectives grilling him like a cheese sandwich.

They let him go home after midnight. He was simultaneously relieved, exhausted, and furious. The detectives both apologized for the work-over but insisted they had to know, that Jennifer deserved the truth. The apology served a number of purposes: one, if Wyche really was innocent, it was a genuine apology to a citizen they were paid to protect. Two, lawsuits against the department were routine. Innocent or not, they didn't want Wyche going home pissed off. But most importantly, if Wyche *was* involved with the murder of either girl, he'd think he had the cops fooled and sooner or later he'd start bragging about it.

The squad room hummed with activity, but in her office Frank quietly sipped coffee while she reviewed Peterson's preliminary autopsy report. The bruising was nearly identical to Agoura's and of indeterminate origin. Peterson's nose, left clavicle, and the second and third fingers of her right hand were fractured. She'd been anally assaulted with no other evidence of sexual assault. This time, instead of an elderberry branch, the perp had used something resembling a yellow broom or mop handle.

Along the path of insertion, Crocetti's eyes had found minuscule fragments of yellow paint that had been sent to the lab for analysis. The trajectory of the path was similar to Agoura's, indicating a left-handed assaulter. Like Agoura, Peterson had bled to death slowly enough to know she was dying. Several major organs had been shredded, and again the perp had rammed his victim hard enough to pierce a lung. The coroner's team had found fibers similar to Agoura's, as well as what appeared to be blue nylon fibers and additional short brown hairs. They were on their way to the lab with the paint frags and tox samples.

The prints from the shooting gallery had come back with a lot of partials and unknowns, offering only two solid leads. Later in the day, Frank and Noah found one of them at a corner mart a block away from the high school. She was a nineteen-year-old black female, a strawberry. She was chain-smoking Kools, searching for someone to blow for a hit off a crack pipe. They worked her for about an hour, but she was useless and barely able to stay in her skin. Next they chased down a seventeen-year-old black male. Noah knew him. He had a crook in his nose and hustled ass, so everyone called him Hooker. He insisted he hadn't been in the gallery the night Jennifer Peterson died. Noah assured him they didn't want anyone in the shooting gallery for criminal charges.

"We're just looking for witnesses, and it ain't a gang thing. In fact, it's probably a white guy dumpin' his shit in your 'hood, makin' it look like somebody inside's doin' it. You'd like to see that mother caught, wouldn't you?"

"Be alright wit me," Hooker answered noncommittally.

"Besides, if you cooperate now, maybe we could cut you some slack later on down the line."

"Right," he said, disbelief written all over his face.

"I'm straight up with you, my man, I ain't lyin'."

"Ain't yo *man*."

"Look," Frank broke in, "even if you weren't there, just give us some names, tell us who shoots there regularly."

Through the GREAT sheet that the LAPD gang details generated, they'd already made a list of Hooker's homies. Noah spat them out.

"Does Dr. Dread hang there, or Little-Kool or maybe T-Square?"

At first Hooker looked surprised, then confused, and finally resigned.

"Sometime," he said, and supplied the detectives with the names of over a dozen junkies and crackheads.

It would take weeks for Frank and Noah to contact all the leads, but so far no one would admit to seeing anything the night Peterson's body had been dumped at Carver. And no sound of crowing from Randy Wyche, either.

Using the major incident list Noah had compiled from in and around the rec area, Frank had found some two dozen rapes and eight murders that might match their perp's MO and time frame. She spent Saturday morning poring through four of the thick rape folders. She discounted the first case because the rape victim was older, knew her attacker, and hadn't been raped anally. The second case was a woman who hadn't seen her assailant even though he'd talked to her, growling obscenities and directions while holding a gun to her neck. After careful consideration Frank put the folder in the reject pile in spite of the fact that the victim had been anally raped.

The next two cases had a lot of similarities. Both victims had been young teenagers, neither had seen their assailants, but they reported he was "strong" and "big" and hadn't said a word to either girl. After examining photographs, diagrams, victim statements, police reports, and hospital reports, Frank put the two folders in a "keeper" pile.

Pleased, she tipped back on the rear legs of the dining room chair and ran her fingers roughly through her hair. She watched the rain pissing down furiously on the other side of the sliding glass doors; it was the first good storm of the season. Gough'd be happy. So would Ike and Diego. They were on call, and good weather lent itself more readily to homicides than bad, so hopefully they'd have a quiet weekend. She thought about calling Noah but hated bugging him at home. Instead, she changed out of her sweats and headed down to the Alibi. Maybe Johnnie'd be around, and if not, at least Nancy could serve her a brew and a burger. But to Frank's surprise, neither of them were there. She straddled a seat at the bar, quickly dousing a tiny flicker of disappointment, and asked Mel where Nancy was.

"Called in sick. Got that damn flu everybody's down with. Stout?"

Frank nodded and ordered the hamburger.

"How's the dead body business?" Mel asked, wiping a slip of foam off her mug.

"Better than yours," she replied looking around.

"God, isn't that the truth. It's the rain. Keeps people home."

"Guess so."

Frank gazed onto the grimy, wet street, glad to be inside and dry. A gas fire glowed in the hearth opposite the entrance and cast warm light on the bar's dark wood. All the lights were on, and behind the jeweled bottles a huge mirror reflected them back.

"That's a damn shame 'bout all those dead girls, huh?"

"It's a shame, alright."

"You think it's the same guy?"

"Mel, how long have I been coming here?"

"A long time, Frank."

She nodded. "And have I ever discussed an open case with you?"

Mel shook his head, laughing. "And have I never not asked?"

Frank smiled softly, sucking the dark beer through its creamy foam, eyeing the football game playing over her head.

"Who's winning?"

"Trojans, six to three."

"Sounds like a baseball score," she noted, glancing back down at the jeweled mirror. Johnnie was jogging outside the barred window, head tucked into his jacket against the rain. He ran inside, shaking himself out of his wet coat like a dog.

"Goddamn, it's cold!" he bellowed, pulling out the stool next to Frank's. "Mel! Hit me with a whiskey beer back," he ordered, his voice husky.

They discussed the day's college games while Mel poured. Then Mel drifted toward the other end of the bar to take care of two uniforms Frank recognized. Johnnie said, "Heard Fubar reamed you a new asshole yesterday."

Johnnie was talking about a newscast the mayor had heard where the anchor claimed LAPD sources confirmed Agoura's and Peterson's murderers were, indeed, the same person. He'd gone on to make some other erroneous claims, and the mayor had called

Foubarelle in a tizzy to find out why he hadn't been told about this first. The captain, in turn, flew into the squad room, fed up with always having to ask for information, and shot at Frank with both barrels. When he'd finished his tirade, Frank had tactfully pointed out that had any of what the newscaster said been true, she personally would have informed her boss right away.

Frank hissed, "Shit," and wagged her head in disgust. "What I wouldn't give to see that squint on the street for a couple years."

"They're givin' us some heat, huh?"

"Yeah. You know if those girls were black or Mexican and dumped in Beverly Hills or Westwood, the press wouldn't even have slowed down as they passed by on their way to a 'real' story."

Johnnie shrugged, licking foam delicately off his lip.

"What's the latest on 'em? Anything?"

Mel slipped Frank's hamburger onto the bar, and she ordered another stout.

"Let's get a table," she said, picking up the plate.

Johnnie followed, and when Frank had finished her first bite she answered his question.

"I got an interesting string of rapes from around that area and a stack of case folders two feet high. So I'm plowing through them this morning—"

"Don't you ever do anything fun?" Johnnie interrupted.

"—and at least three of them so far are similar to what we know about our guy. He was big, maybe left-handed, restrained them with a towel around the throat."

"Kinda grasping at straws, aren't you?"

"Got a better idea? We know there's at least one rapist in that area, our guy's into rape, we know the girls were in that area. Weak lead's better than no lead."

Johnnie shrugged again, a typical gesture for him. "Hey, Mel," he held up his empty mug, "I'm dying over here."

After Mel brought another shot and chaser, Johnnie asked if the whitecoats had revealed anything useful.

"For the DA, but not much right now."

Frank told him the rest of the details from the case folders, then settled up her tab, throwing Johnnie's in, too. She slapped his back and dodged through the raindrops to her Honda. She cruised easily along the slick, gray highway, grateful for the weather keeping everyone home. Upstairs at the station, she started a pot of coffee and slid Beethoven's Fourth Symphony into her little boom box. She closed her eyes while she waited for the coffee and let the Adagio swell over her.

Besides chasing bad guys, music was the greatest passion Frank allowed herself. The singular exception to her general denial of sentiment, she allowed Mozart and Bach to sweep her off her feet like lovers, Sinatra and Fitzgerald to soothe her. She used AC/DC and Led Zepplin to amp herself up, Getz and Jobim to calm down.

During the pause between movements she lowered the volume, poured her coffee, and got back to the stack of cases. The felicity of the Fourth Symphony gave way to the more stately Seventh, then the tape reversed and started all over again. By the time Frank sighed loudly and stretched against the hard chairback, the somber Allegreto of the Seventh was playing for the third time.

Frank turned it up, regretting she hadn't paid attention to the beginning. She allowed the strength of the movement to divert her from the ugly dossier she'd been culling, and as she relaxed it occurred to her that she was tired—deeply, achingly tired.

The Presto began and Frank snapped the player off, determined to concentrate on the lists in front of her. They might pan out to nothing, but at least they offered a glimmer of hope on an otherwise darkened trail. The clock over her door read 6:24. She hefted the phone receiver, debating, then dialed.

"Hey, Trace, it's Frank."

"Frank! You humma-humma, how the *heck* have you been?"

Tracey Jantzen had a mouth like a sailor in a shipwreck, and it was amusing to hear her curb it around the kids. She was an outgoing, gregarious woman, with a heart as big as the South Pacific, and just as warm.

Frank smiled.

"I've been fine," she replied. "How's the most beautiful woman in L.A. been?"

Tracey came back with the standard reply. "Well, if I knew her Frank, I'd ask her. When are you coming over for dinner? I haven't seen you since forever. Noah says you're working too hard. Why don't you come over next Saturday? We'll drug the kids and play strip poker all night, what do you say? Or at least Noah could barbecue some steaks and I could make a pitcher of margaritas. How's that sound?"

Frank interpreted the slight pause as her chance to answer and she said it sounded real good.

"Go-o-od! Now that I've gone and invited you over, let me go check the calendar and see what we're doing Saturday. Hang on, I'll get No for you."

"Bye, Tracey." But the words just echoed onto a tabletop. After a minute Noah greeted, "Whassup?"

"Hey. You busy?"

"Yeah, I'm playing cowboys and Indians with Markie."

"Who's winning?"

"Man, he is. I'm dead meat, 'cause he's a fierce hombre."

She could tell he was still playing with him.

"Do you have a sec?"

"You bet."

It wasn't unusual for Noah's weekends or evenings to be interrupted by work, but it was unusual for Frank to call. He asked if they'd had a break on Agoura or Peterson.

"No such luck. But I combed through the MI list you ran for me and I've found some spooky shit here."

"Speak to me."

She gave him a synopsis of the information extracted from the rape cases.

"The first one happened on December 8, 1996, at the Culver City Park. It's not far from Kenneth Hahn, and it's a lot like it: both places are surrounded by oil companies. There's a lot of brush back in there where anything could happen. Anyway, a ten-year-old Hispanic female wandered away from her brother who was playing baseball. No one noticed she was gone until she came running back screaming. She was hysterical, and the brother took her home. Turns out she'd been assaulted, anally, but by the time they brought her to the hospital the next day, there was no evidence at all.

"When they finally got her to talk, seems a man had grabbed her from behind and choked her with his arm around her neck. Then he'd pulled her shorts down, rubbed something wet on her with his hand, and penetrated her. She tried to scream even though she could barely breathe, and from the way she described how everything was looking gray she was close to passing out. Then he dropped her and she got her breath back. She looked behind her but no one was there and she ran to find her brother.

"Upon questioning, she said the color of his arm was lighter than hers. The detective, evidently a Caucasian, had rolled up his sleeve and said, 'Like my skin?' To which she replied, 'Yes, but not so much hair.'"

Frank continued reading excerpts from each report.

"The second case was about six weeks later, January 22nd, again at the park. This girl was older—thirteen, Hispanic again. A man, a tall man, abducted her on her way to the restroom, choking her with a towel. He dragged her into the surrounding shrubs, pressed her down onto her stomach, fell onto her, and masturbated against her fully clothed. He did that for a while, then eventually lifted himself off and she could breathe better. Then he proceeded to rape her exactly as the first girl had been raped, with the exception that he kept banging his head into her shoulder blades. This time the girl went straight to the ER and somebody was thinking. They did fingernail scrapes and semen swabs, and CCPD determined the assailant was a white male, A-type blood. Collected pubic hairs were light brown."

Noah interrupted, "Okay, so far we've got two prepubescent Hispanic girls who've gotten raped in Culver City. Before Markie graduates from high school, is this going to somehow be connected to two white girls murdered in South Central or am I missing something?"

"Hold on. It gets better. March 25th, a white, twelve-year-old brunette is attacked at Kenneth Hahn. Same MO, on her way out of the restroom, but this case had a witness. A man entering the men's side noticed a tall, slightly overweight man, maybe late twenties, early thirties, peering into the women's restroom. He assumed the guy was waiting for his wife or girlfriend. The wit said this guy was big, broad-shouldered. He was wearing jeans and a dark T-shirt. Straight brown hair. No facial hair or obvious tattoos. No glasses.

"Three weeks later, on Texaco property just southeast of the CC park, a fourteen-year-old white female was smoking dope and drinking tequila with her friends. The girl became nauseous and went into the bushes to vomit. She crawled out later—bruised, scratched, sodomized.

"May 12th, fifteen-year-old white female, sunbathing with her sister and two friends at Kenneth Hahn. The girl was sent back to the car for sunscreen. She was grabbed at the edge of the parking lot, raped. Her left shoulder was dislocated. Not even two weeks later, another girl, fourteen, brunette, was raped outside of Kenneth Hahn, again on oil property, followed by two more in June. But get this, the June girls are fifteen and sixteen, Hispanic and white, a blonde, respectively, but the Hispanic girl is assaulted near Crenshaw High and the white girl's done near Culver City High. Same MO on all of them. A towel was pulled over their heads and twisted under their throats. Their assailant was big, strong. All were forced into the surrounding shrubbery and subdued by strangulation.

"Here's the kicker. During these last four attacks, the perp repeatedly rammed each girl with his head and shoulders while he was raping them. The second girl was lucky and passed out from the force of a blow to her diaphragm, the third girl suffered a concussion, and the fourth girl had two broken ribs."

Frank paused.

"Gotta be the same guy, No. Where he attacks them, how he attacks them...it's pretty consistent throughout all these cases."

Noah interrupted. "How do you make the jump from these last rapes to murder?"

"Look at his style. He's evolving through each attack, becoming more and more aggressive. We can expect that as he gets more practice and more confidence. The earlier victims were mauled and handled pretty roughly, but as he learned he could get away with that much, he graduated to battery. This battery is as clear as a calling card. It's his signature, and even though his MO might vary according to circumstance, this battering's going to remain consistent."

"If it's so consistent, why wasn't he more aggressive earlier?"

"Probably not enough time. If he'd never done this before, he was probably nervous, didn't know how much he could get away with. By the time he gets to the fifth girl he's got things worked out. He's experienced, more secure, knows what he's doing and how much time he's got."

Noah could hear the excitement in Frank's voice, but skepticism forced him to play devil's advocate.

"Isn't it a broad jump from raping girls in parks to kidnapping and killing them?"

"Remember we haven't had a reported rape in that area since...," she quickly scanned her notes, "...June. And Agoura showed up in late October. Maybe he's gone underground for some reason. Maybe he got arrested for something else. I'm going to run a query on arrests for that time frame, see what we get."

"Well, it's something," Noah conceded. "Are you gonna talk to these girls?"

"Going to have to. The witness, too."

"That oughta be fun."

"I know, but something might shake loose."

The line was silent until Noah finally sighed, "I hate this guy."

There was a long silence between them, then he said, "Why don't you rent a video and go home. Get some rest."

He heard the long intake of breath, then the lie on the other end.

"Yeah. Maybe I'll do that."

His father liked hanging out at Gil's Pub. It was a sports bar, with a wide-screen TV and two smaller sets perched over either end of the bar. It wasn't uncommon for him to bring his son to the bar and brag to the other patrons about what a great football player he was while the boy ducked his red face down to his Coke. What was uncommon was the night he got really drunk just before the boy's fourteenth birthday and paid a woman at the end of the bar for a little action in the hotel a few blocks away.

She was drunk and willing enough. A little kinky, she thought, but hell, the boy was big enough and he was pretty cute. Everything was amiable until the father slammed her down on the bed and ripped her skirt up over her ass. She tried to protest, but he yanked her head back by a handful of hair and told her to keep her mouth shut unless she wanted to get hurt worse.

The boy watched his father, curious about this shift in power. His body was starting to harden into a man's, and though the father hadn't done that to him for a while, he was still wary. But now it was almost as if he were being treated as an equal. When the father finished, he growled, "Get on," and the boy did. The woman tried to talk to him, but he jerked her head back like his father had and told her to shut up. The boy didn't want to hear her, see her, smell her. He just wanted to hurt her. And he did. His father leered approvingly. The boy had never been happier.

9

She lay still for a moment, grateful she couldn't remember any dreams. In the soft cradle between sleep and wakefulness, Frank was peaceful. Before anything could ruin that she jumped out of bed, pulling on baggy sweats and a T-shirt so old she could read through it. She interchanged *Sticky Fingers* and *Abbey Road* on the CD player, and rocked and sweated and pumped cool steel for two hours. After that she filled the Mr. Coffee with water and French roast and left it dripping while she showered. Frozen croissants baked in the oven as she spread an arrest printout on the dining room table. The Stones and the Beatles had been replaced by Delibes' *Lakme*, and wedges of apple and Brie waited on a glazed ceramic plate for the croissants.

Frank's painstaking attention to detail checked any intrusion of discord, and she was almost happy. An hour later she rolled south on the Harbor Freeway, whistling the "Flower Song" and looking forward to the Chiefs' game. By the time she got to the Alibi, Johnnie and Ike were already at a table in front of the large-screen TV. Lifting a hand toward Mel, she noticed Deirdre McCall filling in for Nancy and Johnnie already on at least his second beer. It wasn't even ten o'clock. She ordered coffee as Boy-red joined them, joking with the boys and excluding Frank from the banter. Around noon they started ordering pitchers, and Frank helped with a couple more as the Niners trounced the Panthers. After the late game she drove carefully home through the November dusk.

Frank made a chicken sandwich and took the arrest printout into the living room. Listening absently to the news, she scribbled notes in the margins, brushing crumbs away while she worked. A handful of records fit the time frame she was looking for, and three of the perps had priors for assault and/or rape. Between the rape victims, the murder books she'd yet to read, and this list of possible suspects, she had wiggled out a few more leads. Frank yawned widely. She and Noah could start on them in the morning. She hoped like hell they wouldn't fizzle on her.

But Frank's plans to follow up on the Agoura/Peterson leads got shelved, and she spent all the next day working a drowning with Diego. By six that evening, they had a suspect in the locker downtown. Frank celebrated, leaving the office in time to catch all of the Monday night game. She even managed another good night's sleep. Tuesday she was in meetings and at court, but late in the afternoon she finally was able to dig into the rec area murder books. They were cold cases, and Frank had borrowed them from the Culver City PD and LASD without anyone breathing down her neck to get them back. In fact, both agencies had been surprisingly cooperative.

She picked up the first binder and pulled out the pictures and the coroner's report. A handful of scene sketches corresponded to the photos, and Frank spread those in front of her. They were the next best thing to being on scene. She studied them, formulating her own ideas before she was prejudiced by the investigating detective's report.

Jane Doe, fifteen or sixteen years old, Hispanic. Her body was on its stomach in a ditch. She was missing footwear, pants, and underwear. She still had on a white bra and T-shirt, but they'd been pushed up around her collarbone. She showed bruises, too, but they seemed more evenly distributed around her body, especially around the arms and breasts where the perp had grabbed her. The coroner's report indicated anal as well as vaginal rape. She was asphyxiated, but manually. The bruising was obvious on her neck.

Frank closed the file. It was too inconsistent with the profile she was expecting. The same for the second report, a sixteen-year-old Korean girl who'd been found off the 405 near Huntley. The third case was Cassandra Nichols.

A twelve-year-old black girl. The first picture caught her spread-eagled near a dumpster in an empty parking lot. Pink skirt bunched up around her waist, underwear around her knees, blood stains and bruises on her legs. Her bra was pushed above tiny breasts.

Frank's first impression was that this case was also unrelated, but she kept circling around, making notes on a legal pad. The coroner's photos showed consistent bruising. Ligature marks around the neck indicated asphyxiation. Frank held one of the pictures up, squinting into it. It was a morgue shot emphasizing scattered posterior bruising. She searched it carefully, then restudied the photo of Nichols in the lot. Frank unconsciously stroked the empty spot on her ring finger.

The coroner's report told her that Nichols was found shortly after she'd died, roughly 7:00 P.M. The autopsy revealed anal assault and significant contusion of the dorsal region. Cause of death was asphyxiation; the manner was strangulation by ligature with an object similar to a leather belt. The internal exam discovered nothing unusual.

Frank sat back and pulled her Ray Bans off, nibbling on one of the ear stems. This had a lot of similarities to their boy, but it might just be coincidental. Frank kept trolling through the photos. She stopped when she distinguished a thin line under Cassandra Nichols' breasts. Pulling the picture closer to her face, she focused on the strap mark from Nichols' bra. She must have been wearing it throughout the assault. When he raped her, the perp hadn't even displaced her bra. *That* was consistent with the rape profile Frank had compiled. All of the victims on her list had been raped while fully clothed, and the type of sexual molestation was exclusively anal intercourse.

Frank scrutinized the pictures even more closely. Nichols had bloody abrasions on her knees and thighs. Frank guessed she'd been on her stomach while she was being raped, and that the scratches came from being thrust against whatever surface she was lying on. Frank noted there were no abrasions on her upper thighs, which could have been protected by her skirt.

If she was right, the abrasions might have trapped particles of the surface she was raped on, indicating whether Nichols was raped indoors or outdoors, and on what type of ground. Asphalt? Dirt? Grass? Nothing in the coroner's report described more than the presence of the abrasions, nor was there any evidence from forensics. Frank found the property sheet and was pleased to see that Culver City had at least retained Nichols' clothing as evidence. She scrolled methodically through the investigator's notes and reports.

Nichols had never made it home from summer school that day. The last time her father had seen her he had handed his daughter a lunch bag. The case detective had felt it important to note that the lunch consisted of a bologna and cheese sandwich, chips, and an apple, which corresponded with the protocol notes on her stomach contents. That lunch sounded pretty good to Frank and she remembered she hadn't eaten all day except for two jelly donuts on her way in to work at 5:00 A.M.

She leaned back in her old chair, wondering if she'd found another connection to their perp. It seemed possible, but Frank had learned never to view anything as a certainty except for the fact that there would always be dead bodies. Her eye once again caught the picture of Cassandra Nichols splayed on the ground. This time Frank studied it with a prejudiced eye.

She'd been a beautiful little girl, a good girl, the notes indicated. No trouble. Her mother was dead; her father, still widowed, was a high school teacher. That he had packed his daughter a lunch indicated she was a cared-for little girl. Frank was far too familiar with the anguish of loss, yet she still couldn't imagine losing a child. Telling parents their children were dead was almost the hardest thing about being a homicide detective. Not being able to tell them who killed their son or daughter was the worst.

Who did this to you? she wondered, staring at a smiling, gap-toothed school photo.

That Nichols was black was inconsistent, but because their perp intermingled whites with Hispanics, it wasn't a gross anomaly in his choice of victims. And it was a similar MO in the right geographic area. Nichols had been dead for three months. She was a Frigidaire by homicide standards. To her father, she was still his baby. To her killer, if it was the same man, she was an ecstatic memory whose thrill had no doubt faded. Frank fingered the photo, considering the ramifications.

It was tempting to think they might have another link to their perp, but Frank was cautious about attributing this to him yet. And while she wanted the same man to be responsible for all the assaults and all the homicides, the possibility was daunting. If it was true, there was a very dangerous man out there who was able to rape and kill at will. He was smart, and no doubt getting smarter with each successful crime, his intensity level escalating. And it was Frank's job to apprehend him. The immensity of that caught up with her as she stared at Cassandra Nichols.

A rumbling in Frank's gut broke her concentration. Reluctantly, she put the photo away. She massaged her face for a moment, reorienting herself to the world beyond three-ring binders. She stuffed the last one into her briefcase and walked downstairs, out to the parking garage. Traffic on Figueroa was stop-and-go, and Frank let the chill air blow the cobwebs out of her brain.

It was warm and lively at the Alibi as she walked around the tables, dipping her head in rough greetings. Frank raised a hand, caught Deirdre's eye, and settled into one of the small booths. Deirdre delivered drinks to a nearby table, asking Frank over her shoulder, "Stout?"

"Double Dewar's, no ice."

Frank waited until the drink came before she opened the remaining murder book. She was beat, but she was almost through the daunting pile. Besides, under the tiredness she had to admit to curiosity. Sipping her drink, she held up a crime scene photograph, not wanting to lay it out for public display.

This girl was white, blonde/blue, a Jane Doe, fifteen to seventeen years old, and the picture made Frank put her drink down. The vic was lying on her side, eyes open to a concrete sidewalk. She was dressed in tattered blue jeans, a T-shirt, open wool shirt, worn Doc Marten-style shoes. The top of her pants was pulled down around her thighs and soaked with blood. A stick projected from between the cheeks of her ass. The lack of blood at the scene indicated she'd probably been dumped there.

Frank stared at the bloodied girl, the bruised face. She didn't bother with the rest of the photographs but quickly read the autopsy protocol. Cause of death, massive internal hemorrhage. Manner, rupture of internal organs by tree branch inserted through anus. The investigative reports confirmed the Doe had been dumped.

Cursing silently, Frank drained the Scotch. Black electricity was zinging through her. What if the rapes had never stopped? What if they'd turned into homicides instead?

Frantically, she pulled notes out of her briefcase and followed the progression of assaults. The first one on her list was in December, and they occurred on a regular basis after that—January, March, April, May, June—then the rapes ended. But Nichols was killed in August, this girl in September, Agoura in October, and Peterson just weeks ago. Like clockwork. The son of a bitch had never stopped, just progressed. She reviewed the assaults, fully aware of their escalating brutality. As his skills had increased, so had his satisfaction threshold. It made sense. With each subsequent attack the perp had raised his bar a little higher. Murder would be a logical, inevitable benchmark. Meaning there would be more and their horror would increase. And he was almost due.

"Need a refill?"

Frank jerked her head up at Deirdre.

"Geez, you look like you've seen a ghost."

"Yeah, maybe I have. How about another double. And something to go, uh, a BLT."

"Toasted?"

"What?"

"Do you want your bread toasted or not?"

Frank was so preoccupied she had trouble understanding the simple question.

"Yeah. Sure."

Frank felt in way over her head for the second time that night. When the sandwich came she jogged out of the Alibi and drove back to the brightly lit station. Taking the steps to the second floor three at a time, she once again pulled her Quantico books, the BLT slowly congealing in its styrofoam box.

After that night at Gil's, it was common for them to cruise the red light strips. The father would drive, they'd both look. When he found a hooker he liked, usually a young girl, the father would make her get in the car. The hookers hated that, but they were usually hungry enough to go for it. If one refused, they'd find another, then park in a secluded lot. The first couple of times the father had gone first, taking the girl in the ass. Then he'd jerked off while he watched his son with her. Soon he stopped fucking the whores and just got off on watching. The rougher his son was, the more he liked it. If the girl complained too much, the boy tightened his shirt around her throat until she shut up. Then he'd bang into her as hard as he wanted. It felt like flying.

10

When Noah walked into the squad room next morning, Frank was waiting impatiently for him at the coffee pot, eating last night's french fries and sandwich. Her hair was slicked back, dripping occasionally against her burgundy turtleneck, and Noah greeted, "Dudess. Another all-nighter?"

Frank tilted her head toward the office. Noah followed in the wake of her coffee steam.

"Close the door."

"Oh, a good one."

She indicated a city map she'd pinned to the wall above the couch.

"Red pins are rapes, green pins are homicides. I finally got to those murder books yesterday. Here. Take a look at this, too."

She handed him a copy of the report she'd made of the pertinent rape and murder cases.

"Wow."

"No shit."

"So you think he never went underground, just switched to murder."

"Yeah."

"But if it's the same perp, how do you explain this sudden switch from rape to sticks up the ass? Isn't that kinda drastic? I mean we didn't see anything like that with the assaults."

Frank shook her head excitedly, water falling off in fat drops. Her color was high and she was animated, not her regular laconic self.

"Easy. Let's start at the beginning. Look at the ages of these girls. Let's say he's never committed a rape before December, or at least not one he's planned out and thought about. He's out there trolling and wants someone easy. So he picks a little girl. The first one, Aguilar, was only ten. How hard can it be to handle a ten-year old? We know he's a big man. It would be easy to overpower her.

And a little girl's not threatening, you know? She's not street smart, she's not tough, she's an easy mark.

"So Aguilar goes down easy, and he does another little girl in January. That'd be Menendez. She's thirteen, right?"

Noah nodded at the paper in his hand.

"Okay, so she's easy too, and he's getting the hang of this thing. It's simple. He's feeling confident, feeling good. In March he does an eleven-year old. Then in April he graduates to a fourteen-year old, Troupe. That goes down easy too. He's a master now. For the rest of these rapes he stays consistent with fourteen to sixteen-year olds."

"But this Nichols girl is only twelve."

"You're right. But look where she lives...," Frank pointed to an area near a cluster of red pins, "...and where she's found."

She tapped a green pin just above the red ones, saying, "Two blocks from Baldwin Hills Elementary."

Frank pawed through an assortment of notes.

"Look at how he's alternating here," she said, indicating the red pins. "Girls one, two, and four are done at or around Culver City Park. Girls three, five, and six, at or around Kenneth Hahn. With six under his belt he must be feeling pretty confident, and he's smart, too. He must know he can't keep doing this in the same spots and not get caught. So on number seven he goes out of his territory and over to Crenshaw. Number eight is still about as equidistant as seven, but it's west, over at CC High. Do you see?"

Frank swirled her finger above the clustered pins.

"This is his home base. This is where he feels most comfortable. If he's never raped before, and we have no indication he has, he's not going to do it in an unfamiliar place. I'll lay even money he spends a lot of time at these parks, and that they're close to where he lives. This is his 'hood," Frank stressed.

"By the time he does Nichols, he has a long and successful string of rapes behind him. He's got to be feeling pretty good, pretty confident. So let's say he accidentally sees Nichols, he's got a perfect opportunity to take her, and he does. See, he's never *taken* anybody before, so he must feel very safe here. He's familiar with this 'hood and its rhythms."

Still tapping the cluster of pins, Frank stated adamantly, "I'm willing to bet my left tit that we'll find him somewhere in this area. He does Nichols because, again, she's an easy mark. A little girl. Easy to handle. It's his first abduction. He's excited. He can spend time with this one. We don't know exactly how much time, but from when she left school until seven that night. And where does he dump her? Behind a sandwich joint, a barber shop, and a trophy store, all closed by five. Someone from that area would know that the parking lot behind all those shops would be deserted by seven o'clock—around the time he dumped her."

Frank paused, but started again almost immediately as Noah began to speak.

"He might not even have meant to kill her. He could've gotten carried away, which is what I think happened."

She handed Noah the pictures of Cassandra Nichols.

"If you look carefully you can see the marks from her bra. Look at the lines there," she pointed. "I think he got a little panicky, didn't know what to do, messed her up a little to throw us off his track, make it look like a hundred other rapes, and dumped her. When I was looking at this picture I almost dismissed this as an unrelated case, because of the clothes, and the fact that she's black. But the marks from the bra tell us he never had her clothes off; she was dressed the whole time. We know he likes that."

"Yeah, but what about her being black? I mean that's pretty inconsistent with his pattern."

Noah was asking good questions. Frank had been up all night asking them too.

"Right again. But one, I don't think he was really trolling for Nichols. I think he happened upon her somehow, saw his opportunity, and took it. That would explain why he panicked. And two, I went through my notes from that residency I did at Quantico. A serial perp will usually have an ideal victim that fits his fantasies, but it's not unheard of to sacrifice ideal for opportunity. That could explain Nichols."

Still staring at her pictures, Noah said, "She's just a baby."

Frank didn't tell him she'd felt the same thing, continuing instead with her case.

"Nichols is young. He's back to practicing on little girls, but she goes down so smoothly, and he's confident from all his rapes, so his next girl is closer to his ideal."

Frank gave Noah the Jane Doe pictures.

"According to the coroner's report she's between sixteen and eighteen. But look at her—she's small. He's not IDing these girls.

He doesn't know how old she is, and she could easily be fourteen, fifteen, sixteen. Another thing. She was a runaway. Autopsy showed alcohol and crack in her system, grass, no food in her stomach, looked like it had been days since she'd eaten. She'd be another easy mark.

"Now, I'll bet with her he was totally prepared. He'd tasted blood with Nichols and he liked it, so he was prepared to waste this girl. When he was done with her. Remember, this is the first time he's had these girls for as long as he wants them. I think he killed Nichols accidentally, maybe while he was raping her. He used a belt on Nichols instead of a towel, which would be consistent with a lack of planning. Maybe he put more force on it than he realized, then poof, she's dead and he's kinda freaked.

"But with the Doe he's more careful. No belt marks. He's gone back to using a towel. He's playing with her. He's in his element. She has all her clothes on. He likes that. He's punching this girl around like a boxing bag. You can see in the coroner's pictures where a button and a seam on her jeans left marks on her flesh."

Frank's eyes were shining, her voice excited as she added, "This is one interesting boy, No. He's slamming these girls, but he's not getting off on degrading them, he's not making them sex slaves. He doesn't like anything except anal sex. He's not getting off on torturing them per se, though if some mother were doing this to me it'd go down in my book as torture. It's more like he's angry.

"Look at the way he's battering them," she said, jabbing a finger into one of the autopsy photos. "And only anal sex. He's not looking at these girls when he rapes them. He's barely touching them, but he's exerting his dominance in no uncertain terms. I'll bet that somebody's done this to him. He wants to hurt these girls like he's been hurt and he's running on pure rage while he's doing it. It's common for serialists to escalate the intensity of their attacks, like junkies needing progressively stronger hits to get high. With each assault this guy's fantasies get stronger and stronger. At this point, a rape without murder would probably be very unsatisfying for him."

"Which means he's going to get worse."

Frank nodded. Her enthusiasm suddenly vanished, and she looked like what she was—a cop who'd been up for forty-eight hours, working on the hardest case of her career. She sounded weary when she spoke. "We're going to reinterview all the girls, the parents, the responding officers, Culver City homicide. It's going to be a pain in the ass, but at least we've got a track on this guy. I want to get composites done, plaster his mug all over town, go to the parks and see if anyone recognizes the composite."

"Does the captain know about this yet?"

"Nope. He's in Sacramento. He'll be back tomorrow."

Noah chuckled. "I wanna be there when you tell him."

Frank smiled tightly, unable to derive pleasure even from the thought of Fubar's jaw falling to his feet.

11

The phone rang.

"Homicide. Franco."

It was the assistant DA, and she unloaded. Within twenty-four hours, two of Frank's detectives had tried to steamroll her into taking three separate cases based on practically no cause and with equally little supporting evidence. She explained that this was L.A., not some Podunk backwater town, and she needed compelling evidence to get a criminal to trial. Priors and circumstance wouldn't do it.

Frank listened patiently. Pissing off Lydia McQueen was not a good idea. And she was right. If they didn't have solid evidence the detectives shouldn't have gone to her, but it was easy when they were carrying dozens of cases to show the ADA what they had and hope she'd go to bat with it. Frank spent almost half an hour trying to mollify The Queen and then had a talk with Gough about his case. She knew he was suffering from a big case of burnout. He was still a good cop—after all, he'd been doing it for so long—but he'd taken to cutting corners that were best left whole. Frank played on his loyalty to the squad, pointing out that long after he was gone the department was going to have to keep working with the DA's office, and that it would help his colleagues if he went by the book while he was still badged.

Back in her office, the light was blinking on her phone. Hodges, Homicide from the Culver City PD. She returned the call. He was antsy that she was poking around in their cases. She reassured him that she wasn't going behind his back, or being asked to get involved by higher-ups. All the while she was thinking what a paranoid mother he was.

At last she returned to the rape folders. Reluctantly, she dialed the phone number of the first girl on the list. Alissa Aguilar. Frank studied her picture while the phone rang. Finally a machine picked up and Frank left a message saying it was very important that Mr. or Mrs. Aguilar call her back, no matter how late. She left her beeper number.

Making the calls in the chronological order of the rapes, she reached Claudia Menendez' father on the next try. After introducing herself, she explained that since Claudia's assault, they believed her attacker had raped seven other girls and might well be responsible for the murder/tortures of four more. Frank was encouraged by Mr. Menendez' sounds of anger and disbelief, and asked if it would be possible to talk to Claudia again in light of this new evidence.

He was understandably hesitant, and Frank assured him she wouldn't be asking if it wasn't crucial. She had no wish to reopen Claudia's wounds, but his daughter might be able to add something critical that she'd forgotten the first time. Frank heard the frustration in his voice when he said he'd have to talk to his wife, but that they could probably talk to Claudia when she got home from school. Frank left her beeper number, with the appeal that they call her back as soon as possible.

She squeezed the back of her neck. Frank had never worked rape, but she didn't think she'd be very good at it. Handling pain wasn't her forte. Dead was dead, and in homicide she didn't have to deal with the victim's wounds.

An answering machine at the next number took her message. Before she could dial again, Diego came in about an extradition case. Frank was getting him started on the forms when Bobby leaned into the doorway.

"We're all going to the Sizzler for lunch. Want to go?"

Diego nodded, but Frank indicated the case folders stacked next to her.

"Can't," she said, pulling a ten out of the wallet in her back pocket. "But bring me back something, a salad."

"What sort of salad?"

Bobby was very thorough. He would want a detailed list.

"Anything green."

"What sort of dressing?"

"I don't care. Surprise me."

"What—"

"Come on," Diego said, snatching up the money. "I'll get the friggin' salad."

The squad room was suddenly quiet, and Frank picked up the phone. The fourth girl was Jessica Orenthaler. The girl's mother answered. She started crying before Frank could even tell her what she wanted. Frank waited her out, listening to the phone ring in the squad room. When Mrs. Orenthaler quieted down, Frank started to explain the circumstances. Mrs. Orenthaler hung up almost immediately.

Contemplating Claudia Menendez, Frank found nothing remarkable about the child's appearance. She was slight and doe-eyed, with a suggestion of a pallor, and Frank wondered if she didn't go outside much anymore. She and Noah sat at an angle from Claudia on plastic-covered chairs, while the girl nestled between her parents on a matching couch. The only hint of her recent trauma was the way she snuggled into her mother like a much younger child might.

Frank made the introductions, explaining why they needed to ask more questions. The previous interviews had dealt mostly with physical factors about the assault, but because she and Noah were interested in constructing a psychological profile of the assailant, they needed to ask some different questions. Frank pointed out that they wouldn't be nice questions. The parents agreed, and Frank let Noah start. There was a gentleness about him that put people at ease, and maybe because he had three of his own, he was especially good at interviewing kids. The girl looked reluctant, but her father patted her leg and she gamely launched into a quiet recounting. Noah had a list of questions, but he waited for Claudia to finish before asking them. He explained that although the questions might seem silly or dumb, each answer told them something about the man they were looking for.

"Can you remember him touching you anywhere else, except for where he grabbed you and hurt you? This is real important, so take your time and think about it. Don't rush."

Claudia pulled her teeth over her bottom lip and gazed at the coffee table. She shook her head no.

"You're sure?"

Claudia nodded.

"Okay, that's good, that's real good. Another thing that we need to know is if he pulled your pants up before he let you go."

They could see she was struggling to remember, but Mr. Menendez answered for her.

"When she came back to us her clothes were all on. We

thought she'd just fallen down or something."

"Do you remember pulling your pants back up, Claudia?"

She wagged her head, still puzzled, then said almost in a whisper, "I think he pulled them up."

"You think so?" Noah encouraged.

Again she nodded, but they could tell she was uncertain.

"Okay. You're doing great," Noah smiled. "Can you handle some more questions?"

He waited for her assent before asking if the man had said anything to her, and her answer was certain.

"I tried to scream, but he had his arm around my throat so tight I couldn't breathe and he told me to shut up or he'd kill me. I was scared so I didn't say nothing else. And I couldn't hardly breathe," she added apologetically.

"Did he say anything else to you besides shut up or he'd kill you?"

Her brown hair shook emphatically.

"Did he ask you to say anything?"

Again a shake of the brown head. Mr. Menendez was getting restless. Noah said, more to him than Claudia, "Okay, darling. Hang in there, you're doing really well and we're almost done. Can you answer a few more?"

Again Claudia glanced up at her mom for reassurance and was heartened by a warm smile. The last questions were the hardest for everybody. Noah asked ugly questions as gently as he could, but finally the fear and shame and horror caught up to Claudia. Tears slid down her face, but Noah pressed on, promising her he was almost through.

At last, he reached across the table and cupped her face in his long hand. "Alright, honey, that's all. You did a really great job. You told us a lot about the man who hurt you. You helped us a lot."

The girl buried her face against her mother while Noah looked expectantly at Frank. She rose and extended her hand to Mr. Menendez.

"You've got a fine daughter. We're awfully sorry to have stir this all up again, but she's been a big help."

Mr. Menendez followed the detectives to the doorway, asking specific questions that they weren't free to answer.

"This must be very frustrating for you, not having any answers or resolution. I promise we'll keep you advised one way or another."

Mr. Menendez was grateful, and so were the detectives once they were in their car and on the highway.

"Jesus, that was *fun*," Noah said bitterly.

"Want me to drive?" Frank offered.

"No!" he snapped. Pointing through the windshield to an economy tire store decorated with tinsel and Christmas greetings, he ranted, "Look at all this shit! Can you believe it? It's not even Thanksgiving yet and everybody's got their fucking Christmas stuff up already. Jesus! Whatever happened to the pilgrims and turkeys and fall leaves?"

Frank started to return her beeper calls but thought better of it. Noah was letting off steam, and she decided to humor him even though all she wanted right now was to go home, box for an hour, slam a six-pack, and slip into a torpor.

"Well, let's see. First off, this is L.A. There aren't any fall leaves and it's been a long time since I saw pilgrims around here. More importantly, though, there's no money in Thanksgiving. Even Halloween's a bigger moneymaker than Thanksgiving."

"That's my whole goddamn point!" Noah banged on the steering wheel. "Fucking prick. I swear to you, Frank, if anybody ever so much as touches a hair on one of my daughters I'm gonna kill him."

Frank nodded solemnly. "I'll help you."

They drove in silence for a while, both processing the interview with Claudia Menendez. Neither would come right out and say it had been hard to watch her, and harder for Noah to ask the questions. There was a code of silence about seeing pain or feeling it. Pain was part of being a cop and it was expected to be borne stoically and without complaint. This was the LAPD—whiners were not allowed.

Frank sighed quietly, then punched a number into the cell phone. She cut a glance at Noah, who seemed somewhere else.

She poked him in the arm.

"Five bucks says you can't eat two Big Macs and a large fries."

"Five bucks says how can you be that dumb and still be a lieutenant?"

Frank introduced herself to Heidi Troupe's mother on the cell phone. She reluctantly agreed to let them come over after dinner. The second number was busy. Noah picked up on his Christmas tirade again. Just before they reached Alissa Aguilar's apartment Frank redialed and received permission for another interview.

"Two more after this," she said to Noah, handing him the phone. Want to call Tracey?"

"Goddamn this job," he bitched, entering his number.

The halls of the building where Alissa Aguilar lived were filled with the smells of dinner, making Frank salivate and Noah whine some more.

"Man, I can't wait to get to those Big Macs."

Frank smiled to herself. If Noah was hungry, he was alright.

"Maybe if you're nice, Mrs. Aguilar'll give you a bowl of *menudo*."

"Hey, I'm so freakin' hungry I could even eat that brain shit at this point. Let's get this over with quick, huh?"

But the interview with Alissa Aguilar didn't go smoothly. Mr. Aguilar paced around the living room, frequently interrupting the questioning, or answering for Alissa so that Noah had to get her back on track and have her answer in her own words. The interview took longer than it should have, with both Alissa and Mrs. Aguilar ending up in tears and Mr. Aguilar bellowing at the detectives. They let him. They'd heard what they wanted.

Alissa's story mirrored Claudia's, except she'd struggled when he caught her and ceased as the towel grew tighter around her windpipe. She clearly remembered the man pulling her pants up after he'd raped her and thinking that was really crazy. And no, he hadn't touched her anywhere else, which she thought was kind of crazy, too, 'cause she knew guys liked "girls' other parts." More importantly, and this was a bonus neither detective expected, her perp hadn't said anything to her except, "Shut up or I'll kill you."

"Are you sure that's what he said?"

"Do you think my daughter's lyin' to you?"

"Mr. Aguilar," Frank explained, "we have to know if he said something like that or exactly that."

She looked at Alissa.

"No. It was exactly that. I was so scared 'cause I thought he would, too."

The detectives thanked Mr. Aguilar, and Frank handed him a card, asking him to call if they had any questions or if Alissa remembered something else. Mr. Aguilar ripped the card into tiny pieces and threw them in Frank's face.

They drove on to the next interview, but at least this time they both had Mr. Aguilar to use as a whipping boy.

He was tall and strong and fast. He was an outstanding tight end. His father wanted him to get a scholarship, but his grades were mediocre at best. So he just got better and better at football, hoping that would be enough to get him into a good college. He never thought beyond playing football. It was all he knew.

Now as the defense took the field he pulled his helmet off and rested on one knee apart from the other players. The cheerleaders caught his eye, and he watched them jumping up and down inside their little outfits, trying not to think about that now, trying to watch the opposing team, to concentrate on the game. There'd be plenty of time for the other later, when he was home tonight, alone in his bed. He felt himself stirring and frowned, forcing himself to focus on the other team's receivers. Waiting.

12

Foubarelle was fifteen minutes late for his meeting with Frank. When he finally showed, he kept his lieutenant waiting with a phone call. Frank glanced at several small but carefully hung pictures of fleshy, billowy nudes. She'd been to a party at Foubarelle's house, where his penchant for nudes was unmistakable. His walls were lined with reproductions of Renoirs and Botticellis, all showing carefully posed women in various stages of disarray.

She studied one of the pictures from her chair, wondering how it differed from a pin-up. Frank was pretty sure that if someone of a lesser rank had these tacked above their desk, they would be considered sexual harassment; in a captain's office, it was art.

At last Foubarelle hung up and smiled broadly.

"How are we doing, Frank?"

She felt like she was in a dentist's chair. Slapping a progress report on his big, clean desk, she announced, "We've connected the Agoura perp to what looks like at least nine rapes and two other murders, besides Peterson."

Foubarelle had been about to pick up the report, but now he froze, as if the fat folder on his desk had suddenly turned into a rattlesnake. Frank artfully concealed her amusement.

"What did you say?"

"I think our boy's got a whole string of assaults behind him."

"In our jurisdiction?"

Frank shook her head. "A rape at Crenshaw, but the rest are in Culver City."

Foubarelle sagged with relief, then he jerked up again. Like a fucking puppet, Frank thought.

"Is this on the streets yet?"

Again she shook her head, and again her boss was obviously relieved.

"What are you doing?"

"There are gaps in the case reports. If this is the same guy, we're dealing with a major offender. And he's crafty. I want to do some profiling on him, use what I learned at Quantico. I submitted a Request for Information to VICAP and I want to talk with Richard Clay, the shrink at Behavioral Sciences, get his input."

Frank paused, waiting for objections, but there were none.

"We're going to have to reinterview everyone. That's going to take a lot of time. Plus I'd like to recanvass the area where the original incidents took place, see if we can't come up with something new, find someone that wasn't hit before. We're going to need additional manpower if you want us to move on this with anything resembling speed. There was a witness to the third rape. He's coming in this morning to do a composite. I think we should plaster this guy's image all over L.A. We'll need extra staffing just to handle phone calls on that, and then we're going to need help following up on all the leads."

Foubarelle was nodding as if his neck had just gone elastic.

"Do we know what the perp looks like?"

"Maybe. The wit didn't actually see the assault go down, but he saw a man who fits our description peeking into the women's room right around the time the rape went down."

The captain's face clouded. The DA would throw that back in their face like spit in a headwind. Frank explained it was the best lead they had and that she didn't intend to use the witness as supporting evidence.

"And this is going to raise a shit storm, but we need to get the physical evidence from the two prior murders transferred into our custody. The forensic work was minimal on each of the cases, and I'm going to submit them for everything. I hope we can pull some DNA off their clothes that will match what we've got. If we could get a fire under CCPD's ass, that'd be helpful."

"I'll make some phone calls," Foubarelle said pompously, adding, "I know you're going to burn me for overtime on this. Aren't you?"

Frank shrugged. "It's your call, but more people makes better odds."

"Alright. How soon do you think we can get this wrapped up?"

Her wooden expression didn't change, but Frank wondered if Foubarelle had just dropped down into his seat from Mars.

"I really can't say, John."

"Give me an estimate," he wheedled.

She knew he wanted a number for the press.

"I can't. We could get a call right now from someone who turns us on to the guy, or we might look for years and never catch him."

"*Never* is not an option, Frank."

"All I'm saying is I can't tell you we'll have a suspect in custody by noon next week. We're doing the best we can with what we've got. Get the extra personnel, get the perp visible, show people we're moving on this, and it'll look good."

Being a man who easily confused sound and motion for action, Foubarelle liked that.

"Alright. You'll get your people. What else?"

She wanted to say, "A boatload of luck," but answered instead, "Dedicated hot line."

Foubarelle nodded, jotting a note.

Joe Girardi, her predecessor, had fought tooth and nail with the previous captain, and even though Foubarelle didn't know shit about homicide investigation, Frank had to grudgingly admit he knew how to pull strings to get what he wanted. Especially if he was in peril of looking bad. She played on that fear of his, and it usually gave her what she wanted—case resolutions—and that made Foubarelle a happy man.

Leaving his office, Frank wondered why she didn't feel more victorious. In the squad room she told her detectives to have a good weekend because they were going to be spending the rest of their careers going door to door in Culver City.

A couple of hours after their shift ended, Noah and Frank were creeping along Manchester Boulevard. An injury accident had shut down two lanes of traffic on Florence, and Manchester was getting clogged with the overflow.

The detectives were on their way to interview the last rape victim. Five out of the eight families had consented to having their daughters reinterviewed, which Frank considered pretty good odds. If the testimony of the remaining victim was similar to that of the other girls, it would corroborate what they already knew: it was looking more and more like the same man was responsible for both the rapes and murders.

But where are you?

Frank had taken to spending downtime inside this guy's head.

She'd fallen asleep last night on the couch in the den, imagining him lurking in the park, patiently waiting for just the right girl to hit on. While Noah drove, Frank again indulged in her new pastime.

We've established a lack of confidence, so you're probably not going to be economically successful. But you do have a car. Have to the way you're moving these girls around. It's probably an older car, a practical model. You're a young man, so maybe it's your parents' car. Probably not a sibling's car—that would be harder to get hold of. You need more dependable wheels. We've ruled out friends and girlfriends. I bet you're a loner, that you spend more time with fantasies than people—

"Hey," Noah interrupted, "did I tell you Les made two jump-shots last night?"

It took Frank a moment to pull her thoughts together.

"What?" she asked, rather dreamily, and Noah cut her a quick glance.

"Are you alright?"

"Yeah. Why?"

"I don't know. You look...weird."

She ignored him even though she felt weird. Frank was trying to clear her head by studying the two men in the car next to her. A song with a hard bass line beat inside their car. She wondered what percentage of hearing loss they were incurring. The driver felt her staring and turned to glare. Frank's arm was resting out the open window, and the driver rolled his window down too.

"What you lookin' at, bitch?"

He had two blue teardrops under one eye and a partially shaved head with a gang tat on the back. Frank grinned widely, showing teeth, and smoothly pulled her hand in under her jacket. The *cholo* must not have liked what he saw in Frank's eyes because he just sneered and looked ahead, but he made sure to roll his window up.

"Friend of yours?"

"They're all my friends, No. I'm sworn to protect and to serve."

Practice hadn't gone well, and his father had snarled at him all the way home.

"You think you're smarter than me now, don't you?"

"No, sir."

"Think you know more than your old man?"

"No, sir."

"Well I'm not too old to take you on and you're not too big."

They pulled into the garage. His father tossed the keys at him.

"Wait for me in the office," he growled before slamming into the house.

Had it not been for dread, the boy wouldn't have felt anything as he dragged himself into the little locked room. He'd stopped crying years ago and had never imagined fighting. His father joined him after ten long minutes, his scowl replaced by an excruciating smirk.

13

Richard Clay welcomed Frank with a gentle handshake and an honest, open appraisal. Frank respected Clay. He'd been with the Behavioral Science unit for a long time and knew a lot. Unlike some of the other head-shrinkers who were just crawling toward their pensions, Clay was genuinely helpful.

"I appreciate your time, Dick."

"This sounds like an interesting fellow you're chasing. I'm curious to see what you've got on him."

"Well, not much. That's part of the problem."

Frank outlined their perp's MO, showed Clay all their photographs, and briefly justified her reasons for tying the eight rapes and four murders to the same perp. He asked a few questions, then took his time studying the information.

Clay was soft-spoken, and Frank had been sitting on the edge of her chair to hear what he said. Now she relaxed, absently observing him. Although Clay was close to retiring, he looked fit and wiry. Trim white hair encircled a tan bald spot. His eyes, behind wire-framed granny glasses, were warm and dark. Frank had consulted with him before and enjoyed his thoughtful collaboration. As was his habit, he wiggled a pen through his fingers like a drum majorette manipulating a baton. Frank wondered if he did magic tricks for the grandchildren lined up in photos on his windowsill.

After examining the data, he cleared his throat and proceeded to quietly enumerate his thoughts. He corroborated Frank's theory that their man didn't have a lot of confidence, ticking his justifications off on his fingers. Clay paused and asked, "Are you following my train of thought?"

Frank summed up: "A physically indistinct person can indicate an emotionally indistinct person which may indicate a lack of confidence."

"Exactly."

"Which," she continued, "supports his blitz style of attack. He doesn't have the confidence or charisma for a direct confrontation."

"Yes."

Clay looked slightly disappointed that Frank had already reached that step. He was a methodical man and liked laying theories out in baby steps.

"I think this might be one of your greatest insights into his character. If we agree your fellow has a lack of confidence, we can make a number of generalizations about him."

Clay put down the pen and started counting on his fingers again. He listed things Frank had already considered, such as low income and average intelligence. Probably no higher education. If he worked, Clay suspected, it would be at menial jobs, and probably alone or with few others around him. Clay didn't think he'd have good social skills, and partly because of this, he'd be single, though he might have a girlfriend. He suspected that any mutual sexual encounters would probably not be satisfactory for either partner, more discouraging than fulfilling.

Neatly aligning the victims photographs, Clay scanned them through the lower half of his bifocals. Frank was taping their conversation, but she glanced up from the notes she was scribbling as he asked, "Has anything I've said meshed with your calculations?"

"A lot. It's hard to slip him into a specific category—organized/disorganized, nonsocial/asocial—because his characteristics overlap. But I agree with your assessment of his personality. It fits well with his basic MO."

"Did you submit a report to the FBI?"

"It's not back yet. I know an agent there who's going to work it up their list, but it'll still take a couple of weeks."

"Do we have that long?"

"Hey, you're the doctor."

Clay smiled, then looked perplexed as he picked up Nichols' picture.

"I wouldn't think she fit in here."

Frank explained why she thought Nichols had been done by the same suspect and asked Clay what he made of the preference for clothed victims.

"That's an interesting aspect." Clay swiveled his profile to Frank, furiously working the pen in his hand. "Why would you keep clothes on an assault victim?"

"Maybe he's embarrassed," Frank offered. "Doesn't like women. Maybe he's afraid of them, maybe they're dirty. A clothes fetish?"

A smile tweaked Clay's lips. He was in his element and loving it.

"First of all, they're not women, only girls. And to me, why he's assaulting the girls isn't as telling as how he's doing it. Do you ever have dreams that you're naked?"

Caught off-guard, Frank chuckled self-consciously.

"Sometimes," she admitted.

"And how do you feel?"

Frank had to think for a moment. "Like I need to get some clothes on."

"Why?"

She'd worked with Clay enough to know he was going somewhere with this, so she humored him.

"I don't want anybody to see me."

"What would happen if somebody saw you?"

"It'd be embarrassing."

"So if someone took your clothes off how would you feel?"

"Pretty pissed," she responded quickly, but knew from Clay's penetrating gaze that he wanted more. She felt sympathy for his patients.

"I'd be..." Frank ran a list of adjectives through her head and settled for "...vulnerable."

The doctor nodded happily.

"It would be very demoralizing, and it would place your attacker in a position of power. He'd have the advantage and be superior to you."

"Which I would think this guy would like to do to his victims."

"But he's *not,* is he? Think about it. Taking someone's clothes off is a highly personal act. Whether it's consensual or not, it's a very profound intimacy."

Clay sat back, waiting for Frank to make the leap.

"So he doesn't want that."

He nodded, encouraging her on to the next step. He could see she was struggling.

"Okay, this...detachment from his victims is more important to him than making them feel vulnerable."

"Right."

"Why? I don't get that. I would think he'd want to impress them with his power."

"How big did you say our suspect is?"

"Probably around six feet, maybe over, weighs maybe around two hundred pounds."

"Alright. And how much did his heaviest victim weigh?"

Frank shrugged. Agoura was around one hundred twenty pounds.

"And how tall?"

"About 5'4"."

"So he's already got a considerable size advantage over these girls. If we assume he's taken them all by surprise, he has that advantage as well, and he maintains that advantage by choking them, rendering them even more helpless. These victims are very nonthreatening. He has them completely at his mercy and he knows it."

"So why doesn't he take it a step further?"

Clay leaned across the desk at Frank. In his enthusiasm his voice became louder and he gestured with open palms. Frank sat back, intrigued.

"He doesn't need to. What's critical to him is to assault these girls. He's very physical. He's not looking at them, he's not talking to them except to keep them from giving him away, he's not touching them. What does that tell you?"

Frank pushed her lips together and draped an arm around her chair, aware of Clay's scrutiny.

"Well," she finally answered, "I'd guess our boy doesn't want to make any emotional connection with his victims. He just wants to physically dominate them. What I wonder, though, is what that lack of connection means—I mean homicide is a very emotional business."

Clay nodded, adding, "For your average murderer. This guy you are dealing with has bounced far out of the norm. Serial offenders, the good ones, can only do this because they are so unable to relate to people. They don't have what we call normal emotional connections. What your offender is doing to his victims is highly satisfying for him. Through his physical actions he's achieving some kind of an emotional release. Because he's not engaging his victims at all, I'd be inclined to say he's reliving something that's happened to him, something intensely personal and private. Only now he's on the giving instead of the receiving end, and that's where his satisfaction comes from. Now he is indisputably in control."

Clay held up pictures of Agoura and Peterson, going on to explain the rage evident in the assaults. He suggested that pent-up rage might have come from the suspect's own abuse.

Frank puzzled, "Then why not assault boys if he's trying to relive it, or choose victims more closely resembling his attacker?"

"Okay," Clay said patiently. "One of the things we know about this man is that he prefers teenage girls. For some reason, at some point in time he became fixated on them. Yet this fixation is not personal. Look at the variety of victims he's selected. White, black, Hispanic, blonde, brunette, thin, plump. He's all over the place. I think his lack of focus indicates more concern for an abstract image than a real one. Girls this age represent some *thing* to him rather than some *one*. What I suspect drives him is visions of himself with so much power. The fantasy of him abusing these girls is far more important than who the girls actually are."

Clay paused before adding, "You asked why he's not choosing boys to relive this. There could be a number of reasons. If he was assaulted, I think it was by someone older, definitely someone with considerable power, a parent, teacher, close older relative. It could have been a female, but I think again we'd see him assaulting a specific stereotype, someone that resembled his abuser. That leads me to think it was a male who abused him, an older male, someone he doesn't feel able to strike back against. If this person raped him, that would explain his anal fixation."

Frank shook her head.

"Also, attacking boys could be too confrontational, too personal. It would be harder to disassociate from a boy," Clay continued. "Whoever he is, he is crazy like a fox."

"He's smart," Frank agreed. "Careful."

"This could go on awhile, couldn't it?"

"Maybe," Frank said coldly, "but sooner or later he's going to trip up. And when he does, I'll be right there waiting."

*They made it into the district play-offs. His team had fought hard
all season, and they were finally here. He had fought harder than anybody, knew the rest of the team was riding in his wake, but he didn't
care. It was his junior year, and he needed this moment. Dressing in
the locker room, he remembered his father's face in his this morning.*

*"There's going to be a scout from USC at the game today. This is
your chance, boy. Don't blow it," he'd warned, and the boy had no intention of that. He dressed quietly, and alone, not sharing in the nervous, pregame banter caroming off the locker room walls. He stayed
focused, reviewing over and over in his head, like a prayer, the play signals. He saw the team reacting to the quarterback's calls, thought of
his moves in response to his teammates, the defense. He was ready. He
was so ready he was almost getting a hard-on. No one better get in his
way because there was no stopping him today.*

*This was finally his moment. At last his father would be proud.
This was it. Do or die.*

14

The days that followed were monotonous and frustrating. Frank and Noah had followed up on all the assaults they could and were glad when they wrapped up interviewing the girls. Lisa McKinney was the last girl they talked to, a gangly blonde sporting a healing scar for her fifteenth birthday. When Noah asked her about it, she shot him a look full of misplaced venom, vehemently declaring, "That's where my face was pressed against a rock when he was pounding on me."

"What did he pound you with?" Frank asked easily, thinking it might be better if she took over the questioning.

"He was ramming his head and his shoulder into me the whole time he was...," the girl's defiance faltered, "...doing what he did to me."

Her account was much like that of the later victims.

Based on the limited recall of their one possible witness, Frank had a sketch drawn of their perp. Two of the girls confirmed that their assailant had brown hair and one remembered him wearing dun-colored workboots. The sketch was widely distributed, and a special task force was set up to handle the subsequent load of phone calls. The majority of calls were ridiculously unrelated. One woman reported a man with the same height and weight, but he was black. It turned out he was her ex-boyfriend and she wanted to get back at him for breaking up with her. Another caller was sure she knew the man and took Bobby and Jill straight to him. He was a Vietnamese grocer, stood barely taller than Jill's big tummy, and couldn't have weighed more than one hundred thirty pounds. The caller accused him of tipping the scales, and the detectives left them screaming insults at each other.

But the call they all liked best, the nine-three decided after a late afternoon round of pitchers, was the old Mexican guy who pointed to his stocky neighbor next door, insisting he was the one. "I know he don't look like the description," he assured them, "but I seen him change. He don't know I know, but I can see it," he confided. He explained to Gough and Nookey how the neighbor could shift shapes, that he could become anybody or any animal he wanted to be. The old man said he'd seen him turn into a bat, a black dog, even a beautiful woman one time. After the interview, Nookey spent the day howling like a werewolf and Gough eagerly counted his remaining days on the force.

After several weeks of back-to-back interviews, the nine-three had followed up on some solid leads, even arresting two felons with outstanding warrants, but none of them had led to their perp. Frank spoke with the lead detectives on the Culver City cases, questioning their methodology and generally pissing them off. She didn't understand how they had missed the connection between the assaults at the parks and the dump at Culver City High.

To their credit, they *had* seen the connection. But it still hadn't given them anything new to go on, other than they were looking for their man in a wider area, making their search even more difficult. They justified not putting up posters because they didn't have the personnel to handle the additional work it would entail.

Returning from CCPD, Noah drove and Frank checked out the deteriorating scenery. Storefronts were gaudy with tinsel and canned snow. Someone, maybe a wishful kid, had chalked a crude Christmas tree on a crumbling block wall. A banger had scrawled his *placa* through it, but a rival had rubbed him out, spraying his name and affiliation over the original message. The city impressively whitewashed graffiti as it occurred, but in South Central they'd conceded the battle.

The afternoon was cool, somewhere in the fifties Frank guessed, but she still had her window down. Once a cop always a cop, hyperalert for the anomaly in the scenery, the thing that didn't belong.

"Tracey wants you to come over for Thanksgiving dinner. You'd better come, 'cause you know she'll kick my butt if you say no."

"How's she doing?" Frank asked, by way of side-stepping the invitation.

"She's good. I think she's mellowing with age. She's cranked about all the hours I'm putting in lately, but at least I'm not sleeping on the couch or banging on your door at 2:00 A.M."

Both detectives grinned.

"And the kids," he continued, "when was the last time you saw them?"

"Labor Day?"

"You're kidding. Man, that's way too long. You gotta come over. I'm telling her you'll be there. One o'clock."

"Hmm. I'll call and find out the time myself. Last time you invited me it was three. I thought she was going to kill me until I told her you said five, and then you were almost the dead man."

"Three, five, whatever."

"I'll call."

They drove in silence for a while before Noah said, "Hey, Frank?"

She glanced at him.

"What do you think about setting up a decoy and trolling for him?"

Frank shifted in her seat, chewing slightly at the inside of her lip.

"Crossed my mind."

"And?"

"Too many drawbacks, not enough potential."

"Yeah, but there's a lot of drawbacks to being dead, too. I mean, how many bodies we gotta go through before we can catch this guy?"

"Where would you start?"

"The area where we found Nichols. We know that's his 'hood—"

"We *think* that's his 'hood."

Frank consistently reminded her detectives when they were speculating. The worst thing they could do was get locked into an idea. If it was wrong, they'd lost valuable time on a fool's errand, and the more committed they were to an idea, the harder it was to see other options. Noah continued impatiently.

"We know he's got a thing for schools, right? Am I safe in saying that? He's dumped two bodies at high schools, he's raped at and around two high schools. I think we should set up a decoy, maybe a homeless girl like the Jane Doe he did. Plant her around Nichols' walk to school."

"It's not in our jurisdiction."

"I know—we'd have to get cooperation from Culver City or cut them in on it."

Frank shook her head.

"No way. We're already brass heavy and soldier light," Frank said, in reference to the endless memos, meetings, and conferences that had been generated by involving Culver City in the investigation.

"Besides," she added, "it's just too big an area. We have no way of knowing if he'd see us."

"Well, what are our options right now, Frank? Sit around and wait for another Cassandra Nichols to turn up with a tree branch stuck up her ass?"

Noah tossed his boss a challenging look.

"If you're right, we've got a fistful of rapes, four dead girls, and not one solid lead to follow."

"I *know* what we have."

"Everything's petering out. The captains are all over us to close it so they can have their cops back, none of the cops want to be here, the chief's on Fubar's ass. I guess the only good thing is that it just isn't big enough for RHD yet. But at this rate that'll only be a matter of time. So what do we have to lose except the case and more girls?"

Continuing her perpetual street scan, Frank answered sarcastically, "Oh yeah. Fubar'll love it when I request additional manpower for a stake-out. And where exactly do we find a fifteen-year-old undercover cop?"

"I've been thinking about that. I got some ideas," Noah answered enthusiastically.

Frank was silently stroking her ring finger where she used to wear a thin gold band. She hadn't worn the ring for years but she still reached for it when she was mulling something over. Noah pressed his tiny advantage.

"I think I might have the perfect girl...woman," he corrected. "She's in Narcs at Parker Center. I met her a few weeks ago. I don't know how old she is, but I was really surprised when she told me she was a detective. She looks very young. Whaddaya say I talk to her, see if she'd work?"

Frank rubbed thoughtfully at the empty spot on her finger. It was a long shot, but at this point it might be their only one. She nodded, not breaking her stare out the window.

"You talk to your narc and I'll feel the Fubbie out. He won't want to share this anymore than I do, and I doubt CC will either."

"Atta girl, Frank, atta girl," Noah congratulated, punching his boss lightly on the shoulder.

"Are we any closer to finding out who he is?"

Foubarelle was hoping Frank wanted to see him because she had big news.

"Not really. Based on the way he's hit these girls and the way he's dumped them I feel pretty confident narrowing him down to a section of Culver City, but so far we haven't generated anything specific on this guy's ID."

"So technically this is Culver City's problem, but because Agoura and Peterson were dumped in our jurisdiction we're stuck with it."

Foubarelle grimaced, and Frank suspected he was weighing the merits of hanging on to this case or trying to dump it into the lap of the Culver City police. Foubarelle was a political weasel. If he thought this case was going to make his office look bad, he'd hand it over in a heartbeat. On the other hand, solving four homicides and nine rapes in one swoop would be an impressive coup. She figured this was a good time to hit him with their latest plan.

"Speaking of Culver City...we've been playing with the idea of setting up a decoy and doing surveillance for this guy. Take a look at this."

Noah had made a computer chart showing where their perp had committed his assaults, where he'd abducted girls from, and where he'd dumped them. Frank explained the plan, and the captain frowned.

"Now you're definitely out of your jurisdiction."

Frank nodded, deftly conceding a sense of control.

"If you wanted to run with this, we'd have to work with CCPD, get them on our side. It only benefits them in the long run—clears two homicides and a score of rapes for them, and they wouldn't even have to lift a finger. Good deal."

"But we still get credit for it," Foubarelle said absently.

"You still get credit for clearing two murders and a rape, not to mention bagging the Culver City Slayer."

The papers had taken to calling him that and it pissed everybody off. CCPD had to answer a lot of ugly questions and intensify their investigations, which basically meant assisting the LAPD carte blanche. This infuriated McNaughton, the CCPD chief. His mayor had ordered him to work with LAPD because the chief had hinted at nasty repercussions if CCPD didn't cooperate. To his own force, McNaughton had done more than hint. He didn't like that the media was having a field day at his expense and he'd made it very clear to his minions that the Culver City Slayer shit had to stop.

"What if it doesn't work?"

Frank shrugged.

"If the stake doesn't work, at least you can say you've taken a proactive stance and aren't just sitting around with your thumb up your ass."

"You know this is costing a fortune."

"I know, but does the chief want to wait until the guy comes knocking on our door, or does he want us to do everything we can before he kills another twelve-year old. God forbid a very well-connected twelve-year old."

Foubarelle reluctantly agreed to the stake. Frank dipped her head in assent, reminding him they'd have to borrow the decoy from another district. Foubarelle agreed to that, too, and Frank left the office having convinced her boss to enact a plan she barely believed in herself.

His father hadn't talked to him since he'd blown it during the championship game. His chances for a scholarship had slipped away with that intercepted pass and now the old man completely ignored him. The boy thought even the pain from the old days was better than this. He had to find a way to make things right again.

15

The guts of three case reports were spilled across Jill's desk. She and Bobby were looking at similarities between an old shooting of Gough's on 87th, the Mackay case, and a shooting Jill had picked up on 51st. Frank poured a cup of black coffee that smelled like burnt rubber and perched on Jill's desk, poking through the evidence with them.

All three looked up at the blonde girl Noah walked in with. Frank thought she must be a witness and glanced back down at the murder books, but Noah stepped up to her, waiting expectantly.

"What's up?" she asked.

"Detective Kennedy, meet Lieutenant Franco."

Frank was nonplused. Kennedy extended her hand, drawling, "How ya doin'?" around a mouthful of gum.

Frank thought Noah was joking. The young woman before her looked more like a Malibu party girl: shaggy, sun-streaked blonde hair around vibrant brown eyes; tanned and toned arms dangling out of a sleeveless T-shirt with a purple sports bra underneath; baggy, purple harem pants ending in Teva-clad feet. Frank didn't see a detective anywhere in the get-up. Cracking and popping her gum, the woman smiled placidly between Noah and Frank, the latter staring quizzically at her detective.

"She's interested in being our decoy," he explained with his usual boyish enthusiasm.

Frank snorted a dismissive laughing sound, sure now that he was kidding. When he didn't laugh back she became apprehensive.

"I need to see you in my office."

He followed her in and she told him to close the door.

"What the hell's that all about?"

"What's what all about?"

"The girl. She barely looks old enough to cut her own food."

Noah laughed.

"*Exactly.* She'll be a perfect decoy."

Frank adamantly shook her head, "No way."

"Why not?"

"She's a *baby,* No. I'm not putting her out there. She'd blow it and get somebody hurt in the process."

"Frank, she's twenty-nine years old. She was a street cop in Corpus Christi for five years, got her shield and worked Narc before she moved out here. She's done undercover. You don't get where she's at by being a baby," he protested.

"Uh-uh." Frank was still shaking her head, and Noah flapped his hands in exasperation.

"Why not?"

"She's too young."

"That's the point, Frank! Who do you want out there, Grandma Moses?"

The higher Noah's voice rose, the lower Frank's got.

"I don't like it, No."

Frank was entrenching herself and Noah took a deep breath, settling on the edge of her desk.

"Alright," he spoke patiently. "Tell me exactly what you don't like."

Aware she was being mollified, Frank thought about pulling rank. But she trusted Noah and was aware of her tendency to be overly conservative. She answered instead, "She's just a kid. How do we know she didn't get promoted for political reasons—"

"Like you did?"

"Like I did. But I was a damn good cop. If she is qualified for this kind of work she sure doesn't look like it or act like it."

Noah grinned. "You're right. She looks like she should be hanging off a surfboard and getting faced on mai-tais every night. But hey, what sort of cop were you at twenty-nine?"

"Let's say I had a little more respect for the position. Look at her."

With a bluntness earned from years of friendship, Noah said, "Frank, everybody knows you were born with a baton coming outta your ass, but she's a narc, for Christ's sake! She can't run around in a suit and badge, so she's a little casual. Big deal."

"Is she on a stake now?"

When Noah shook his head, Frank shrugged, "That's my point. I can't look at her and say, Yeah, I want to trust a whole undercover op to this girl. She just doesn't strike me as very professional. This is a big op, No, and I'm not sending someone out there who doesn't totally have her shit together."

"Okay. I don't know her that well, granted, but her record speaks for itself, and just talking to her you can tell she's bright. I wouldn't say she doesn't have her shit together, and I don't see how you can just by saying hello to her."

"I've been a cop for a while. I think I know a little something about people."

"Well, I think you're wrong here. You're making a snap decision based on very little information. I don't think you're being fair and, frankly, I'm surprised. That's not like you." Noah paused, his sincerity evident. Then he asked, "Would you be so resistant if this was a man?"

Frank clamped her lips together. Her jaw muscles bounced. Noah was right—she wouldn't be nearly as resistant if Kennedy were a man. She knew that she resented it like hell when her colleagues had thought that way about her, and she had to admit the injustice of her attitude.

Nine times out of ten, a woman in a difficult law enforcement position was just as effective as a male. Both were trained to react in a specific manner, both knew what had to be done. Problems happened if a man started feeling responsible for his female partner, for fear of either his own safety or hers. This weakened his reactive instincts, interfered with hers, and put both partners in peril. Frank was irritated to find herself behaving exactly like that.

She propped her elbows under her chin and covered her face with her hands, lightly moving her forehead up and down against her fingertips. When she stopped, she looked at Noah and asked, "What's with the gum? That just really tops her whole image."

"She's a pistol," Noah agreed, leaning forward eagerly. "I like her, Frank. We talked on the way over. She seems really smart, steady, confident. I think she'd be great. We've got somebody out there banging away at these girls like they're bumper cars. If you're right, this guy has murdered four of these girls. I'd hate to see a fifth one go down because you were afraid to try an option."

"A pass play," she said.

"What?"

"Never mind."

Noah studied Frank, gauging her stance.

"Just talk to her. Give her a chance. If you can't get over it, we won't do it. You're the boss."

Frank lifted her eyebrows dubiously, and in the ensuing pause both cops tried to read each other. A good detective knew a lot of body language, and Frank figured she was probably speaking volumes. Her clasped hands were like a row of soldiers guarding her mouth, the thumbs and index fingers posed like sentries between chin and mouth. Frank finally pulled her face from behind its barricade, sighing, "Bring her in."

When Noah and the young detective returned, Frank asked her sharply, "Why do you want this assignment?"

Kennedy smiled and casually flicked her shoulders, loosely holding Frank's piercing gaze.

"It sounds fun."

Frank threw Noah a quick I-told-you-so glance.

"I assume Detective Jantzen told you what the job entails?"

"Yeah. He says you've got a real fuck-up on your hands."

Around a thick hick accent, Kennedy snapped her gum for emphasis. Frank stared coldly. She detested Southern accents and allowed herself her prejudice. In men they reminded her of ignorance and inbreeding; in women they suggested incompetence and illiteracy. In Kennedy they sounded like all those things. But there was an edge to the drawl that suggested it was more affect than actual. The young detective stood comfortably, her hands held loosely in her deep pockets. Her hair was pushed back behind her ears, revealing three diamond posts sunk in the cartilage of her right ear and two in the left. A small gold cross swung brightly from a hole in the left lobe. Her shoulders were bronzed and well-muscled.

"Where'd the tan come from?"

Kennedy grinned hugely.

"Surfing. I moved out here for the waves."

"Do you manage to squeeze in some time for work?"

"We've been workin' a lotta nights, which is kind of a drag, but it gives me time in the water, so that's awright."

Jesus Christ, Frank thought, Annie Oakley meets Brian Wilson. She asked smoothly, "Noah said you're in Narc. How many collars have you had?"

"Dang," Kennedy said, looking absently at the ceiling. "I'd have to check, but I reckon around one-twenty or so, mostly in Corpus Christi."

Frank was impressed, although she gave no indication of this.

"Have you ever worn a wire?"

"Yeah, it's pretty cool."

Frank just stared, but Kennedy remained unfazed by the cold scrutiny. Her playful insouciance was aggravating, and Frank said sarcastically, "You realize this isn't Beach Blanket Bingo, don't you?" When Kennedy looked puzzled, Frank continued. "We've got a psycho on our hands. A big, dangerous man who likes killing girls after he's battered the shit out of them. Someone who wouldn't think twice about snapping you in half like a twig and then jamming a stick up your ass to watch you die. This isn't about fun and games. It's about little girls dying."

Frank had spoken with more heat than she intended. Without a trace of accent, Kennedy calmly parried, "I understand that, Lieutenant."

Frank knew she'd given away her hand. Locking eyes, she discerned a steel resolution beneath the easy facade. Frank looked away first, casually picking up a pencil.

"Who's your supervisor?"

"Lieutenant Luchowski."

"Have you talked to him about this?"

"No, ma'am."

Frank concealed her sharp irritation. She hated being called ma'am under normal conditions, and from Kennedy it was almost too much. She tersely asked Kennedy for his phone number.

Frank looked at Noah, who'd been watching silently, and said, "Alright." He grinned and gave Kennedy a low-five.

"I want to try and wrap up those interviews today, so don't disappear on me after you return Detective Kennedy to her—" Frank almost said tiki-hut, but realized that would not be politic—"office."

"You got it."

Frank watched the two detectives leave like they were going to play football together and she hadn't been invited into the game. She pulled the phone toward her and pounded Luchowski's number into it. He was pretty dedicated to playing by the rules, and Frank didn't think he'd be happy about loaning out one of his detectives. But that was alright, because Frank suddenly found herself eager for a good fight.

"I worked my whole goddamed life for you people and what do I get back from you? Nothing! Nothing, goddamn you!"

His father had called in sick again and spent the day drinking. The boy could hear him in the living room, could hear his mother trying to murmur her way out of the deadly salvo. It wouldn't work, though. Why couldn't she see that? He was only a kid, and even he knew better than to talk back to the old man. She was just making things worse.

The boy sat huddled on his bed. Every muscle was rigid, every nerve stretched taut. He sat waiting. Waiting for the old man to yell his name.

16

Beer-thirty?"

Johnnie leaned eagerly in Frank's doorway, like Greg Louganis entering a swan dive. She glanced at the clock.

"Yeah, I'll be there."

Johnnie exited, clapping his hands. Frank knew his enthusiasm wasn't for her company but for the rounds she'd buy. Though she should be last in line to point the finger, Frank briefly worried about Johnnie's drinking. He drank a lot, every day, but if she excluded his frequent hangovers, or sullen distress when he had to work beyond quitting time, it didn't obviously affect his work. She realized that buying him beer only contributed to whatever problem he might have, but it wasn't her place, yet, to advise him on his drinking habits, nor did she want to disrupt tradition.

When Joe Girardi had been lieutenant of the ninety-three, he'd always popped for rounds on Friday afternoon at the Alibi. It was an informal way to end the work week, swap stories, blow off steam. More importantly for Frank, it was an opportunity to engage in the squad's good-old-boy camaraderie. Amid the continual whirl of razzes and quips that passed for conversation, through undeclared drinking contests and suddenly declared fistfights, Frank had held her own. She'd earned her spot on the nine-three as much at the Alibi as on the streets.

Concentrating on the paper under her nose, she heard Gough and Nookey talking. Most of the squad was still out, though, and Frank was determined to get more work cleared off her desk. Poking his head in, Nookey asked, "See you at the Alibi?"

"In a bit," she nodded. Nook left with Gough, but a few minutes later the silence of the squad room was interrupted by the rest of her detectives. Frank gave up the notion of any more work and followed them out.

Because the Alibi was the cop-friendliest bar closest to the station, it wasn't uncommon for it to be jammed on a Friday night.

Gough and Nookey possessively defended a large table while Johnnie arm-wrestled at the bar with a uniform in his street clothes.

"'Bout time you got here," Gough grumbled. "I thought we were going to have to call the Guard to help us save the table."

Johnnie was bigger than his opponent, but as she took a chair Frank saw his arm go down. He motioned for Mel to buy the victor a beer and joined the nine-three table.

"Where's the Fire Truck? And the Taco Loco?"

"Girl-red's tired and Diego's at a niece's birthday party."

"Those Mexicans are always going off to some damn party," Johnnie pointed out amiably. Bobby deftly changed the subject, asking what had happened to the guy on the 405 who was threatening to shoot himself.

"He did it, man. Blew his brains out all over the right-hand westbound. Helicopter news crew was broadcasting it live. They got the whole thing."

"Son of a bitch still has the highway closed," Ike complained, appraising the crowded room. Like Johnnie, he was divorced and always looking for an available woman, though they were as rare at the Alibi as a clear day in July.

"What was his problem?"

"Them. Us. Little green men. Who knows. He wasn't playing with anything near a whole deck."

"Where's No?"

"Said he'd catch up to us," Johnnie answered, as Nancy came up. He tried to pat her ass, but she blocked his hand with a hard forearm and resumed writing in her pad, standing safely between Gough and Nookey.

"That's right, darling, we won't hurt you. Johnnie there just doesn't have any manners," Nookey crooned.

"Don't I know it. Hey, guys," she greeted the late arrivals. "Pitcher?"

Knowing the tab was Frank's, she smiled, directing the question at her.

"Hey, Nance. Start with two and keep 'em coming."

"You got it."

Frank absently watched her whirl away while the conversation turned to jabs at Fubar. As their supervisor, Frank had made it clear a long time ago that she wouldn't tolerate ethnic or minority slurs while they were on the badge. Except for Johnnie and Gough, this prohibition was still respected after-hours, so Foubarelle and the rest of the brass became their favored focus of derision. Although Frank didn't usually contribute to the conversation, she rarely defended her higher-ups and was restrainedly amused, knowing her own back got covered with shit when she wasn't around.

Nookey was moaning about a 60D Fubar had sent back because of spelling errors. "Man, I feel like I'm in sixth grade with Mrs. Beaman again." He shuddered. "I still have nightmares about that bitch."

The word *nightmare* made Frank wince at the involuntary images that her own had conjured up for her: Mag's bewilderment, Frank's helplessness, and blood everywhere. Frank jerked her head up to find Nancy approaching and distracted herself by focusing on the waitress.

She'd been at the Alibi almost as long as Frank had been a cop. Watching Nancy twist agilely through the crowd, Frank noted the sprouts of gray at her temple and the lines that weren't there twelve years ago. Then she chided herself, *Look who's talking.*

Nancy set the pitcher down next to Frank and whispered, "I saw that look. Is this finally gonna be my lucky night?"

Frank grinned slightly into the fist against her mouth, the clouds blowing out of her eyes for a moment. Nance had been offering for years, and many times Frank had been tempted.

"Huh?" Nancy laughed, though they both knew the answer.

By the time Bobby and Johnnie got to trading gridiron stories, only Frank was left with them at the nine-three table. She was relaxed and easy, her long legs up on a chair. She'd heard all their stories before but was mildly entertained by their one-upping. It crossed her mind to lift her pant leg and show them the fat scar under her patella where Junior Kensington had tackled her.

She'd been playing football in the street with her cousins and their friends. Junior had hit her hard and laughingly clambered off her, then got white when he saw the blood staining her jeans. Afraid she was going to throw up from the pain, Frank had peeked at the tear in her pants and seen a gash exposing her bone. She'd told her cousin to help her up, but she couldn't step on the leg. The world had started getting gray and narrow, and Frank had bit down on her lip to keep from passing out. Her younger cousin had run to get his mother, who had rushed Frank to the hospital, cursing all the way. They'd stitched the tendons back together, but it was months before Frank could walk on that leg again.

A hint of a smile played across Frank's mouth as the boys moaned about being tackled on Astroturf, but her nostalgic languor vanished when Noah walked in with Kennedy. Reluctantly, she pulled her legs off the chair and sat up straight.

"Hey, Lieutenant."

The drawl was like nails on a blackboard. Frank clenched her back teeth, acknowledging Kennedy with a quick bob. Noah clapped Frank's shoulder and took the chair next to her. Within seconds, Nancy appeared.

"Hi, No. I haven't seen you in ages. Did they kick you off the squad for being too handsome?"

"Yep, that's it. How'd you know?"

"It's obvious. Bring another mug?"

"You got it."

"And you, hon?"

Nancy's smile to Kennedy was returned.

"Ma'am, a Coke, please."

"Sure you don't want a shot of rum in that?" Johnnie asked

"I reckon straight'll do me just fine."

"Only sober cops I've ever seen have got God," Johnnie said challengingly.

"Or a wife like Leslie," Bobby muttered. She hated him drinking after work, but once or twice a month he'd go out on Friday night anyway. He and Noah had swapped plenty of sleeping-on-the-couch stories.

"You're not gonna get all preachy on us are you?" Johnnie dogged.

"Darlin', what was your name again?"

"Johnnie."

Kennedy nodded. "Tha's right. Johnnie." Then she leaned toward him and said, "Son, I don't even *know* you yet but you're already gettin' on my nerves."

"Wait'll you get to know him," Noah laughed, "then he'll *really* piss you off."

Johnnie waved disgustedly, muttering something about uptight bitches, and moseyed off to the men's room. The young narc turned her attention back to Noah. "So, tell me more about this dickhead I'm gonna be freezin' my ass off for."

"Not a whole lot to tell. We could be barking up the wrong tree, but it's more to go on than nothing. Just keep in mind that much of what we've got is theory, and be flexible."

Kennedy nodded her understanding. Noah explained their logic while Frank watched the young woman. The hick act was good, but twice now Frank had seen daggers winking under the guise.

"We've got some physical evidence on this guy. Size, weight, hair—not much else. Most of this is from the description the girls gave us, and we had a witness who saw someone matching this description where the third girl was raped. The wit estimated his age as somewhere between late twenties to early thirties. Frank likes the younger end of the range."

"How come?" she asked Frank, who shrugged and addressed her beer mug.

"He's smart but he's not confident. That usually comes with experience and/or age. He's eluding us but he's not mocking us. That says he fears us to some degree, respects us. You see that more in younger perps. The level of anger in these attacks would be hard to sustain for years on end. He's probably been holding this in for a long time and can't anymore. This guy's canny, though. I think he'd do it more often if he thought he could get away with it.

"As it is, he's committing these perps on a fairly regular basis. For the most part his assaults are premeditated and inherently risky, suggesting his caution is overruled somewhat by his compulsion. Again, we can look at the escalation of his attacks—as his confidence increases he spends more time with each victim and becomes more brutal. An older man might have already plateaued out, not exhibit such a steep learning curve. He'd probably be more aggressive from the git-go, take much larger risks. And I'd expect his vics to be more carefully considered. Our guy seems to settle for whoever comes his way, also characteristic of a younger personality."

"And you think he's going to go for me just because I'm young?"

Noah looked at Frank. He sighed when she didn't answer and picked up the slack. "Young, and in the right place at the right time. And if you act right, he'll sense that you're tentative, vulnerable. Hopefully he'll be attracted to that. Almost all the girls we talked to were real hesitant and uncertain. Somewhat afraid of us."

"Don't you think that's just normal for a girl who's been traumatized and is talking to the police?"

There was the merest hint of a challenge in Kennedy's questions. It irked Frank, but Noah didn't seem to notice.

"Sure, but you can see it's a basic part of their personality, too. It's their vulnerability that appeals to him. It makes him feel confident and in control. It doesn't look like he's actually stalked any of his vics, but he definitely prefers a certain personality, so he must be watching them at least for a little while."

Nancy paused at their table and poured the rest of a pitcher into Noah's glass.

"You guys ready for another round?"

Frank nodded and Nancy asked, "Who's your friend?"

Kennedy smiled, and before Noah could answer she shook Nancy's hand and introduced herself. Frank watched the women boldly appraising each other. Their mutual interest was suddenly clear to Frank. She drained her mug, chagrined she hadn't picked up on Kennedy sooner.

Nancy smiled, "Nice to meet you."

"Likewise," Kennedy replied with disarming attention.

Nancy blushed lightly as she wiped at the table, asking Frank if she'd eaten today. Frank thought for a moment before answering no.

"Are you going to?"

Nancy smiled down at her, but Frank was intent on Kennedy's wide grin.

"No," she said grimly.

"Fra-ank," the waitress chided, then turned to Kennedy. "How 'bout you, hon? You want something to go with that Coke?"

"I reckon I would," she said, raking Nancy's solid figure just long enough for the innuendo to register. Then she sat back and asked nonchalantly, "Ya'll got 'ny french fries in that there kitchen?"

The way she said *there* sounded like *they-uh* and Frank was amazed anyone could think that sticky inflection was charming. Kennedy's blatant flirtation was equally astounding. Nancy wasn't even a member of one of the most homophobic police forces in the nation and she was more discreet.

"I reckon we could rustle some up for ya," Nancy teased, playing with the accent.

"Well, that'd do me fine. An' how 'bout a salad, ma'am? Could I get one a them, too?"

"Only if you start callin' me Nancy. *Ma'am* sounds so old. I'll bring you a menu."

"Tha's awright. Just gimme your house salad, with ranch dressin', an I'll be happier'n a pig in a sty."

Just when she thought Kennedy couldn't get any lower, she impressed Frank by taking out a shovel and digging deeper. Noah chuckled, and Frank cut him a withering glare.

"Where were we?" Kennedy asked, innocently crunching an ice cube.

Frank pushed away from the table.

"I'm out of here. See you in the morning."

"Aw, come on," Noah protested. "We just got here."

Despite his pleas to stay, Frank slung her jacket over her shoulder and walked away, suddenly inexplicably angry. If she had turned around, Frank would have seen Kennedy smiling curiously at her retreating figure.

They didn't joyride together anymore. The boy missed that. He and his father had fun then, cruising, picking out the whores. The old man always let him pick whichever girl he wanted. The boy liked the younger girls, the younger the better. His father was really good about that. They'd drive for hours until the boy found a girl he liked.

But now that all was gone. The boy was alone with only his magazines and his memories.

17

The next morning, Frank looked out the rainy window and thought briefly about going back to bed. She was cold but refused to turn the heat on, rationalizing that this was *southern* California. She settled for a hot shower and upped the heat in the car as she drove in to the office. Walking into the squad room, Frank was disconcerted to find the *enfant terrible* scrunched in Noah's chair, surrounded by open case folders.

"Hey," Kennedy yawned, circumspectly taking Frank's measure. Faded jeans, old boat shoes, and an LAPD sweatshirt gave Frank a deceptively laid-back appearance. With her hair messed from the wind and her cheeks flushed by the cold, Frank looked almost sexy. She shattered the effect by grunting, "What are you doing here?"

"Shy and hesitant isn't my normal MO," the younger detective replied lazily. "I was just goin' over the reports on all these girls, trying to absorb as much of their personalities as possible."

Frank nodded, unlocking her door. Then she did an unusual thing: she closed it behind her, leaving Kennedy staring and tapping a pen against her teeth.

An old sax man wailed plaintively as Frank pressed through her notes. Oblivious to Kennedy's Circean presence on the other side of the door, Frank was doing what she did best.

As a rookie, Frank had been fascinated by what she saw on the streets and she'd quickly learned what they didn't teach at the police academy. How to feel fear and work around it. How to shoot with your left hand while you were moving. How to watch a cop die and not go crazy. How to turn all your senses up when you were out there. How to know, without knowing how you knew, when a lie had gone down. She'd enjoyed the theory in the academy, and the rigorous mental and physical training, but the street was reality. There should have been a sign on the way out of the academy that read: *This is where the training really begins.*

Frank believed in procedure but had learned to entertain other options when necessary. The chances she wouldn't take in her personal life she took through her work. She was physically unafraid, at ease with leadership, and willing to sacrifice personal comforts. Her patience and determination lent themselves well to police work, but one of her strongest assets as a detective was her curiosity. If a case wasn't closed, Frank wasn't happy. She *needed* to know who'd done it and why. Frank had spent her life fixing problems and couldn't relax until they were solved. The hide-and-go-seek for clues, the hunt and chase for the perps—this was as close as Frank came to being playful—and profiling particularly intrigued her.

It was a stretch to look beyond the physical evidence. That's what cops were trained to rely on. But an eleven-month fellowship at Quantico had showed her how to use the available physical evidence to gather intangible psychological clues. Part craft, part science, profiling was particularly helpful in tracking down repeat, violent offenders. Scientifically, profiling utilized behavioral clues the perp left at the crime scene, clues that indicated a perp's unique behavior patterns. For instance, a sloppy, disorganized crime scene could often be traced to a sloppy and disorganized offender, suggesting possible physical and behavioral distinctions about the perp.

And because people were capable of infinite permutations, the parameters for one sloppy perpetrator would not exactly match the profile of another. Being able to assemble the clues and predict the most likely set of behaviors for a given offender was part of the craft. Its inherent ambiguity made profiling an imprecise tool, but one that could be used with excellent results to narrow a list of possible suspects, hence narrowing the scope of the investigation and concentrating resources where they had the best chance for success.

Frank had no suspects in the Agoura case. Just plenty of victims. She needed to learn as much as possible about them before being able to fathom their perp. Frank laid out their pictures in the chronological order of the crimes. The most immediate distinction was the racial heterogeneity—three Hispanics, eight Caucasians, one Black. Serial perps usually targeted a specific race and stuck to it. This guy didn't seem to care. That he was hitting outside strict racial lines said something in itself.

The girls were all pleasant and average-looking. There was nothing exceptional about any of them, and that very blandness was suggestive. Maybe the perp didn't want anyone too extreme, too threatening. This would indicate he had a narrow range of life experiences and would be put off with unfamiliarities.

The assaults were not personal. None of the living victims knew their attacker, and apart from his direct assaults he had not engaged them in any other manner. She kept searching the display of photos, pausing to read each girl's pedigree. Nothing stood out as connected. She couldn't pin a common association, activity, or person to all twelve girls. None of their bios matched. They were from low to middle incomes, and though two-thirds of them had been accosted in a park, the other third were assaulted near high schools or in urban settings. Some were in junior high, some in high school, some in elementary, one was a runaway.

Frank sighed and stretched. She got up to change the music, absently trading the jazz for Fauré's *Requiem*. She turned up the volume, bowing her head as she listened to the first stanza.

Requiem aeternam dona eis, Domine, et lux perpetua luceat eis thundered though the small space, and Frank thought, grant them eternal rest and let perpetual light shine on them, indeed. She lost herself in the grandeur of the introduction, and when it ended, she opened her eyes. The girls stared up at her.

Cassandra Nichols smiled doe-eyed and gap-toothed. Claudia Menendez smiled too, contrasting sharply with Frank's memory of her heartbreak and puzzlement. Even the ones he'd left alive he'd managed to kill somehow.

Alright, buddy. Let's go one on one. You and me.

Frank was finally ready to get into his head, but first things first. Frank pulled out a VICAP form and started filling in the offender information section.

"Always start where you are," she muttered outloud. Joe Girardi had told her that her first day in Homicide. Answering the questions on the FBI form, she ended up with a long list of the perp's data. Armed with that, Clay's tape, and her own limited knowledge, she played with the information and the options it suggested, starting with a physical description of their perp. He was a big man with brown hair. None of the girls could remember anything remarkable about his body or the feel of it against them, so he probably wasn't too skinny or too fat. If he didn't have a good image of himself, he probably wasn't concerned with keeping up his physical appearance. The Troupe witness had said maybe he was slightly overweight.

His hair would be unkempt. He'd only cut it when it started to draw attention, but then he wouldn't cut it too short. He'd just have the barber trim him, keep him from feeling conspicuous. Their witness had described a man in jeans and a T-shirt. In Los Angeles that was standard attire. Frank bet his clothes had small holes or stains. Again, nothing too noticeable, just ordinary enough for a man who didn't care much about his image.

Frank looked at the notes she'd made while talking with Clay. All the assaults had happened between mid-morning and early evening. All of them were on weekdays. This made Frank feel that the perp worked evenings and weekends, most likely as an unskilled laborer. That would fit with his workboots, and explain his wearing blue jeans in the summer heat. He would be unassuming enough to keep a job, would probably never make waves, but he would most likely never be promoted. She figured he did what he had to to get by but didn't have the incentive to further himself. He probably worked alone, or with minimal contact with other people.

Frank continued in this vein, rearranging facts and figures into the logical behavior pattern critical to good profiling. She used her ability to slip into the perp's head, to see what he looked at, hear what he heard, feel what he touched, taste what he licked, loathe what he loathed, love what he loved. Ultimately, Frank needed to know how it felt for him to rape, batter, and finally kill a young girl. If she knew why he was doing this, maybe she could stop him.

"Yeah," Frank answered to a knock on the door.

Kennedy opened up. "I'm gonna go get something to eat. Wanna join me?"

Frank had glanced up from her work but looked back down as she replied, "No thanks." End of conversation.

"You sure?"

"Very."

"Want me to bring you somethin' back?" Kennedy pressed.

Frank patiently sat back in her chair, giving Kennedy her full attention. Slowly and evenly, as if dealing with a simpleton, she replied, "No."

With concentrated detachment Frank noted that Kennedy's eyes were brown. They caught the cold fluorescent light and warmed it. A warning flickered in Frank's gut. And in her brain. The flicker became cognition: Maggie's eyes had looked like that.

Frank blinked like a lizard.

"Is there anything else I can do for you, Detective?"

"Well...I've got a couple questions that maybe you could help me with."

Kennedy took an uninvited seat on the couch. Frank was sorry she'd asked.

"You seem to have an angle on this guy we're lookin' for—"

"Which is all speculative," Frank warned.

"Right, but still you've thought a lot about this. So I'm going through the books, and I'm trying to figure out what's the hook for him? What's gonna make me stand out from any other chick out there?"

Frank considered the question. She started to reach up and stroke her chin but stopped, almost as if she were being interrogated. She refused to give Kennedy even that much.

"A lot of things," Frank shrugged.

Kennedy was unrelenting.

"Like what?"

She leaned forward eagerly. Frank noticed she'd lost the accent.

"Could be any number of things." Frank outlined her sketchy victimology, stressing his apparent preference for passive, vulnerable victims.

"So basically, I should be a rag doll," Kennedy concluded.

Frank nodded. "Be innocent. Be vulnerable. Make yourself as visible as possible."

"Kind of contradictory, isn't it?"

"Do you feel like you can't handle it?"

"Not at all. I just want to make sure I do it right."

Frank's stare was the narc's only reply, so she asked, "Sure you don't want lunch?"

"Positive."

At the door she turned and asked, "What's that music?"

"It's a requiem. Fauré's."

"Hmm. I don't reckon I know what a requiem *for A's* is, but it shore is perty. I like it."

"I'm so very glad," Frank answered coldly.

He was yelling again. He'd lost his job, his pension, everything. And it was the boy's fault. What were they supposed to do now that there was no scholarship? Who was going to take care of things? The old man was crying. The boy stood with his ear pressed to the door.

His mother was crying too.

And a new, nameless fear gripped the boy.

18

Frank knocked on Tracey and Noah's door on Thanksgiving Day, wondering whose truck was in the driveway. Her blood chilled when she noticed the surf logos and parking sticker.

Tracey threw the door open, overflowing her flowery one-piece and screaming. She wrapped her arms around Frank's neck, mindless of the wine and flowers she was smashing between them, then yanked Frank inside, yelling, "Goddamnit, you old hama-zama, where the hell have you *been* all my life?"

Frank had to laugh.

"Well? Where you been?"

She threw a couple of punches at Frank who raised her offerings, pleading, "I come in peace."

"Yeah, well, you come that way but I'm not gonna let it stay that way," she said, taking the flowers, then sweetly asked, "For me?"

"Nope. For No. We got a thing going, didn't he tell you?"

"I should be so lucky," Tracey heaved her eyes dramatically. "If it would get him out of my pants for a while, he's all yours."

"You guys bad-mouthing me already?" Noah wandered into the living room in his bathing suit, holding a plate of grilled sausages. He held it toward Frank while Tracey moved like a warship into the kitchen.

"What's your poison tonight, babe? I've got margaritas in the blender."

"Sounds good," Frank called after her, snagging a piece of meat. She looked flatly at Noah, chewing.

"Tell me whose truck's in your driveway."

Noah grinned, "Hey, you're the lieutenant. You tell me."

"You didn't tell me she was going to be here."

"Ah, relax, Frank, it was a last-minute thing. Don't get all nutted up about it. Come on, let's get you oiled so you don't squeak so loud."

She followed him into the kitchen, dreading hearing Kennedy's drawl, but there it was, screeching through the sliding glass door of the backyard. Frank lingered with Tracey, who slammed a frosty, salt-rimmed glass into her hand and raised her own.

"Skoal, sister."

"Skoal, Trace."

They swallowed, and Tracey's eyes admired Frank up and down.

"You are hard like a rock," she said, squeezing Frank's arm. "Ouch."

"And you're as soft as one of those clouds the angels sit on. I can see you've been taking your gorgeous pills every day."

Tracey flopped a hand against Frank's chest and said, "Oh, stop teasing. I'm a fat old cow and you know it."

"You're gorgeous, Trace. Noah's the luckiest man in L.A."

"And don't think I ever let him forget it," his wife laughed boisterously. "Come on, come say hi to the calves."

Reluctantly, Frank let Tracey lead her out of the kitchen. Kennedy was in the pool playing Marco Polo with the kids.

"Leslie!" Tracey bellowed, and they all stopped. "Come say hello to Frank!"

Leslie waved happily and hopped out of the pool, all long legs and innocence. She reminded Frank of Cassie Nichols and she felt a quick, hot pang of sympathy for Cassie's father. Leslie gave her a big hug, shocking Frank with her frigid skin and dripping suit.

"What did you bring me?" she asked brightly.

"Les," Noah warned.

"How do you know I brought you anything?" Frank frowned.

"'Cause you always do."

"What if I forgot?"

Leslie turned on her heel, tilted her head in the air, and said with an imperious flourish of her hand, "Then you'll have to leave."

"She got that from her mother," Noah commented, basting the turkey on the barbecue, and Tracey snapped a towel at him. Frank sighed and stood up, resigned to her banishment.

"No! Don't go," Leslie squealed, wrapping her dripping blue arms around Frank's legs.

"What's in your pockets?" she asked curiously as Frank shrugged unknowingly.

She pulled her wallet out and handed it to Leslie.

"Not that."

She pointed silently at Frank's front pocket and Frank hauled out her keys. Leslie shook her head. Then Frank pulled out a new Hot Wheels truck and Leslie shook her head again. Frank reached in and found a package of animal stickers. Leslie examined them, but Frank said, "I brought those for Jamie. I don't have anything for you."

"What's that?" Leslie poked at something hard in Frank's back pocket.

"Oh that," Frank said dismissively. "That's nothing."

"What is it?" Leslie insisted.

"You don't want that. It's nothing."

"Let me see!" Leslie jumped up and down, hugging her goosebumps.

"You sure?"

"Yes."

"Alright. But you won't like it."

"I don't care. Let me see!" Her eyes were glowing with expectation and her brother and sister had joined her. Frank dipped into her pocket and slowly took out a bottle of purple nail polish. As Leslie grabbed for it, Noah whined, "Jesus, Frank. You tryin' to make my daughter look like a hooker?"

Frank grinned defenselessly, but Leslie was already sitting and drying her toenails off. Kennedy joined them, wrapping herself up in a towel.

She drawled, "Hey, Lieutenant," and the rare joviality evaporated off Frank like spit off a red iron. She took a large swallow of her drink and nodded curtly. Mark and Jamie had cursorily examined their toys and begged Kennedy to play Marco Polo some more. To Frank's relief, she agreed. And why wouldn't she, Frank thought acerbically, she's just a kid herself.

Tracey slapped Frank's thigh.

"Remember that psych tech at work who had a crush on me?"

Frank nodded, and Tracey launched into an animated account about how he'd pinned her against the wall a few days ago and tried to kiss her. Tracey took the bouquet of wildflowers he'd offered, then gave him a dislocated shoulder and testicles the size of oranges.

"And they say the cops are rough." Frank shook her head.

"Let me tell you," No said earnestly, "don't be puttin' the moves on Trace when she doesn't want 'em, man. Uh-uh. You'll be lucky to wind up dead."

"Oh, hush. Don't listen to him, Frank. Let me get you another drink."

She sailed off. It pleased both Frank and Noah to watch her walk. Noah grinned, and Frank spread her hands.

"I'm telling you, you make her a widow and I'm stepping in."

"She'd have you in a heartbeat, and you'd be begging for mercy."

They shared a smile as Tracey returned with a pitcher and another raunchy tech story. By the time Noah declared the turkey done, Mark and Jamie's teeth were chattering, and Kennedy was shivering uncontrollably. Leslie's nails gleamed like ripe grapes, and neither Frank, Noah, nor Tracey felt any pain.

Sitting beside her at the table, passing potatoes and green beans, Frank was almost civil to Kennedy. Dinner meandered through a couple bottles of wine and endless stories. Before the adults ate dessert, Tracey and Noah put their nodding kids into bed. When they left the room, Frank started clearing the table. Kennedy helped her, trying to make conversation but getting no encouragement.

Finally, after Frank handed her a rinsed plate for the dishwasher, she stated, "Lieutenant, I get the feelin' you just about des-*pise* me. Is that at all accurate?"

"I don't think I care enough about you to despise you," Frank said coolly.

Kennedy grinned into the dishwasher. "So I take it it's nothin' personal, and that you always act like you're chewin' on glass?"

Frank stopped rinsing and focused intently on Kennedy. "Detective," she said quietly, "you can take that anyway you like. However that is, I really couldn't care."

"Yes, ma'am," Kennedy drawled.

The women barely spoke to each for the rest of the evening, but their eyes met often. Kennedy's were sparkling and relentless, while Frank's appeared glacially indifferent.

Frank and Noah were eating lunch in a Chinese restaurant, working on the details of their undercover plan. Frank had spread a map on the table showing where their boy had struck. Around a bite of lo mein, she asked, "Where's he going to hit next?"

Noah frowned at the map as if it were deliberately withholding the answer from him.

"I think he'll hit somewhere around the parks again."

Frank nodded, but said, "Okay, why?", wanting to hear his reasoning.

"Well, look. You've said he's comfortable in this area, confident. He spread out for the rapes, but abduction's still a new thing for him, so he's still working on his confidence in that area. If he's insecure, he'd want to be in as familiar an environment as possible."

Noah poured green tea into their little cups, asking, "What say you, Sherlock?"

Frank dexterously grabbed the slippery noodles with her chopsticks and said, "I think we'll find him where we found Jane Doe and Nichols."

"Why there?"

"Elementary, Watson. He might plan on hitting the parks again, but two things might thwart that ambition. One is fear and the other is circumstance. He's got to know he can't keep going there and getting away with it. Some perps become so good at what they're doing that they start to mock the police, but I think our boy's a long way from that kind of self-assurance. That's why he branched out to the high schools for the last rapes."

Noah protested with his mouth full. "But Agoura and Peterson were from the parks."

"Exactly. Let's assume Jane Doe and Nichols were accidental, chance moments of opportunity. If he's scared to deliberately go out and grab a girl, he's going to do it where he's most comfortable, which I agree is the park areas. But he's hit them twice now, so between all the previous assaults and now the two murders, he's got to know both parks are hot for him. He's sick, not stupid."

Frank put her chopsticks down and wiped her mouth. "Point two, again assuming Doe and Nichols were just opportunities he couldn't pass up, he had to have been in their vicinity to catch them, someplace centrally located around the parks. We know he takes advantage of circumstance, so let's put one—Kennedy—in his path. If we do the parks instead, how do we know which one to pick? I think we've got a better chance of running into him on the street."

"Alright. I can see that. How do you want to play it?" Noah asked.

"Make Kennedy a homeless girl, a runaway. Put her out on the streets."

"Oh, that's nice duty in the middle of winter."

The idea amused Frank but she didn't show it.

"Well, this guy has a pretty consistent time frame. All the assaults have been on weekdays, in broad daylight. So we dump her predawn and pick her up after dark. Six A.M. to six P.M. Could be worse."

Frank finished her tea and asked Noah what he thought.

"Glad it's her and not me," he grinned.

Later that afternoon, Noah slowly chauffeured Frank, Kennedy, and two officers from the Special Investigation Section, around downtown Culver City. Cruising the neighborhood where Cassandra Nichols and the Jane Doe had been found, they searched for an optimal stakeout area.

Lieutenant Hobbs was a bull of a man and looked like the poster boy for the LAPD's swat team. In an incongruously high-pitched voice, he said, "Here we go," pointing to a corner off Sepulveda. Kennedy had to perch on the edge of the seat to see around Marquez, the other SIS officer.

On the southwest corner, facing onto the boulevard, was a squat, concrete building with three store windows. An electronics shop fronted Sepulveda and Venice, and next to it were an auto parts store and a barbershop. An alley ran down the barbershop side, and where the building ended, a six-foot chain-link fence closed the alley off behind the shops. The alley dead-ended against a two-story building. A long drugstore dominated the other side. It was a cul-de-sac accessible only from the opening on Sepulveda. A laundromat on the far side of the boulevard offered an unobstructed view down the alley. They drove around the block to see what the alley dead-ended against. It was a lighting fixture store and a sign-making shop.

"Whaddaya think?" Kennedy asked, firing off a round of bubblegum.

"Looks good," Hobbs said, and Marquez nodded.

"Go around again, No. Let me and Hobbs off at the corner. Marquez and Kennedy, see how it looks from the laundromat. We'll meet you at the Shell down the street."

The two lieutenants carefully moved past plastic garbage dumpsters pressed against weeds and shrubs that were taking over the alley. They checked for holes in the fence and unexpected doors or windows. Frank searched the ground for drug paraphernalia, not wanting to set Kennedy up in a shooting gallery. There was no access from the roofs, except for jumping straight down, and the vegetation would afford a homeless person adequate cover.

"Looks good," Hobbs repeated, hands braced on his slim hips.

Frank nodded reluctantly as they left the alley, their long steps evenly matched as they walked down the street.

"I want to wire her. If we lose her visually I still want to be in contact. I know it's a little extreme, but our perp's extreme. We don't know who he is, where he'll be coming from. I just want this as covered as possible."

"You got it."

Frank listened as Hobbs described how he'd fit her for sound.

"Good?" Noah asked when they were all back in the car.

Their alley was situated almost dead-even between the Nichols and the Jane Doe sites. They had their decoy, they had their surveillance team. Now all they needed was their perp.

"Green light," Frank answered. Kennedy started whistling "Back in the Saddle Again." The slight narrowing behind Frank's Ray Bans was the only hint of her irritation.

Hobbs was pleased. Technical surveillance was his baby. The smaller the chips, the thinner the wires, the happier he was. Kennedy stood before him, decked up and tricked out like a terrorist package, but no one could tell by looking at her or patting her down. They tested the wire until Hobbs was satisfied, then they reviewed their game plan for the dozenth time.

Weather, the brass, placement, the wire—all of that was going through Frank's mind as she watched Hobbs delicately unhooking Kennedy. She and Noah were chattering like Heckle and Jeckle, Hobbs and the techs were joking around, but Frank stood apart, nibbling at the scarred tips of her sunglasses.

She was nervous about this op, didn't like how many elements were out of her control, but after hours of guesswork, hunches, and plotting the odds, they were finally ready to roll. No matter how much she tried, Frank couldn't come up with a better plan. At this point, with so little to go on, and knowing that the perp would be out hunting soon if he wasn't already, the gig with Kennedy was their best bet. Frank had marginal confidence in the young detective, questioned the odds of encountering their guy this way, and second-guessed her own profiling skills. She was extremely uneasy pouring this much resource into an operation based almost entirely on conjecture, but unless another body turned up offering more clues, it was their only choice.

Compounding her frustration was the increasing attention from the media and RHD. They'd been sniffing around the case, and Foubarelle was about ready to drop it in RHD's lap. The only good thing about the attention was that no one wanted to look like the bad guy. All the agencies were cooperating, and manpower was being thrown at them like lifelines to a drowning man.

Frank sighed, feeling the pull of the muscles in her neck and shoulders. She wanted to knead them but thought better of it in front of Hobbs and his crew. Just as she discarded the notion, an obscure memory leapt from a dark corner: the end of the day, sitting on the couch, talking with Mag, Mag's strong fingers digging into her neck, easing all of Frank's knots.

Frank forced her mind to become a blank screen. Returning to the management of a homicide investigation, she asked brusquely, "We ready to roll here?"

Kennedy bellowed, "'Roll o-o-n, Big Mama,'" cracking up Marquez and Noah, who thought she walked on water. Feeling like she was in charge of a kindergarten class, Frank stood icily apart from the merriment.

He was deeply into one of his fantasies, playing it out behind his locked door, when he heard the shot. His mother started to scream as he tore his helmet off. She was still screaming by the time he got downstairs. He took one look and couldn't move. His father was sitting on the couch, half his face chewed off by shotgun spray. The son remained fixed to the carpet, as if he'd sunk roots. His mother just went on screaming. Eventually a neighbor came over and let himself in after his pounding went unanswered.

The neighbor quickly backed out the same way he'd come, gagging on his words. The police came and took the body away, and the boy's mother retreated upstairs to her bed. The boy tied the sofa to the top of the car and dumped it in a trashy alley. His mother was still in bed when he returned home. He eventually asked if she was going to make dinner. There was no answer, so he fixed a bologna sandwich and ate it in front of the TV, where the couch used to be. Spots of blood had soaked into the carpet. He thought about trying to clean them up but dismissed the idea as too late, though he did wipe the wall behind the couch with some water and a sponge. He didn't want the living room to start smelling.

19

rank pulled into the parking garage at half past five. A light drizzle had misted her windshield all the way to work. As she yanked her briefcase out of the back she wondered if the rain was going to intensify. The Weather Channel called for morning drizzle turning to rain, but Frank wasn't about to call off an op based on TV weather coverage. Glancing around the garage, she noticed Kennedy's truck wasn't there yet.

Frank slammed the little Honda's door. She wouldn't be surprised if Kennedy was late. Taking the stairs two at a time Frank felt a smug justification. She noticed lights on in the squad room and was surprised when she entered to find Kennedy standing at the coffee pot.

"Mornin'," Kennedy chirped.

"Morning."

Kennedy poured and asked Frank if she wanted a cup. Frank shook her head.

"Any problems last night?"

She was worried the perp might somehow get wise to their con and follow Kennedy home.

"No, ma'am," Kennedy grinned. "The surf was great." She extended a steaming mug. "Sure you don't want some?"

Frank's first instinct was to say no and walk away, but she *did* want it. She checked her vexation and accepted the mug without thanks.

"You should come out with me sometime. I've got an extra board. It'd be good for you—the ocean's very therapeutic."

Frank stared hostilely at the cocky young woman. Normally when she drilled people with her icy blues, they tended to turn away, but the smile in Kennedy's brown eyes never wavered. Her happy-go-lucky boldness continued to irritate Frank. Feeling slightly off center, she swallowed her annoyance as Kennedy said, "I heard it's supposed to rain today."

"Might," Frank agreed tersely.

The plan was for Kennedy to go into the drugstore if it started raining heavily. An undercover stationed at the laundromat would drop off clothes and a wig so she could change in the bathroom and leave undetected, and later that morning, that was exactly what happened. The bottom fell out of the sky, and Kennedy barely had time to cover her wired torso with a garbage bag before seeking the Rexall's shelter. She came out a few minutes later with long dark hair, a raincoat and umbrella. The van picked her up at the Shell station.

"Yeehaw," she said yanking the wig off her wet head as Noah drove away.

"Hey, don't get water on this," Marquez yelped. Kennedy pretended to shake her head over the instrument panel, and Marquez defended it with his body.

"Gotcha," she grinned. They were still in high spirits as they walked into the station house. Marquez playfully asked Kennedy out for lunch, and Noah ribbed that the Lady Godiva wig had turned him on. Kennedy retorted that the burly tech really had a thing for peeping toms and it was the trenchcoat that had done it. They were still goofing off when they strolled into the homicide room.

Frank looked up from the bulletin in her hand. "How did it go?"

"Quiet as a church on Monday morning," Kennedy volunteered.

"Except for that old lady who told you to get a job and almost hit you," Noah snickered.

"Oh, Lord," Kennedy groaned. "I'm out there worryin' 'bout serial killers and meanwhile little grannies are tryin' to bash my head in!"

Kennedy's *head* sounded like *hay-ud*. Frank had become used to Kennedy's accent coming and going: the better the story, the heavier the accent. Frank debriefed with the op team, and just as she was about to send Kennedy back to Parker for the day, Johnnie slammed down his phone and jumped out of his chair.

"Hey," he rasped, "I don't know who that was, but somebody that's pissed at the Tunnel. Says he's back in town, dealing out of a crib on," he grabbed the back of a receipt he'd written on, "Reston. 5500 Reston, Apt D."

"You have a warrant?"

Johnnie pawed a big hand around the layers of paper on his

desk and came up with the necessary document.

"Got two days left on it."

"What else did your tip say?"

"Asked if we were looking for Timothy Johnston. I said, 'The T-man? The Tunnel?' He said, 'That's the man.' I said, 'Yeah, we're interested in him.' He said, 'I know where he was.' I said, 'Where's that?' He gave me the address and I asked him why he was telling me. He said, 'Do we want this mo-fo or not?' I said, 'Yeah,' and he said, 'Now you know where to find him,' and hung up."

The fifty-five hundred area of Reston was deep with Bloods who hated the LAPD, and Frank considered the possibility of an ambush.

"Did you recognize the caller at all?"

"Yeah, Frank. It was my dead grandfather calling from the grave...I don't know who it was."

Johnnie slapped the warrant impatiently and said, "Are we gonna move on this or not?"

She thought a moment longer, then replied, "Suit up. Everybody roll. Check out the Kevlar and thigh holsters. Get some jackets. Johnnie, put that warrant in your pocket."

He rolled his eyes, "Yes, mother."

Two years ago they'd gone out to bust a dealer who'd killed three kids who were working for him and ripping him off. As they were scrambling out of their units, Johnnie had patted his pockets. No arrest warrant. They had to call the bust off, and their man walked. They were still looking for him. Frank wouldn't let Johnnie forget it.

Noah, Jill, Johnnie, and Frank were the only detectives in the office. And Kennedy.

"Suit up," Frank said to her.

"Naw, Frank. She doesn't need to go on this," Noah interjected.

Frank turned to him.

"Why not?"

"Yeah, why not?" Kennedy echoed, facing him, fists on hips.

"It's not her gig. We got enough people from here, we don't need to be dragging in narcs from Parker."

Frank tilted her head toward Johnnie's retreating back and told Kennedy to go help him. She readily followed. Noah asked again, "Come on, Frank, leave her out of this."

Frank had already started walking to her office. She had to let Foubarelle know what was going down, but now she paused.

"Is there something I should know about? A problem?"

"No. It's just that this guy's a bad dude, and Reston's a really bad place. She shouldn't have to help us with our dirty work. The four of us can handle it. And we'll have back-up, too."

Frank seemed to mull it over, but then hoisted him on his own petard.

"Would you be this concerned if Kennedy was a man?"

"Touché. But maybe I would. Hell, *I* don't want to go there and it's my case. I'd just rather leave her, that's all."

Frank shook her head.

"She's going. I want to see Gidget in action."

Frank went to make her call, hearing Noah hiss "Shi-it" behind her. She was amused by his concern, but Frank was eager to see Kennedy under pressure. Truth to tell, she wouldn't mind seeing Kennedy sweat a little and have that damn cocky smile wiped off her face. It briefly crossed Frank's mind that she was being petty again, but she didn't pause to examine the thought and dialed her captain instead. When he didn't answer, she stalked back into the squad room. Noah, on the phone arranging for back-up, looked grim. Jill seemed worried.

Frank crossed the room and asked her quietly, "Okay, Fire Truck?"

Jill smiled wearily, "Right as rain."

She slipped into an extra-large flak jacket and Frank gave her a quick pat on the shoulder. Glancing at Johnnie and Kennedy, she recognized their excitement. Though her own composure was still unflappable, Frank was excited and slightly apprehensive. Busts like this were inherently risky and made the adrenaline flow. She mentioned her concerns about an ambush, briefly scanning Kennedy's reaction, but the young cop's enthusiasm didn't waver.

"Can we try and draw him out of the apartment?" Noah asked.

"Are you kidding? Into this weather?" Johnnie laughed at the idea. "I say we just go in and take him."

Frank sided with Johnnie. "We don't know enough to draw him out. It's a pretty mellow day, and he's probably just hanging inside, chillin'. Unless it's a set-up, I think we've got surprise on our side."

Noah made a wry face as Frank outlined their strategy. The Reston Arms was a concrete, two-story apartment complex, with walk-ups and a balcony around the front. The front door was the only entrance, and depending on how Apartment D was situated, the back-up would cover the windows to the rear and/or side of the building. Technically, Noah and Johnnie would go in first because it was their case, but Frank wanted a better shooter up front. She and Johnnie would flank the door, with Noah and Kennedy behind them. Jill would back up the uniforms behind the apartment.

"Alright. Questions?"

Moving, Johnnie said, "Yeah. You buying lunch afterwards?"

"I thought you were on a liquid diet," Jill shot back.

Filing out in their navy windbreakers, with LAPD stenciled boldly across their backs, they looked like a ball team taking the field. Outside, the rain fell straight and steadfast, a resolute army of droplets streaming unwaveringly to the ground.

"You sure these apartments aren't inside?" Jill asked in the Mercury, squashed between Kennedy and Briggs.

"Don't worry, you ain't gonna melt."

Frank could see the radio units following them in the side mirror. It felt good. They had the advantage of surprise and lots of manpower. Frank's stomach rumbled. She was looking forward to lunch. She cut Noah a glance and could tell he was still upset. His knuckles were white on the steering wheel, and he hunched over it in bleak determination. He hated busts.

"What's for lunch, Watson?" Frank asked.

He just shrugged, concentrating through the flapping wipers. Frank twisted around with a sharp glare for Kennedy. "Are you ready for this?"

"You know it," Kennedy grinned, making three loud pops with her gum.

She apologized sheepishly when Jill said, "If my kid does that, he'll never chew gum again."

"How come he's called Tunnel?" Kennedy asked.

"Cause he's long and black," Johnnie chimed.

As they approached Reston, Frank went over the plan one more time. The detectives squinted through the rain at the crumbling apartments. Five units stacked over five, spalling gray concrete dotted with bullet holes, rusted stairs at either end providing access to the upper apartments. Some of the windows were covered with tin foil or cardboard. Some were intact but cracked. A few held sagging Christmas decorations.

They parked on the street and scrambled through the maze of crumpled lawn chairs, sprung couches, and garbage. It was hard not to step on shattered Olde English or Cobra bottles. While Jill and two of the cops scrambled around to the back of the building, the other two stayed with Frank's group. They took their positions under the balcony at the apartment's door, hands loosely next to their holstered weapons, radios on. Johnnie pulled the warrant out with a flourish and winked at Frank.

She knocked loudly, and a woman's skinny face peered from behind a sheet in the window. They heard muted voices, then after an inordinate amount of time bolts were slowly drawn back. The woman who'd appeared in the window opened the door a few inches and peeped out from under a chain lock

"We have a warrant for the arrest of Timothy Johnston," Johnnie growled.

"He ain't here."

"We have reason to believe he is. Unchain the door and step outside."

"I gotta get my coat," she said fearfully, starting to close the door.

"STEP OUTSIDE NOW!" Johnnie bellowed.

The woman glanced over her shoulder, then closed the splintering door and fiddled with the chain. Like a high-speed computer, Frank's brain processed reasons for the delay—getting rid of a stash, trying to get out the back, hiding, positioning for fire. The former seemed the most likely scenario. As the door started to open, the radio blared that a black male, not the suspect, had jumped from a rear window and was in custody, but that there was at least one more black male inside the apartment.

As the woman stepped through, Frank flung the door open. It bounced against the wall. In slow motion she saw Johnnie step inside. Frank followed. They'd walked into a small entry in front of a kitchen. A figure—black/male, Frank registered—had slipped down a hallway off the cluttered living room to their left. Johnnie yelled at him to freeze, but his shadow slid down the hall. He and Frank drew their pistols at the same time. She was vaguely aware that Noah and Kennedy had done the same. Her peripheral brain acknowledged a greasy pile of rock on a coffee table. A cold drop of sweat splashed onto her ribs as she stepped long-legged across the open doorway to the hall. Their suspect had turned, facing them. He was unarmed, but not Tunnel. Where the hell is he, she wondered?

Frank's adrenaline rush made each word coming from the radios crisp and distinct. "We have a second black male in custody. Not the suspect."

Two, she thought, neither Tunnel. Stealing a terrified look to his right, then back at the cops with 9mms drawn on him, the man at the end of the hall slowly raised his hands.

"I didn't do nothin'," tumbled breathlessly out of his mouth. Outside, the skinny woman started crying, wailing to be released.

"Okay," Johnnie soothed, walking toward him with gun lowered. "Be cool. Just keep your hands behind your head and kneel down for me."

Frank held her gun on the man until Johnnie cuffed him. Noah was just inside the hall, gun drawn. Kennedy was next to him, a step behind. Johnnie hustled his man between them, out to a waiting cop. The skinny woman's wailing increased. Frank distinctly heard her scream, "Timmy! Come out, baby," and the hair on Frank's neck stiffened.

He's still in here.

She motioned Noah to take the door to his right, and Kennedy the room to her left. Frank stepped into the bathroom. Rain water was blowing in from the open window. She reached toward the closed shower curtain.

"GET OUTTA HERE MUTHA-FUCKAS! GET OUTTA HERE OR I CUT THE BITCH! GET YO FUCKIN' ASSES OUT NOW!"

Frank froze, but her brain screamed, *Kennedy. Fuck! He's got Kennedy!*

The woman was screaming louder now. Frank heard Noah say very calmly, "Okay. We're gone. We're outta here. Just relax, man."

"GET OUT! GET OUTTA HERE! GO ON, MUTHA-FUCKA, 'FOR I CUT YO' ASS TOO!"

Frank stood in the little bathroom, barely breathing. Automatically she clicked off her radio, abstractly noting the cracked, faded linoleum, the dirty white towel hanging on the bathroom door, the old toothpaste scum in the rusty sink. She heard scuffling in the hallway, Noah's easy voice, in the living room now. She couldn't hear him clearly, the woman's crying was drowning him out.

"GO ON! GET OUT!"

Then Noah's voice, louder than it had to be, for Frank's benefit. "Okay! We're all gone! We're all out of here, man. It's okay now."

A door slammed and the woman's screams receded. Through the open window radios bleated for back-up. In the living room, a man she assumed was Tunnel was repeating, "Aw motherfuck, aw Jesus, aw fuck."

"Hey, it's alri—"

"SHUT UP BITCH! I WANT YOU TO TALK I'LL TELL YOU. SHUT YO' FUCKIN' MOUTH!"

Kennedy said something quietly, then Frank heard Noah talking through the door. It sounded like he was trying to reassure Tunnel that he was going to be okay, that this could be worked out if he just stayed cool. Frank strained to hear him asking Tunnel what he wanted.

"JUST BACK OFF!" Tunnel shouted, then said more to himself, "I gotta think 'bout this."

Noah replied they couldn't back off without Kennedy.

"You understand that, don't you? You wouldn't leave one of your homies and we can't leave ours. So what do you want us to do? Talk to me, Timmy."

Noah was engaging him, keeping him occupied. Tunnel had no idea Frank was in there with him. Her gun hand started to shake and a completely irrational memory flashed through her head of driving up Highway 101 in the sunshine, Mag laughing and getting whipped by her own hair.

Okay, she ordered, *steady up, goddamnit.* Despite a clamoring heartbeat and an incredible desire to take a leak, Frank forced herself to breathe deeply and smoothly, focusing on the present. Noah was talking soothingly through the door, and she thought, Good boy, No. She was glad he was out there.

Stepping carefully and without sound, she peered around the door. The hall was clear. She couldn't see Kennedy or Tunnel in the living room. She was grateful for the commotion in the apartment complex—anxious neighbors talking to each other, catcalls and insults, sirens, radios, cops in motion. A chopper was thumping overhead, and the rain fell on, a somber motif to the cacophony. Frank was acutely aware of sights and sounds, the smells of old grass and cigarette smoke, fried food and musty carpets, the texture of the 9mm, warm in her damp, cold hand.

Tunnel was telling Noah that he wanted a car, a black Explorer. Frank could hear him by the door, explaining he wanted a fully loaded vehicle.

Frank sucked in a deep breath. No one was in the hall. She darted into the bedroom on her left. It was dim and windowless and she froze beside the door. Holding her breath, heart thudding, she listened for Tunnel. He was still talking to Noah, who asked how Kennedy was.

Tunnel said, "Your bitch be fine unless you fuck wit me."

"How do I know you haven't cut her?"

"Fuck that. She my insurance. I cut her when I'm good an' ready."

"Then how come I can't hear her?"

"Tell your homie, you alright."

"I'm fine, Noah. I really am."

Kennedy's voice was strong and steady. Her confidence encouraged Frank. *Okay*, she ordered again, *breathe easy*. Willing herself into a quiet spot amidst the chaos, Frank envisioned herself moving up the hallway, hugging the wall. She remembered the sheet hanging over the window in the living room. No reflection. Good.

Tunnel was nervously telling Noah that this was bullshit, like the cops were really going to let him get away.

"Hey man, I'm not saying we're gonna let you get away, but at least in a car you got a chance. I gotta tell you it's not a good one. The best thing you can do right now, the safest thing for yourself, is to send her out, and you follow, hands up."

"I can't do that!" Tunnel pleaded. "I can't be locked up again."

There was a pause, then Noah, ever patient, saying, "I understand you gotta do what you gotta do. It's on you, man. Do you still want the car?"

"Hell yeah! What other choice I got?"

"You can come out, man. End this right now, before you get hurt or a cop gets hurt. You know that'd be as good as the chair, Tim. If you stop now it'll go a lot easier."

"I done it now, cain't stop. Done set it rollin'," Tunnel said pragmatically.

That was when Frank made her move to the edge of the hall. Now Tunnel was talking softly to Kennedy.

"I should just bleed you just like I'd bleed a Crab, and let your brothers take me out. Yeah," he said wistfully, "I go out a ghetto star and there be one less pig bitch in this fucked-up world."

Again Frank felt the panic brush against her, like a huge, winged shadow, and she knew she had to do something. She knelt quietly and peeked around the wall. Tunnel was standing with his back to her, facing the door and holding Kennedy against him. It looked like he was holding something to her neck, but from her angle Frank couldn't see what it was. She retreated behind her corner, weighing her options. Sneak out the bathroom and continue negotiating. Stay hidden and continue negotiating. Pull a gun on him and hope he'd surrender. Not likely. Johnston's rap sheet was extensive and included numerous aggravated assaults and two murder charges, both of which he'd beaten. Clearly he was capable of violent and aggressive action.

"Get me that shit," he was ordering Noah. "And I want it now, like in ten minutes and—"

"That's impossible, Tim," Noah interrupted.

"DON'T TELL ME WHAT'S FUCKIN' IMPOSSIBLE!" he exploded, "CUZ IF I DON'T HAVE ME A FUCKIN' RIDE IN TEN MINUTES I START CUTTIN' THE BITCH! SO DON'T TELL ME WHAT'S FUCKIN' IMPOSSIBLE!"

Frank squeezed her eyes shut. His height made his head a clear shot. There'd be no wounding him, only the one clean shot. It would kill him. *Oh Jesus Christ.* She thought about aiming for his right shoulder and disabling him, but Kennedy was too close against him. *Christ, if she'd just step a little to the side, I could get his arm.*

She held her breath for a moment, trying to hear where Tunnel was.

She had to look again. Johnston still had his back to her, was still hugging Kennedy against his chest. *If I go wide I hit Kennedy to the left, to the right I go straight through the front door.*

Frank resumed her squat against the wall. Shivering threatened to overtake her again and she backhanded drops of sweat off her brow. *Fuck, this is so sideways!* She heard Noah's assurance that a car was on its way, but because they didn't have enough time it wouldn't be a black Explorer.

"What is it?"

Noah's reply was muffled. Frank couldn't hear it, but Johnston seemed satisfied.

"Alright. Yeah, that'll work." Then to Kennedy he said, "Yeah. You an' me gonna go for a long ride, baby."

Frank could see this getting out of hand, another OJ ride down the freeway, but the difference was OJ had everything to lose and Johnston had nothing. The fear in her gut told her to just end it, take him out while she still had a smooth, clear target. *Only one shot.* Part of her wanted to giggle insanely as Robert DeNiro's face from a scene in *The Deer Hunter* swung crazily before her. Underneath her agitation, an older voice born of years of training and experience urged her to be calm and wait it out, get the negotiators in to slowly diffuse the situation with no one getting hurt. The problem was, she didn't know if Johnston could be reasoned with. While she weighed this she could still hear Noah's soothing voice and Johnston's tense one. Then she heard another sound, like scuffling, quick steps, and Johnston swearing. Then with a hint of panic, he urgently whined, "Bitch, don't *fuck* with me."

She thought for a moment that Tunnel had seen her, then realized Kennedy must have broken free. Frank heard more steps, then Kennedy saying, "Come on, man, you're not stupid. You gotta know this ain't gonna work."

In a freeze-frame moment Frank would never forget, the earth stood perfectly still and every clock in the world stopped ticking. Words and sounds murmured around her, but all she could distinguish was the rush of blood in her brain, like surf breaking smoothly on sand. Summoning a breath and holding it, she harshly willed her body to cease its trembling. She wiped the sweat out of her eyes and stood swiftly. In one smooth motion she swung a leg into the living room and took a stance, aiming the 9mm with both hands. Frank's vision had narrowed and all she could see was Johnston closing in on Kennedy in the small kitchen, an open pocketknife in his hand.

She heard herself say, "Drop the knife," and her voice sounded like someone else's, from far away. She hoped he'd heard. He must have because he turned toward her. As he did so, Kennedy moved in on him. Johnston swung back, slashing the knife toward her. Frank moved when Kennedy did but stopped when she recognized the bright red spurt of arterial blood and saw Johnston reaching again for her. In slow motion she saw Johnston trying to drag Kennedy back against him, saw Kennedy grasping at her neck, the too-fast flow of blood, Kennedy suddenly white.

"LET HER GO!" Frank commanded. Johnston's face was in her sights. He stared at her, still grappling with Kennedy, and Frank squeezed softly on the trigger. Like a girder in an earthquake, the tall man buckled and swayed as the right side of his brain flew into the ceiling.

Kennedy made a startled, incoherent sound and started to go down.

"Get an ambulance, get an ambulance!" Frank screamed to whoever was kicking on the door. Noah and Johnnie tumbled inside, drenched, hair plastered on their faces. They paused involuntarily, taking in Tunnel and Kennedy on the floor.

Frank had whipped off her jacket and was pressing it against Kennedy's neck. Kennedy looked at her, eyes wide and dark against the sudden paleness of her skin. She tried to say something, but Frank hushed her. "You're gonna be alright. Just be still, okay?"

Kennedy barely nodded, and Frank said quietly, "Atta girl."

Noah knelt next to Frank. He took Kennedy's hand. "You're supposed to stay outta the way, idiot."

Kennedy grinned weakly. She tried to shrug.

"Hang in there," he crooned, "You're doin' fine, just fine."

Kennedy glanced at Frank, as if for verification, and Frank smiled reassuringly, telling her to stay still. "It's just a nick. Don't worry. Ambo's on the way."

"What happened?" Noah asked. Their eyes locked over Kennedy, sharing a flicker of dread.

"They were scuffling. He cut her. I shot him. Where was he?"

Noah looked sick. "Behind the door," he said pointing his head toward the hall.

Frank looked perplexed. She glanced at Tunnel, realizing he was skinny enough to have gone undetected on the other side of the hall door. For a second she thought she was going to puke, but she took control and said softly to Kennedy, "How you doing, sport?"

The young cop blinked a few times and shivered. Frank barked, "Get me blankets!"

A uniform covered Kennedy with a ratty bedspread, while Johnnie yelled on the radio for a fucking ambulance. Jill burst through the crowd, completely soaked, and gasped, "Oh, my God."

Frank looked up to see her propped against the stove, almost as white as Kennedy. Too much blood was soaking through Frank's wadded jacket, warm and slippery on her fingers. It was too familiar, and Frank felt the dark panic flapping toward her again. She was ready to bolt from the room, but Kennedy was staring at her. Not cocky anymore, but bewildered and pale.

"You're doing great," Frank assured, wondering where the goddamn ambulance was. With her free hand she smoothed Kennedy's forehead, smearing even more blood on her. A siren grew closer and Frank silently exhorted, *Hurry, hurry, hurry, fucking hurry.*

Cops had gathered like flies on shit around the apartment.

"Get everyone out of here," she said to Jill who seemed grateful for an order. Two EMTs rushed past her, and Frank and Noah scrambled out of their way. The techs wedged a foam block around Kennedy's head and slid her onto a backboard, rising together on the count of two.

Frank and Noah followed them to the ambulance.

"I'm going to ride with her," Frank shouted over the rain. "Get back to the office, find out who her next of kin is, brief Foubarelle."

To the ambulance driver she shouted, "Where are you taking her?"

"King/Drew," he yelled.

"No, tell Foubarelle where we are," Frank said, as she jumped into the back. An EMT banged the doors together. She left Noah standing in the rain and swearing.

20

Everyday, in milliseconds, people make decisions that put them on specific paths with destiny. Some are good decisions, like taking the stairs instead of the elevator only to find later that the power went out just as you walked out of the building, or choosing tuna salad at lunch and watching all your co-workers who ate the egg salad get salmonella poisoning. Some decisions don't have such good outcomes, like taking the freeway instead of the interstate and hitting gridlock that makes you miss an important meeting. Or doing something seemingly trivial that creates a fatal domino effect, like Frank did when she spitefully ignored the half-and-half on the grocery list.

Mag and Frank had been lucky enough to work the same shift that day. They'd gotten off late, as usual, but Mag had been done earlier than Frank. On the drive home she'd asked Frank to run into the liquor store for a pint of half-and-half for Angie.

Angie was Mag's best friend from high school. A pilot with American Airlines, sometimes Angie stayed with them for a night or two on a layover. She and Mag would be up till the early morning, laughing and catching up on news from home while Frank fumed in bed. Despite the fact that Mag clearly adored Frank, and that Angie was happily married with two kids, Frank always felt second best when the two friends were together.

Angie was so much like Mag—outgoing, vibrant, adventuresome —all the things Frank wasn't, and she had convinced herself that sooner or later Mag and Angie would end up together. Frank would sulk jealously throughout Angie's visits. If Mag couldn't tease Frank out of her sullenness, she'd just ignore her. She'd explained often enough that Angie was like caviar and champagne, but Frank was pot roast and mashed potatoes. Her friend was extravagant and funny; Frank was daily life with all its stable, reliable comforts and pleasures.

Smacking Frank's thigh, Mag had double-parked in front of

the liquor store. Trying to humor Frank out of her funk, she'd teased, "Come on, old pot roast."

But Frank had whined, "Why can't she just use milk in her coffee?" and slouched further in her seat.

"Because she *likes* half-and-half. And I had it on the list yesterday, so don't give me any crap."

Frank had retorted, "She's not even here yet and you're already fawning all over her."

Sighing patiently, Maggie pointed out, "One, I'm not fawning. Two, if you could read a simple grocery list, this wouldn't be a problem. Come on, honey, I'm double-parked here."

"She's *your* friend," Frank muttered sullenly. "You go get it."

Seeing Frank was serious, Maggie had grabbed her purse, swearing, "Goddammit, Frank! When are you going to grow up?"

She'd slammed out of the car leaving Frank churlish but unrepentant. She was still hunkered in her seat, building an even bigger case against Angie, when she'd heard a boom and saw a kid running out of the liquor store. He'd run right by the car, toting a sawed-off. Frank had bolted after him and caught him almost immediately. He couldn't have been more than fifteen. He was terrified. As she'd cuffed him to a stop sign he'd stammered, "I didn't mean it."

She'd glanced behind her, expecting Mag to be running up, but there was only a crowd growing at the liquor store and a man shouting. Frank had raced back, feeling like her feet were glued to the sidewalk. Shoving people out of the store's entrance, she'd seen Maggie on the floor, surrounded by bright, colorful candy bars. A hole foamed pink air just above her left breast. A man had scurried around her, ranting in a language she didn't recognize. He'd tried to blot Maggie's blood with paper towels. Frank had stepped toward her, wanting to touch her and afraid to, sure if she just let this play out she'd wake up to find it was only another nightmare.

She'd heard someone yell, "Call 911!" and realized she'd said it. She'd tried staunching the wound as she knelt next to Maggie, but it was too big and the blood flowed freely around her fingers. Frank gently and uselessly wiped the froth off Maggie's lips. Her lover's face blurred and shimmied as Frank viciously cuffed tears from her eyes. She'd whispered, "Hold on, baby. Stay with me, stay with me."

Mag had stared at Frank without responding. Air had breezed through the hole in her chest. Frank had seen holes like that in other people. Most of them had died. Mag was unconscious when the paramedics rushed in. Frank had prayed in the ambulance for the first time in decades.

At the hospital, she'd paced and paced. When the doctor came toward her she'd read his face and felt herself go into free fall. His voice had been dim and far away, saying Mag had never regained consciousness, the damage was far too massive. She'd literally drowned in her own blood. All over a pint of half-and-half.

Shock, coupled with the deep fatigue of an adrenaline crash, was threatening to settle over Frank. She needed coffee and numbly followed the signs to the cafeteria. Standing in line, she was oblivious to the dried blood on her hands and clothes, or the stares around her. The cashier gingerly handed Frank her change, suggesting there was a bathroom just down the hall where she might want to wash up. Frank's only response was a weary blink. The woman lowered her eyes back to the register.

Frank dragged herself back to the waiting area, where Foubarelle, Luchowski, Noah, and Chief Nelson were waiting for her. The head nurse volunteered her office, and the five of them squeezed inside. Frank reflexively gauged their moods: Foubarelle was livid, Luchowski looked sour, and Noah was still amped. Only the chief seemed calm.

"What happened in there?" he asked as soon as he shut the door. He indicated a chair, and even though she'd have loved to sink down into it, Frank stood. She started from the beginning, with the abandonment of the stakeout. At the part where the bust slipped sideways she paused to let Noah explain. He spoke animatedly with big gestures. Frank envied his energy, but knew it was just adrenaline he was running on.

"It was a clean shoot," she concluded.

"How can you say that?" Luchowski exploded. "You might have killed one of my men!"

Without bothering to correct pronouns, Frank said with barely controlled restraint, "No, Timothy Johnston was killing your man."

"Lieutenant Franco, of course we weren't there, but this looks like a gross overreaction. Was it necessary to mortally wound the suspect?"

Frank couldn't believe these dumb fucks. Kennedy's life was on the line and they were asking if it was necessary?

"With Detective Kennedy bleeding the way she was I didn't feel that exposing her to further risk of injury was prudent. Johnston had clearly demonstrated his intent to harm her, and in my mind he wouldn't have hesitated to kill either one of us if he had another chance."

"With a *pocketknife?*" Luchowski sneered in disbelief.

"Yeah, the pocketknife that put a fucking hole in her throat!" Frank exploded.

"Calm down, Lieutenant," the chief soothed. "What we mean is that with a firearm you obviously had the advantage over a small knife. What we—"

"Yeah, I had the advantage and I used it. Timothy Johnston wasn't a boyscout playing with a Swiss Army knife. This fucker was a convicted felon with a rap sheet longer than my arm and a lot of time in stir. You weren't there, but I can guarantee you he wasn't going back in. And he wasn't going out alone. He'd already cut Kennedy and he was going for her again. I stopped him."

"All we're trying to ascertain is whether this was an overreaction or an absolutely necessary measure. It's possible that in a moment of extremely high stress you overreacted and simply—"

The sound of Frank gritting her teeth was clear to everyone in the room. She spoke each word slowly and with tremendous effort.

"With all due respect, sir, if I had fired out of sheer impulse, I can guarantee you Mr. Johnston would have had more than one bullet hole in him."

She'd seen enough shootings to know that when someone fired in terror, or fury, their victims were usually riddled with bullets. They want the fucker to go down and stay down. But Foubarelle was shaking his head at the floor, and Luchowski was glaring. Noah wouldn't look her in the eye and Nelson wouldn't stop looking at her.

"Did you consider your backboard, Lieutenant?"

Frank patiently explained how she had weighed all the consequences of a bad shot, and how Johnston's head seemed the most reasonable target area, the way he was positioned with Kennedy.

Finally Nelson wagged his head sadly, warning, "You know

OIS is going to have to look into this."

"Of course."

"And that you'll be relieved of duty while—"

"Sir, my squad and I are in the middle of a very sensitive investigation and I can't—"

Now Nelson interrupted. "Oh, yes. That Agoura/Peterson case?"

"Yes, sir."

"That's going to be handled by RHD now. It should've been given to them a while ago," he said, with a scowl at Foubarelle.

Frank bowed her head to conceal her disappointment but then quickly raised it, determined to hold on to her case.

"Sir, I respect your judgment on this matter but I've put a lot of time into this case. I think it would be a mistake to let RHD—"

"Lieutenant, you are ROD and the case is downtown. There is nothing else to discuss."

"But Chief, RHD doesn't know the—"

"There is nothing further to discuss, Lieu-te-nant. Or would you rather go back to de-tec-tive?"

Frank clamped down on her back teeth. "No, sir."

"And, of course, you need to hand over your badge and weapon."

He held Frank's gaze for a moment as she slowly unholstered the 9mm. Satisfied that he'd restored order, Nelson nodded to Foubarelle and left the room. Luchowski followed him, throwing Frank an evil look, and Foubarelle stepped up to Frank with his palm up. Gently she placed her weapon in his hand, then the badge. It felt like giving up a major organ.

"I want this written up by the time I leave my office tomorrow," he warned.

She nodded almost imperceptibly. It was Standard Operating Procedure to get RODed after an Officer Involved Shooting. A statement and a written report immediately after a shooting was SOP also. Frank had been in an OIS before, but she'd never killed anyone. She knew she'd have to talk to Clay or another LAPD shrink before she'd be cleared for work, if and when OIS signed off on her.

Foubarelle left with a parting glare, and Frank crossed her arms. She asked Noah, "You want a shot, too?"

"Nope." He paced the tiny room in two steps, his big hands

jammed tight into his pockets.

There was silence except for Noah's agitated pacing. Finally, he stopped and stared at the floor.

"You know, I should have said something this morning. I mean, it just didn't feel good to me, her going in there. She should have been back at HQ, I mean, it wasn't her bust, or her squad. Hell, even her division. I don't know. It just seemed wrong. But I let you talk me out of it. I gave in. I deferred to you."

Noah said the word like an insult, then he looked squarely at his boss, his friend. "Tell me you didn't have your own reasons for dragging her in there, Frank."

Like a mantra, Frank reiterated her reasoning. "Reston's a bad area. They hate us there. I wanted as much force behind us as I could get. I—"

"That's a load of shit, Frank, and you know it. We had plenty of back-up without her."

"I've got that kid sitting out there as psycho-bait," Frank continued wearily. "I didn't think it was too much to see her in action."

Noah spluttered, "Well, you saw her, didn't you?"

Frank reached around to the back of her neck. Thinking the best defense was a good offense, she tried turning the tables.

"I don't get why you're so defensive about her. You got a hard-on for her or something?"

Noah almost choked. "*Me?* Hey, *you're* the one who's been riding her since day-one. You're on her like stink on shit, man, and you're wondering if *I've* got a hard-on. Jesus, Frank, take a look in the fucking mirror!"

On top of all she'd been carrying for the last couple of hours, that was the straw that finally broke her. Adrenaline spurted into her bloodstream again, and Frank literally saw red. Her hands closed into bloodless fists. In a tight, barely audible voice, she warned Noah that he'd definitely crossed a line.

"Oh, did I? Well maybe it's about time, Frank! Take a fucking look around!"

It was already cramped in the tiny office, but Noah stepped even closer to Frank, mad-dogging her from only inches away. She was solid, livid fury, but he didn't back down.

"Just explain it to me, Frank. For Christ's sake, what the fuck is going on with you?"

Frank knew she could take him. A left uppercut, a right to his gut, and he'd fall like a rock. She held her stance for a long, taut moment. While she deliberated, some of her anger drained off. It felt curiously like standing in the surf as the breakers pulled away. Frank closed her eyes and bowed her head. She sagged against the edge of the desk, knocking over a pencil cup. Noah took up the space she'd left, insisting, "Talk to me, Frank."

Resisting Noah was taking more strength than Frank had. She asked resignedly, "What do you want to know?"

"Why do you hate her so much? What did she ever do to you?"

Frank dropped her face into her hands. From behind them she said, "I don't hate her."

"Well, you sure as shit don't like her. And I *know* you, Frank. She pushed some button in you that I've hardly ever seen go off. You were dead set against her the minute you laid eyes on her. Why?"

Frank worked her fingers against her skin for a long time. Finally she straightened up and combed her hands back through her hair, locking them behind her neck. She looked everywhere, except at Noah.

She wondered how Kennedy was doing, wondered if a doctor was trying to find her. Then she realized the nurse would know where she was. There was nothing to do but wait. And answer Noah. All the fight was out of him now; he looked as tired as Frank felt. She fished around the room again, hoping for something, anything, to distract her. Finding nothing, she settled for the imaginary ring on her finger. It was hard enough admitting to herself how Kennedy made her feel. She didn't know if she could actually say it out loud.

"Look, No. Let's just drop this, okay? I made a mistake. You were right, I was wrong. I should have listened to you. I didn't. I'm sorry."

"Frank, don't placate me. I'm asking as your friend. And I'm asking as a cop. I don't know what's going on with you, but whatever it is it might have gotten Kennedy killed today."

Noah's jabs were right on target, each one a TKO. It was Mag all over again. Frank's fault. If only she'd gotten the half-and-half on the list, if only she'd gone into the liquor store like Mag had asked. If only she'd left Kennedy behind like Noah asked her to.

Frank shut her eyes, running her hand against the tightness in her neck. Walking around the desk she slumped into a chair, wondering how things had gotten so out of hand. Noah was still staring.

"Alright. That first day? I don't know. She just pissed me off. Right off the bat. She was so...young. So arrogant. She didn't have a nerve in her body. She just threw me off, for some reason. And there you were, acting like she was the greatest thing since Mickey-D's."

"You were jealous?" Noah asked incredulously. He dragged the only other chair in the room around the desk and hunkered across from Frank, their knees almost touching. Frank shut her eyes, wishing she could just succumb to the exhaustion pulling at her.

"I wouldn't say jealous...resentful's better. She was so fucking cocky, No, so sure of herself."

Frank paused. "I used to feel like that, seems like light-years ago."

"With Maggie?" Noah asked. Frank shut her eyes against the taboo name.

"Yeah," she finally whispered, and when she didn't continue, Noah coaxed, "Tell me more."

Frank flapped a hand in a futile gesture. "I don't know. Maybe it pissed me off that Kennedy reminded me of all that. Everything I used to have, used to be. Maybe it pissed me off that she still had it and I didn't, almost like she was mocking me. She made me feel stuff I didn't want to feel. She pissed me off. You know, part of me was hoping she'd lose it today. Piss in her pants or something. Anything to wipe that damn cocky smile off her face. I wanted to see her squirm for a change. And know that I was watching her."

Distractedly, Frank rubbed at a doodle on the blotter. This time she continued without prompting.

"I've got things pretty much sewed up, No. The past is gone, it's over. It's all behind me, and I just keep moving on. I don't want to look back. I don't want to remember anything. I just keep looking forward. But I had no contingency plan for Kennedy. She got right in front of me, right in my face. It was like I couldn't go around her, couldn't move ahead. And I sure as shit didn't want to go backward. She stalled me me out in places I didn't want to be at."

"Yeah," Noah agreed softly. "Maybe when she stopped you, she touched you, and maybe that's a good thing. You're human,

Frank, not Robo-cop."

"Don't want to be human, No. Been there, done that."

They were silent for a moment as Frank's finger meandered over the desktop. The gentle motion was hypnotic in the quiet room.

Noah said almost dreamily, "Kennedy said something the other day...she made a crack about you, I forget what, but I busted up. I mean she was dead-on and I thought, man, she reminds me of Maggie, how she used to bust your chops all the time."

Frank stared oddly at her old partner.

"You ever thought about that? Kinda like a tomboyish Maggie? They both got that same look, you know? Just kinda happy and...glad to be alive."

For the second time that day Frank couldn't look at Noah. She nodded weakly at the floor. He pressed, "Maybe that's where she stalled you out."

Frank sat up, and with obvious effort reassembled her impregnable mask. "Look," she sighed. "I owed you Kennedy, but not..."

Noah let it go, placing a hand easily on Frank's knee. "You know, that could've been any one of us in there."

"But it wasn't."

"Would you feel better if it had been me? Or Jill?"

Frank didn't answer. Instead she asked why he'd been so insistent she leave Kennedy out of the bust.

Noah flapped his big hands in his lap. "I don't know. It just felt wrong. What was I gonna say? 'Gee, Frank, I'm like having a psychic flash or something.'"

"Could have."

"Would it have changed your mind?"

Frank thought about it, and Mag's last words zig-zagged in her head: *Goddammit, Frank! When are you going to grow up?*

"Probably not," she admitted, disgusted with herself.

Noah heaved a bony shoulder. "You couldn't have known it was gonna slip."

"No, but I could have listened to you. You've got good guts, and maybe if I hadn't been so hell-bent for Kennedy I'd have heard you."

"That's hindsight. Don't start second-guessing."

A cold smile twisted Frank's face.

"That's my specialty. We should go see how she's doing."

Frank started to rise, but Noah reached over and pushed her back down.

"Hold on. They know where we are."

Frank was too tired to protest. Noah rubbed at a bloody smear on his wrist, and she waited patiently for him to continue.

"You know, I gotta tell you, I was fucking scared."

Frank nodded her understanding.

"When I saw him standing there with his arm around her throat and the knife there...I didn't know what to do. I just felt so helpless. And stupid. I just kept wondering how the hell did this happen? And Kennedy, man, she looked so scared. But she was calm, man, and I remember thinking I had to be calm, too. For her. And then outside, knowing you were both in there...but at least outside I was doing something, you know?"

Noah looked up anxiously, and Frank bent toward him.

"You did good, No. You don't know how fucking glad I was that you were there. You handled Johnston beautifully. I know the commission's gonna try and eat us alive, but you did great. I wouldn't have done anything different than you did."

"Lotta good it did us."

"Hey. There was nothing else you could've done."

The silence settled between them again. Frank tried not to remember the clutch of fear in her gut, or the moldy bathroom, or Johnston's sudden shout. She did not want to remember the fear in the hallway trying to envelop her in its leathery wings or the disappearing white curl on Johnston's do-rag, or him dancing herky-jerky with half his head gone. Least of all, she didn't want to remember seeing Kennedy turn with her eyes too wide and her fingers red, and wanting to run as far and as fast as she could, screaming all the way. She didn't want to and *wouldn't* remember.

"You know what? After sitting in here with you, and with the way you shoot, I think you should get out of law enforcement and become a shrink."

"Man, you're not kidding. If I can get you to talk I can have an autistic kid's life history in five minutes. And wait'll you see my bill."

They shared tired smiles. Frank slapped Noah's leg and said, "Come on. Let's go see how she's doing."

21

rank sat in recovery with a sheaf of papers on her blood-stiffened lap. Jill and Johnnie had brought them for her after she'd sent Noah back to division. He'd wanted to stay and see what the doctor had to say, but Frank had him copying the Agoura and Peterson murder books. She might be officially off the case but she was goddamned if she was going to give it up. Noah tried to talk her out of it, but she'd slapped a wad of bills in his hand and told him to take the binders to Kinko's and copy them there. She couldn't order him to, she was ROD, so she asked him as a favor. Before Foubarelle or RHD got hold of them.

"Frank...," Noah had sighed, trying to protest.

She'd gripped his shoulders.

"If not for me, then for Cassandra Nichols." Cheap shot, she knew, but it worked.

"Shit."

As Noah stuck the money in his pocket Frank told him, "When you're done with that go home and kiss the kids, make love to your wife, and sleep as late as you want. Fuck those IAD bastards."

Noah waved tiredly.

The doctor came out of the recovery room about an hour later and told her Kennedy was going to be alright. A flicker of relief penetrated the emptiness she felt. She asked if she could sit with Kennedy.

"After you clean yourself up," he said.

Frank scrubbed the blood off her hands with her nails, catching a sorry glimpse of herself in the mirror. It was the best she could do without a shower and a change of clothes, but she didn't foresee either of those in the near future. She snagged a tepid cup of coffee from a vending machine and settled into a chair next to Kennedy's bed.

An IV stuck out of Kennedy's hand and a half-dozen leads and wires monitored her vital functions. A large bandage plastered her neck. Kennedy's head was still enclosed in a block, but the doctor was happy. He told Frank it was a damn good thing the ambulance arrived as soon as it did.

"She was this close," he said, holding his fingertips slightly apart. Tunnel's knife had jerked into her carotid artery, causing the massive blood loss and a precipitous drop in blood pressure. Once they'd stabilized her and gone in, the rip was easily repaired, but Kennedy was going to be laid up for a few weeks. Luchowski had called her father, who was too sick to fly out, and there was no one else on her emergency contact sheet. Frank had thought hard about that, finally deciding that Kennedy could stay with her. It was the least she could do.

Despite the fatigue that had settled into her bones like lead, Frank tried concentrating on the statement she was writing. But she couldn't stop replaying the scene in Johnston's apartment. She and Johnnie had been the first ones down the hall. It was hard for her to believe she hadn't picked Tunnel up behind the doorway. If only she had, this never would have slipped out of her hands. She'd be home drinking a cool one, sitting on the couch in clean clothes, ignoring the TV while she wrote far less difficult reports.

And Kennedy'd still be getting to me, she thought. Frank glanced at the sleeping young woman and felt a wave of shame. Bleeding out on Tunnel's floor, Kennedy hadn't looked so cocky anymore. Frank squeezed her eyes against the similar image of Mag amid the candy bars, blowing pink spume. Both days, Frank's pride had been running the show. She wondered how many times she was going to have to do this. How many trips to the hospital would it take before she got it right?

She had no answer. In fact, Frank felt like she had nothing at all. She'd lost Mag, she'd almost lost a cop in her command, she'd lost her case to RHD, and she'd lost her badge. She thought that must be how it felt to drown: words were useless, fighting just made you more tired, there was nothing to see but waves and waves and more waves behind them, and always the dark weight of the water trying to pull you under. At some point it probably felt good to give up. Frank wondered if she was there yet, but then a lifeboat bobbed into sight. It was the realization that Kennedy could be in the morgue instead of the hospital. It wasn't a huge comfort, but it would do.

This close.

Remembering the grotesque spew and suck of Mag's breathing, Frank gratefully watched the even rise and fall of Kennedy's chest. The ride in the ambo, the waiting, blood everywhere—it was all too déjà vu. It was Maggie again, but this time with a different script. Through her hazy fatigue, Frank wondered dimly if Kennedy wasn't some kind of second chance.

Elbows on knees, chin against fists, Frank studied Kennedy's still figure. An uncompromising determination gripped Frank, and the lifeboat she'd glimpsed on the horizon sailed closer.

As Kennedy came out of the anesthesia, a nurse bustled around her, asking how she felt.

"Fine," she croaked, jerking Frank out of a shallow sleep.

"How's the pain?" the nurse inquired. Kennedy seemed to think about it for a moment, then answered, "No pain."

Her doctor joined them, saying, "You gave us a scare, young lady. You lost a lot of blood from a tear in your carotid artery. We patched it together but you're going to have to take it easy for a while, not strain yourself."

Kennedy nodded, and he patted her hand. "We're going to keep you here a little longer, make sure everything's working right, then move you to a room."

"How long do I have to stay here?"

"We'll see. At least a couple of days. We want to give the artery a chance to knit itself together. We don't want you moving around right now and tearing it open."

Frank could tell Kennedy wasn't pleased with the answer though she nodded resignedly. When the nurse and doctor left Frank stood by the bed. "Still sleepy?" she asked.

Kennedy stared up at the ceiling before replying, "More stupid and foggy, really. And thirsty. I feel like I've been running through the Sahara."

"I'll see if they'll let you have water yet."

Frank returned a moment later with ice chips and slipped one into Kennedy's mouth. "This'll have to do for now."

Kennedy glanced at the blood on Frank's shirt.

"That all mine?"

"Sure is. And there was a helluva lot more."

"You must have saved my life."

"How do you figure that?"

"Keeping as much in as you did before the ambo got there."

Frank didn't know what to say. Taking credit for saving Kennedy's life after she was the one who'd endangered it in the first place hardly seemed fair. Kennedy clamped her eyes shut, and thinking she was suddenly in pain, Frank asked, "What is it?"

Kennedy opened her eyes, and Frank was alarmed to see tears. "I almost died in there, didn't I?" she whispered.

Frank swallowed hard, pushing her hands down in her pockets. She nodded at Kennedy, confused by an ugly knot of shame and guilt. Kennedy closed her eyes again as a tear slowly leaked out. Frank watched it slide down her temple, amazed, even slightly envious, at how easily Kennedy let it go. As she watched the tear fall, Frank walked into another part of the day's script. With no warning, she remembered the shock that had hit her when she realized how close she'd been to dying, the pure terror of it.

Frank wanted to get the hell out of there. She wanted to go home and stand in the hot shower and drink a quart of Scotch and not remember anything ever again. A little voice in her head screamed for her to run as fast as she could. She could do that— just walk out and not look back. And she knew if she did, she was as good as dead.

When are you going to grow up?

Barely breathing, Frank took Kennedy's hand. It was warm and smooth, and Kennedy's fingers grabbed tightly. Frank marveled at Kennedy's ability to cry, as if it were as natural as breathing. Before she could think about it, Frank reached out with her free hand to keep the fat drops from rolling into Kennedy's ears. She was surprised and embarrassed by the tenderness of her gesture. She half expected Kennedy to tease her, but the detective only whispered, "Sorry."

Frank shook her head. "Don't be. Go ahead and cry. It's pretty scary."

"He was gonna kill me."

Again Frank was speechless. She looked down at the hand in hers, the blood crusted in the knuckles and nails. She felt a dull justification in shooting Johnston, but it paled next to her regret.

Frank said, "I'm sorry I got you into this." She heard the quaver in her voice and wondered if she was helping Kennedy or just shamelessly seeking her own absolution. Kennedy tried to shrug and winced. Wiping her tears, she said simply, "I'm a cop."

"Yeah. And a damn good one."

Frank squeezed Kennedy's hand and she squeezed back. Frank had to clear her throat before she could ask, "More ice?"

"Yeah."

Frank fiddled with the slippery ice shavings while Kennedy recovered her bravado.

"So," she teased, "are you being my personal slave-girl now?"

Frank considered the question. She didn't think she'd ever be glad to hear Kennedy call her a slave-girl, but as she caught a piece of ice she grinned slightly. "Looks that way."

"You look like somethin' the cat ate and threw back up."

When Kennedy woke up again, Frank was still in her ruined clothes, still working.

"Hey."

Laying the statement aside, Frank noted, "You don't look much better."

Although the nurses had sponged off the worst of it, there was still gore matted in Kennedy's hair. Betadine yellowed her jaw and neck.

"Want some more ice?"

"Yeah."

Kennedy accepted it eagerly. Frank asked how she felt.

"Okay, I guess. Tired."

"It's been a long day."

Frank waited to give her another chip, and Kennedy said, "For you, too. Why don't you go home? You're gonna start to stink the place up."

Frank shrugged. "I just want to make sure you're okay."

"I'm fine. 'Sides, that's the nurses' job."

Frank slipped more ice in her mouth.

"Luchowski called your father, but he said he couldn't make the long flight."

"Yeah. He's got emphysema pretty bad. It's hard for him to get around."

"Is there someone you want me to call?"

"No."

"Then I'll stay."

Kennedy made a face and told Frank not to be silly. "I'm in a hospital, for Christ's sake. What's gonna happen to me?"

Frank didn't know how to explain about the nightmares and cold sweats, or the screams that woke you out of your sleep and the terror that lingered even after you were awake.

"They're probably going to move you soon. I'll just make sure you get there and then I'll go."

Kennedy wisely declined to argue. Shortly after, she was transferred to a double room. The other bed was empty, and Kennedy joked about keeping it empty because she might want to have a party later on. She'd already charmed her nurses. After they settled her in and left, Kennedy told Frank to bring on the dancing girls. Frank had to admire Kennedy. Under all the shock and trauma, there was still a resilient vitality.

"The only dancing girls you're going to be seeing are in your dreams, sport, so why don't you try and get some more rest."

"Not a bad idea." Kennedy started to yawn, but the pull in her neck cut it short. "Only if you go home, though."

Although Frank craved her bed and the merciful oblivion of sleep, she said, "Tell you what, I'll stay with you until you fall asleep and then I'll go."

"Promise?"

Frank nodded.

"Alright."

Kennedy promptly shut her eyes. Frank sat down, propping her bloodied shoes up on the other bed. She started on the statement again, but after a few minutes Kennedy asked somberly, "Have you ever been hurt on the line?"

Frank stared at the last sentence she wrote.

"Couple times."

"What happened?"

"Different things." Frank didn't want to go into details. Kennedy was silent for a minute. Then she asked quietly, "What was the worst?"

Frank sighed, giving up on the report.

"Right after I made detective, my partner and I were talking to a woman and her boyfriend. Her baby'd been thrown out the window. Fell three stories, and they were insisting they knew nothing about it, that he must have just crawled over the windowsill. Problem was, the kid was only a couple months old. So I'm talking to the mother. My partner's standing next to her, and all of sudden he gets this look, and he's looking right behind me. I see him pull at his holster, and just as I'm crouching and turning to see what's behind me, I feel this burn over my hip. Bastard shot me with a .38. My partner blew his fucking arm off. Turns out he'd dumped the baby and decided we were weren't taking him in for it."

Frank shrugged. End of story. But not for Kennedy.

"So what happened to you?"

"I was fine. By some...fluke, it went right through me. Exited the other side. I didn't know that though until after I came out of surgery."

"Did you think you were gonna die?"

Frank had told her story to the wall. Now she turned toward Kennedy, remembering what Noah had said, how she looked like Mag. Her eyes were serious for once, but they still burned. There was a hunger in them that made Frank more comfortable looking at the wall again.

"I saw where it had gone in and figured it was pretty bad."

"Were you scared?"

Frank scanned the smooth white paint for an answer. The shooting was another part of her past that Frank had walked away from without looking back. She'd never talked about it with Joe Girardi or her partner, and had managed to gloss over it during the shrink sessions. She'd acknowledged it only in the dark safety of Maggie's arms after a flashback had sent her reeling, or a nightmare had yanked her from sleep. Slowly she squared the papers on her lap, then closed the folder around them.

"Yeah, I was scared. Not as much when it happened, but later. That's when it hits you, is later, after you think it's all over and everything's okay."

"Like how?" Kennedy persisted.

Frank twisted her invisible ring and took a long time to answer. She was so tired. She wished that Kennedy would go to sleep and quit dredging this shit up, but she bit back her irritation. This was why Kennedy's script was different than Maggie's. This was where Frank had a chance to right wrongs, maybe to grow up. It felt like an atonement, and Frank reasoned that penance was never easy. She'd gotten Kennedy into this mess and she'd see her through it.

"You'll be talking to a wit, or just standing at the sink doing dishes, brushing your teeth—you can be doing anything—and then out of the blue it just hits you. You'll feel where you got shot, you'll see your partner's face. You'll hear his voice, feel the burn where the bullet went in, smell burned eggs and a full diaper pail...you'll be there and it'll be real. It'll be happening all over again. And it'll scare the crap out of you. Then afterwards you'll think you're going crazy, but they say it's perfectly normal. Post-traumatic stress. There's also the nightmares. They're just as real. Sometimes worse than real."

Frank faltered, her profile to Kennedy. She was haggard. Her jaw had softened and her shoulders hung slackly. Exhaustion had replaced tension. Frank's hard veneer had cracked. When she spoke again it was with effort.

"You know you're ROD for a while. You'll have to talk to a shrink before you can go back to work."

Kennedy bobbed her head amiably. "Yeah. I figured as much. Did you go to a shrink after you got shot?"

Frank closed her eyes and let her head fall back against the chair.

"Yep."

"Did it help or was it just bullshit?"

"Let's just say I think you'll be a better patient than I was."

"That shrink didn't get squat from you, did he?"

Frank graced the ceiling with a faint smile.

"You're gonna have to go in this time too, aren't you?"

Frank sighed, arching her back as she got out of the chair. "I thought you were supposed to be sleeping."

"You can go home anytime," Kennedy grinned. "You don't have to stay here."

"I know."

"So why don't you go home, get some sleep."

Frank looked down at Kennedy. Around the jaundiced edge of the betadine, her color was good. Still pale, but not the awful chalk-white of serious shock. Her eyes were bright again. Frank looked away. She was young and strong. She'd be alright physically; it was the emotional fallout that worried Frank. But so far Kennedy was coping well, better than Frank ever had.

She felt an involuntary pang of tenderness. In order to get out of Johnston's apartment alive, they'd had to put aside their mutual antagonism and forge a fragile alliance. They came through it together, and Frank wasn't about to abandon Kennedy now.

"Look. I thought the deal was you sleep, I go. The sooner you go to sleep, the sooner I can get out of here."

Kennedy surprised Frank by closing her eyes and wiggling deeper into the sheets.

"I'm Audi," she murmured, and indeed she was gone, sleep quickly claiming her. But Frank stayed by the bed. A lock of hair, the color of sunflowers, was taut under Kennedy's pillow. Frank freed it, surprised how silky it was. She held it for a moment, then let go, an odd expression on her face. Quietly she backed away. Instead of going home, however, she took off her shoes and stretched out on the empty bed.

A few weeks after his father's funeral the boy picked up a whore. He was nervous. His father had always handled the business, but she seemed willing enough. He asked if it would be okay to do it in the car. When he told her what he wanted she balked and jacked the price up fifty dollars. He didn't have that much money.

"Then I guess you gonna have to settle for what you can get," she said, starting to blow him.

He couldn't do it.

A week later he tried with another whore and a hundred dollars in his pocket. When she got on her hands and knees, he flew again. But he missed his dad.

22

The next few days brought endless visits from deputy chiefs and commanders. OIS came and went with their interminable questions and forms, as did Foubarelle and Luchowski and the suits from IAD. Timothy Johnston's family was calling for an investigation, and Internal Affairs was cross-examining all the detectives involved. At least Frank had managed to avoid the RHD dicks, but they finally cornered her at the hospital. She was less than cooperative. The two detectives left in a snit after a tense fifteen minutes, threatening to nail her with hampering an investigation.

"I reckon that's the least of your worries right now," Kennedy observed.

Frank agreed. "Pretty low on my list of priorities."

Having just come from home and a decent night's sleep, Frank asked how Kennedy was doing.

"Never better. Ready to git on my board and hit the surf."

"Not on my watch," Frank warned.

Kennedy grinned. "What are you, my mother?"

Frank nodded. "As long as you're in here."

"Well, that ain't gonna be for much longer. Doc said he'll probably release me tomorrow."

Frank raised an eyebrow. "Really?"

"Yep. Then it's me an' the long-board."

"I don't think so."

"Oh, yeah? Who's gonna stop me?" Kennedy challenged.

Frank leaned on her knuckles at the foot of Kennedy's bed. She couldn't have imagined just a few days ago that the younger woman's cheekiness would have ever pleased her. But then there was a lot she couldn't have imagined a few days ago.

Except for brief trips home and to headquarters, Frank had spent most of her time with Kennedy. They talked a lot, alternating between friendly sparring and painfully serious discussion. Kennedy was able to switch gears rapidly and easily, often leaving

Frank in the dust; one minute Kennedy made her laugh and the next she felt like she'd been skewered through the heart. Keeping up with her was demanding, but Frank was game. She considered it part of her reparations to Kennedy. Though in truth, she actually enjoyed the young woman's company.

"Who's going to stop you?" Frank repeated, considering what she was about to say, "I'm going to stop you. You're coming home with me."

For once, Kennedy was the one floundering, and she said, "I don't get it."

"Simple. You're going to stay with me until you're okay."

"Well, I'll be dipped in shit and covered with peanuts," Kennedy murmured.

"Hmm. Nice," Frank said sarcastically, flipping through a surfing magazine.

"I don't know if this is such a good idea."

"Why's that?"

Kennedy lifted her good shoulder, glancing out the window for an answer.

"I don't need a babysitter. I can take care of myself."

Frank was getting used to Kennedy's independent streak and agreed, "Yeah, you can. But it'd be better if you took it real easy for a while. So I'm going to take you home and be your slave-girl. Can't ditch your slave-girl just like that," Frank said, snapping her fingers.

Kennedy just plucked at her sheet. Frank reluctantly asked, "What's the matter, sport?"

"I feel like such a geek, like I'm a fuckin' albatross around everyone's neck."

"You're not an albatross," Frank replied awkwardly, touched by Kennedy's candor. She hesitated, then said, "I *want* you to come home with me. It's the very least I can do for you."

"You don't have to do anything for me, Frank. I remember you apologized right after I came out of the anesthesia, and at the time I remember thinking, That's so stupid. If anybody should have been apologizing it was me, for having been such an idiot in the first place."

Frank sat on the edge of the bed.

"Hey. We've been over this. I was the first one in, remember? I should have seen him. I didn't. You're not to blame here,

Kennedy. Now we've all got our 20/20 hindsight, and we'd all do it differently, but we didn't know then. There's nobody to blame," Frank lied, convinced she could have prevented the whole affair.

"So we're going to baby you for the next couple of days, get you back to 100 percent, and then throw you out in the trenches again. Get you on that surfboard. Okay?"

"'Kay."

Kennedy smiled a little, then added, "But you know you don't have to do this."

"Jesus Christ!" Frank blew out in a long breath.

"Frank, really I—"

"I don't want to hear it." Frank stood, holding up her hands. "I'm going downtown. I've got to see the shrink in twenty minutes. He's gonna be a picnic after you, sport."

As Frank reached the door Kennedy called, "Frank?"

"What?"

"Thanks."

Her back to Kennedy, Frank smiled.

"No sweat."

Kennedy had been right. The psychologist Frank was required to see after she'd been shot got nothing from her. Later on, when Mag was killed, she hadn't been forced to see anybody. Instead, Frank had spent a lot of nights with the Jantzens. Long after Tracey had gone to bed, Noah and Frank would sit out on the patio, watching the barbecue coals die. He tried to get her to talk, but they shared more silence than words. He'd nurse a couple drinks, Frank a bottle, and eventually she'd pass out in the lounge chair.

"Hello, Frank."

Richard Clay stepped out of his office, interrupting Frank's thoughts. He held out his hand.

"It's good to see you again. I wish it were under more auspicious circumstances."

"Hello, Dick," she said smoothly, returning the shake. She perched on the edge of a chair in front of Clay's desk while he took the one beside it. Frank recognized the move, she did it all the time. Get close to your suspect. Make her nervous. Invade her body space.

"How's your serial case coming along?"

"Not mine anymore. RHD's got it."

"Hmm. Is that a relief or a disappointment?"

Frank hated this touchy-feely shit, hated it like the plague, but she knew she had to go along with it for Clay to sign off on her ROD. She felt his quiet appraisal and wondered vaguely if he saw what she wanted him to or something else. Frank was a detective. She was a master at projecting whatever attitude was needed. Today called for casual yet earnest cooperation.

"Guess I'd have to say disappointing."

"And how does being relieved of duty feel?"

"It's probably good for me. I haven't taken a vacation in years."

Clay was peering at her over his bifocals.

"Does it *feel* good?"

Frank considered for a moment, wondering how high Clay's bullshit barometer went. As she recalled, it was pretty sensitive.

"I've felt better."

He smiled softly. "I'll take it that's a 'no'."

She shrugged.

"Tell me about the shooting."

Clay remained silent while Frank laid out the mechanics of the story. When she'd finished he asked, "How did you feel going in?"

"The usual. Excited. Tense. Pumped."

"And in the hallway right before Detective Kennedy was seized?"

"Same. Probably a little more concerned. We didn't know where this guy was, but he was in there somewhere with us."

"Were you afraid?"

"Didn't have time to be. I suppose I was. It's hard to remember," she lied.

"How about when you were in the bathroom and heard the suspect screaming at your detectives? How did that make you feel?"

Frank remembered the lurch her stomach had made and the nauseating panic, then the icy calmness that took over, the complete detachment.

"I felt like a machine. My vision and hearing were acute. I could smell the towels on the door. They'd been damp for a couple of days. There were black and brown cracks in the linoleum. It was mustard colored, had some sort of a square geometric pattern.

I was on autopilot."

"Were you scared then?"

"I guess. I don't remember."

"When you shot the suspect, what was going through your head?"

"Not being seen. Being 100 percent accurate. No room for error."

"It must have been tremendous pressure."

Frank shrugged. "I suppose. You don't think about it at the time, though."

Frank was trying to lead the conversation and hoped he'd ask when did she think about it. But Clay had been doing his job for a long time. He bowled her over by asking, "Tell me how you felt kneeling over Detective Kennedy while she was dying on you."

Frank wasn't expecting that one. Clay's vivid description forced the scene into her mind, followed by Mag on the dirty liquor store floor. Frank sat perfectly still. Her eyes narrowed and focused intently on Clay's, warning him not to continue. Clay steadily maintained his gaze. They both knew he'd set the hook. Now she'd either fight it or give into it. He was allowing her time to figure it out. When she spoke it was almost in a whisper, as if sound might shatter her self-control.

"I know I'm supposed to talk about this. I have no intention of doing so. I respect your time and I don't want to waste it."

Clay took off his glasses and thoughtfully polished them with a handkerchief. He took some time doing it, carefully rubbing each lens, redoing them, examining them for smudges. He refolded the handkerchief and patted it back into his pocket. Frank knew he was buying time. Slowly, using both hands, he slid the glasses back onto his nose, adjusting then until he'd found just the right spot. Adopting Frank's casual posture, he leaned halfway out of the chair and rested his forearms on his thighs, fingers clasped between his knees.

"You know I have to sign an evaluation saying you're capable of performing your job."

"I am capable of performing my job."

She spoke evenly, very quietly.

"Are you sure about that?"

"Very."

Silence stretched between them until Clay said, "Unfortunately, I think you're right. I think you'll be just fine on the street. To be honest, it's what you do when you're not working that worries me."

Frank knew what he meant, that sometimes work was the only thing a cop had and when the job was gone there was nothing left but bullets or bottles. She offered him nothing.

"Your consult form says you're single."

"That's right."

"Do you date?"

"Are you asking me out?"

Clay smiled. "Do you?"

"No."

"How come?"

"Too busy."

"Would you *like* to date?"

Frank and Clay were head to head, eyes locked. She hesitated before answering no, and he immediately asked her why.

"Too busy," she repeated with a shrug.

"Doing what?" he pressed.

Frank sighed, conveying a supreme indifference to the barrage of questions.

"I don't know. Working, I guess."

"What do you do when you're not working?

"Sleep. Eat. Exercise. Read the paper, watch the news, football."

Clay sat back, asking what team she liked.

"Chiefs look good. And just to show I have a heart, Warren Moon makes the Seahawks a sentimental favorite."

Clay smiled again, like an indulgent grandfather. "You wrote down that you drink moderately. What's moderate to you?"

"I don't know. Depends on the day."

"Do you drink more on bad days?"

"I suppose."

Frank sat back, stretching her legs all the way out, crossing arms and ankles.

"What's an average day's consumption?"

"Two, three beers. Scotch sometimes, maybe wine if I have dinner."

"Do you ever have nightmares?"

Frank's nonchalant expression wavered for an instant, but

then she said stoically, "It's a package deal. You get a pension, medical, and nightmares for the rest of your life."

"Are they bad ones?"

"Is any nightmare good?"

Clay smiled at his own question, neatly laying the trap. "Do you ever wake up crying?"

The flexed jaw muscle was Clay's answer. He shifted his attention to a thread on his slacks. "I don't suppose you'd tell me what they're about."

He looked back up and searched her cobalt eyes, waiting. Finally he sighed loudly. "Lieutenant, you seem like an intelligent person. I have to admit, I admire your investigative skills and I've enjoyed it the few times we've worked together, but frankly, I sure as shit wouldn't want to be living in your shoes right now. I'd say you're on the edge of a hard place and I'm offering you a hand— no strings attached. I can help you, Frank, but only if you'll let me."

Their eyes dueled while Frank considered Clay's offer. She respected him, he seemed like a straight-up guy, but she just couldn't tell him everything. What she'd endured lately with Kennedy and Noah was bad enough. She wasn't willing to go any further. Not for a stranger. Clay finally realized that.

"Fine. You're right. You *are* wasting my time."

He stood, reseating himself behind the desk. "You know my number and you know where I am."

Frank hadn't expected the abrupt dismissal. She got up and walked to the door, then paused, her hand on the knob. Clay had opened a folder and was sorting through its contents.

"Are you going to sign off on me?" she asked.

Without lifting his head, Clay answered, "Of course I am. Your job's all you have in the world."

Sometimes he'd go out and find a whore before he had to be at work, or sometimes he'd cruise on the way home. He couldn't do it very often. It cost a lot for what he wanted, and his mother always noticed the missing money. After a while he gave it up and just watched the whores, thinking about what he'd like to do to them. He'd sit alone in the car, wishing his dad were with him, missing him.

23

Frank tried to help Kennedy into the Honda after she was wheeled out of the hospital. Kennedy slapped her hand away, complaining she hadn't forgotten how to walk.

"Geez Louise," she drawled, "the way ya'll are fussin' over me you'd think I was a double amputee."

Watching Kennedy get in on her own, Frank commented, "Too bad Tunnel cut your carotid and not your vocal cords."

They went by Kennedy's apartment to pick up some clothes. Frank looked around while the younger woman packed. The place obviously came furnished in used Sears Roebuck. The carpet was the standard chocolate shag, and though worn, it was clean. The kitchen was cramped but tidy. There were some dishes in the sink, and Frank quickly washed them.

Kennedy emerged from the bedroom with a suitcase. When Frank offered to help, Kennedy waved her away. Frank waited against the door, surveying the spartan surroundings. No plants, no books, no pictures. A stereo system and lots of CDs dominated the room, as did a pile of sports equipment. Two surfboards and a mountain bike were propped against the wall. A neat pile of newspapers sat on one end of the couch.

"Okay. That's it."

Frank tugged at the suitcase, reminding Kennedy she was supposed to be taking it easy.

"Oh yeah, it's *really* heavy."

"That's not the point. Easy is easy. You're lucky I let you walk up here."

"Oh, you're so *butch*," Kennedy teased.

Frank headed down the balcony steps while Kennedy locked up. By the time Kennedy got to the car, she was pale.

"You alright?"

"Yeah. I just got a little dizzy."

"You've been in bed for days and your body's been through a lot of trauma. See why you've got to go slow?"

"Yes, mother."

"I ain't yo mama."

"Damn straight. You're way better lookin'."

"Don't you ever quit?" Frank asked, turning into traffic.

"Uh-uh."

Frank checked her mirrors, thinking it could be a very long week. When Frank parked in her own driveway, she hopped out to open Kennedy's door, but of course Kennedy was already out and reaching for the suitcase. Again Frank snatched it from her but this time the younger cop didn't protest. She was busy studying the stuccoed house, the trimmed lawn on either side of the brick walkway, the lush bougainvillea hedges. Frank opened the front door into the big living room, and Kennedy whistled.

"Are you on the take? How the hell do you afford this on a cop's salary?"

"You don't. It was in foreclosure, so we got a great price."

"Who's 'we'?"

Realizing her mistake, Frank said, "Let me show you your room."

Kennedy followed slowly, nodding approvingly at the gym. She paused at the den.

"Dang. Have you read all those books?"

"No," Frank said patiently.

Kennedy smiled as she passed the dining room table, cluttered with the xeroxed guts of the Agoura/Peterson case. Standing behind Frank, she surveyed the guest room.

"This is nice," she said. The room was simply furnished. Pale yellow walls and a couple of large, healthy plants gave the room a sunny, tropical feeling. Fingering a palm frond, Kennedy said, "I never would have figured you had such a domestic streak."

"I don't. My housekeeper takes care of everything. If they die she gets new ones."

Frank opened the door to a small bathroom and said, "Let me know if you need anything."

Kennedy poked her head in, regarding the folded yellow towels on their racks, the new bar of soap in the dish, and a vase of tiny white and yellow flowers.

"Did your housekeeper pick the flowers, too?"

Kennedy reminded Frank of a lioness observing its quarry, carefully noting every weakness and opening. She admitted to having cut the flowers and Kennedy twanged, "Ah knew it. Yer just a big ol' femme under that crusty outside."

Frank knew Kennedy was teasing, but all the butch and femme references still made her uncomfortable. They alluded to a sexuality that was well buried, one that Frank wanted to keep that way.

"You're welcome to use the dresser. Why don't you unpack while I start dinner."

"Can I help?"

"Yes," Frank said firmly. "You can watch."

Frank put groceries away then started the barbecue, relieved by the familiarity of her household chores. Stirring together a marinade for the chicken, she wondered if she had enough fruit on her trees to make a citrus salsa. Kennedy wandered out to the patio as Frank was picking oranges.

"This is a most-excellent house."

"Glad you like it," Frank said through the branches.

"Did you buy it like this or remodel?"

"Bought it."

"Was the gym already there?"

Always the detective, Frank mused. Luchowski was a lucky guy.

"Nope. I did that."

"Who decorated?"

Frank remembered the day the big leather couch was delivered. Maggie had laughed, "*Now* it's a home," and pushed Frank down onto it. They'd made love on the slippery plastic packing.

"A friend," Frank offered.

"You have friends?"

Kennedy was humored with a fake smile. She followed Frank back into the kitchen.

"Sure I can't help?"

"Yep." Frank pulled a beer out of the fridge and asked Kennedy if she wanted anything. She said, "Yeah," and got up, but Frank pushed her onto the barstool.

"You sit. I wait. What do you want?"

Kennedy rolled her eyes and said exasperatedly, "Make it a Coke, slave-girl."

Frank handed her a can, then a glass with ice.

"Do I leave a tip when I go?"

"All gratuities were included in your hospital bill."

Frank disappeared into the den, and a moment later a bossa nova swayed gently from the living room speakers. She resumed her stance against the counter as Kennedy watched her chopping scallions and garlic and ginger. The absence of words between them was comfortably filled by the music. Kennedy relaxed against the bar.

"Tired, sport?"

"A little. It's kinda nice just to sit here and watch you. What's the music?"

"Antonio Carlos Jobim."

"It's pretty."

Frank nodded, pausing her chores to drain a quarter of her beer. Beyond the living room window the sun was sinking red. Pretty soon the lights would flick on automatically and she would get the chicken grilling. The evening's order soothed Frank.

"You like cooking?"

Frank smiled a little.

"Yep."

"Did your mama teach you?"

"Pretty much taught myself."

The two women swapped information about their families and where they'd grown up. The conversation continued casually as they moved outside while Frank barbequed. Returning to eat in front of the TV, Kennedy surveyed her abundant plate and said, "Geez Louise, do you always cook like this?"

"I like to eat," Frank said simply.

"I guess so."

Frank sipped from a wine glass as Kennedy started wolfing her dinner. Frank used to bolt her food too, but Mag had shown her how to slow down and draw out the pleasure. Frank picked up her fork, warning herself not to go there. After they ate dinner and watched a little TV, Kennedy admitted she was bushed. While she got ready for bed, Frank started washing the dishes. She was rinsing a plate and didn't hear Kennedy come up behind her.

Frank jumped and Kennedy said, "Sorry. I just wanted to thank you for everything. The dinner was incredible and your hospitality could make you an honorary Texan."

"That's something I've aspired to for a long time," Frank said wryly.

"I'm sorry to flake out on you so early."

"No, that's good. You need your rest. Get to bed."

"Alright."

Kennedy turned away, thanking Frank once again.

"Sure."

Frank stuffed the flatware in the drainer. She felt ridiculous accepting Kennedy's thanks. If anything, Frank should be down on her knees thanking Kennedy for not having died on her. She couldn't even consider what that would have been like. She wiped the counter, finding comfort in the familiar blue tiles, but she was still disconcerted by Kennedy's gratitude. Staring at the light spilling onto the floor from the guest room, Frank stood drying her hands longer than she needed to. Finally, she walked toward the yellow beam and knocked gently on the open door.

"Yeah."

Frank stepped tentatively into the room, still gripping the dishtowel. She wanted to say something to Kennedy but didn't know what.

"Do you have everything you need?"

Kennedy was propped against her pillows, a magazine in her lap. Fatigue, plus a huge T-shirt, made her look young and fragile, and Frank felt a quick, choking desire to protect Kennedy from every bad thing the night could bring. She wanted to warn her to leave the light on and not close her eyes. Kennedy's smile and contented reply forced the words from Frank's head but did nothing to reassure her. She passed the towel from hand to hand, still groping for what to say.

"How's your neck?"

"It's okay. It's kinda tweaky and tight but nothing I can't live with."

"You going to be able to sleep alright?"

"If you ever quit worryin' about me and get outta here," Kennedy grinned.

"Alright." Frank shifted from her left foot then back to her right. "If you need anything, just let me know, okay?"

Kennedy nodded, her eyes mirroring the trace of her smile.

"I mean, don't worry if you have to wake me up, okay?"

"Okay."

But still Frank didn't leave, and Kennedy asked, "Is something wrong?"

"No. Not at all. I mean, I just..." Frank took a huge breath.

"Look, I don't know, maybe you're...healthier, better-adapted, maybe it won't happen to you, but if you wake up scared, or have a bad dream, I'm just next door, okay? You don't have to go through any of that alone. Just come and wake me up, alright?"

Kennedy's smile faded and she agreed.

"Promise?"

"Yeah," the younger woman said seriously.

"Okay," Frank sighed, hugely relieved. "Get some sleep."

She returned to the dark kitchen and hung up the dishtowel. Pouring the last of the wine into her glass, she noticed the slight trembling in her hand.

On Friday afternoons he watched the football games at Culver City, or sometimes he'd go to Crenshaw or Inglewood, but he never went back to his old school. He drove by occasionally but would have been ashamed to be seen there. That was where it all started to come undone. He played that game in his head every night, and every night, he stopped battering Jimmy Pierce once he was on the ground. In his head he went on to finish the game, neatly straight-arming blockers, flying into the end zone with the crowd cheering and his father clapping. The scout on the sidelines would be incredulous and he'd ask the beaming coach, "Who's that kid?"

He missed the game, missed the contact and the release of pounding into the other players. After the games on Friday, if he had enough money, he'd cruise LaBrea or Washington until he found a whore. Then he'd take her in the back seat and slam into her, a towel around her throat silencing her cries.

24

Frank woke up on the couch in the den, fuzzy and slightly headachy from the wine. It was a familiar feeling, and she dismissed it with a glance at the VCR clock. It's gleaming red numbers mocked that it was only half past three. Dark, relentless dream flashes assured her there would be no more sleep tonight, and Frank was glad the lamp was still on. She straightened her legs over the end of the couch and concentrated on Stan Getz soloing on "These Foolish Things."

When the song ended, she stopped the spinning CD and walked quietly into her bathroom. She shook out some aspirin and brushed her teeth, then got into bed with a pysch text. She closed her eyes, the book unopened, wondering where he was.

You're out there somewhere. Maybe working. What do you do?

Frank made a list in her head of night jobs. She ruled out all the jobs that involved people. If their profile was right, he wouldn't work well with others, too insecure. She considered delivery jobs.

Nope. You're smart and you'd use that. Your assaults and your bodies would be spread all over. No, I think you go somewhere, not too far from home, and you stay there. Probably drive the same route every night. Comfortable, predictable, no surprises. You don't like surprises, do you buddy? We have a lot in common, you and I.

Frank would have smiled if it hadn't been so true.

I lie here thinking about you and you're thinking about...your last girl. Peterson. Bet you didn't even know her name. Bet you never even talked to her. She would have been so scared, so frightened, and I'll bet you just stood mute over her.

Frank thought of standing silently by Kennedy's bed in the hospital that first night, not wanting to console her, crippled by her own fears.

Or maybe you're on to your next girl already. Its been a while. Are you thinking about how you're going to do it next time? Do it better, make it last longer. How you're going to hurt her? Same way, or are you ready for something new? Simple assault, violent assault, murder...where

do you go from here? Do you ever see yourself in the mirror and won-
der who you are?

Frank remembered striking the mirror the night she'd had that dream. This wasn't the first time she had compared herself to a sociopath. She thought cops and criminals were really the same animal; the main thing separating them was which side of the law they stood on. Only one was sanctioned to kill.

Where are you, buddy? I see you working alone, something like night security or physical labor. If you were doing a security gig, that would explain why you know so much, why you're so clever at this game. I think you'd be bragging, though. Security guards are wannabe cops. They talk tough, act tough, swagger. But you seem like a lay-low kinda guy to me. And you're a big guy. Physical labor would be easy for you, effortless. Gives you lots of time to daydream, time alone, nothing too intellectually challenging, quiet, no one in your face except maybe a skeleton crew or night shift supervisor.

She considered making a list of all the jobs in the area that ran twenty-four hours, then realized the implausibility of that. After all, this *was* one of the largest cities in the world. There wasn't even any guarantee he'd work within the area she examined. *If* he had a night job.

Maybe you're a porno freak and spend all your nights in gummy joints and cruising strips.

Frank tried that on, envisioning him in porn theaters, walking down sidewalks, hands crammed in pockets, hunched over, unobtrusive, inconsequential, no one. She put him in a car, an older one, maybe a sedan or import, something practical, nothing flashy. Maybe an older truck if he did manual labor. It would be dusty and in need of waxing. There'd be litter in it. Not a lot, but some, enough to look messy. She could see him cruising, watching the hookers, building up his nerve, probably spending more time jerking off than picking up.

Nope. I like the night job better. It's more consistent with your hours of attack. You could be doing porn anytime. And you'd need a job to pay rent. You're living somewhere. You did Nichols and Agoura and Peterson inside. Jane Doe was an aberration. You might live with your folks, but at your age they'd expect you to have some money at least.

And you spend your mornings cruising. But you won't be at the parks anymore. I know the black-and-whites are scaring you away.

You're not stupid. Going there for the last two was risky enough. But you had to do it, didn't you? And at the end of the rapes you switched to schools, not just one school but two. You're good, breaking it up, moving it around, but you're still in the locus of Culver City. You haven't moved out of there, and I don't think you will. You're comfortable and feeling good where you are. You've got us running all over.

But why schools? Just because you know that's where you'll find girls? Why not just pick up runaways, homeless kids? It'd be harder on us, better for you. Nope. You like them young and innocent. You don't want a street veteran. You want someone who'll offer no resistance, someone who has no clue how to fight back.

Frank recalled the anticipation and pleasure she'd felt after denying Noah's protests and deliberately putting Kennedy on the bust.

The lieutenant opened her eyes to the shadowy ceiling. Usually she enjoyed the challenge of trying to think like perps, especially someone like this with no apparent motive, but tonight the similarities felt too close to the bone. Frank opened the fat book she'd been holding and squinted at it. Not to bring images closer, but to squeeze them away.

Frank glanced up from the sports section as Kennedy stumbled out of the guest room in shorts and a sports bra. Unaccountably flustered, Frank closed the paper and got up for more coffee even though her cup was still half full.

"What are you doing up so early?" she asked sarcastically. Behind her Kennedy mumbled that she was going to get bed sores if she slept any more.

"Coffee?" Frank asked, not turning.

"Sure."

Kennedy slouched against the counter and Frank handed her a cup, careful to keep her eyes above Kennedy's neck.

"What the hell you get up so early for when you don't have to work?" she grumbled good-naturedly.

Frank flipped her wrist over. "It's nine o'clock."

"Like I said, what do you get up so early for?"

Frank shook her head and picked up the paper, muttering, "Kids."

"What's happenin' in the world?" Kennedy asked, standing close enough to Frank to see the paper too. Frank was keenly aware of Kennedy's soft smell, like freshly mowed grass or baking bread. Something ancient and involuntary turned over in Frank's belly; it was small and buried, but it groped at the warm scent. She got up and opened the refrigerator.

"How'd you sleep?"

"Oh, pretty good, I reckon, considering there's a hole in my neck. Your bed's comfortable."

"Hungry?"

"Girl, how do you eat so much and stay so skinny?"

Frank closed the door, still keeping her back to Kennedy.

"Hey. How about I take you out to Sylvester's? Best corned beef hash in the city."

"They got grits?"

"Kennedy," Frank said, fooling around at the coffee pot again, "this is L.A., not Lubbock."

"*Damn.* Ya'll don't know how to eat around here." Then, to Frank's relief, Kennedy went into her room to put on a shirt.

The day was clear and sunny. During the drive they bantered easily, and at the restaurant they both ordered the hash. Kennedy kidded the waitress about putting grits on the menu. Then a comfortable silence slipped between the cops as they assessed the patrons.

"So," Kennedy asked at length, "who's the we you bought the house with?"

Frank stalled, sipping her coffee.

"You've got a mind like a steel trap."

"I'm a detective," she grinned helplessly.

Frank studied the happy eyes and shiny hair. Kennedy's cheekbones were high and strong; her color was good. Her lips were pink, the lower one fuller than the top.

"Who'd you buy the house with?"

"You're relentless," Frank said dismissively, deciding that was a better quality in a cop than a houseguest.

"Who was it?" Kennedy pressed.

"Look, sport, I'd really rather not discuss my personal life, okay?"

"You did in the hospital."

"That was different."

"How so?"

The waitress brought them a basket of biscuits, forcing Kennedy's elbows off the table. Frank noticed her lean right back in when the waitress moved away. Like an animal hunting, she didn't want to lose the trail.

"Why was it different in the hospital?"

Frank paused, appraising the handsome face again. She decided it wasn't the packaging that made Kennedy appealing, but the enthusiasm behind it. She was so damn...vibrant. Kennedy was staring at her, waiting for an answer. Frank knew she wouldn't quit until she got it.

"That was all stuff I thought you should know."

"I see."

Frank watched her open a biscuit and draw butter and honey across it.

"Pretty good," she said around a mouthful.

"As good as mama's?"

Kennedy laughed and mumbled, "Mom couldn't cook for shit. It got so that if something wasn't raw or burnt me and my brother wouldn't eat it."

Frank smiled in spite of herself, infected by Kennedy's high humor.

"So, did you decorate the place or was that the mystery guest?"

Frank's jaw muscle jumped. She'd been willing to share about the nightmares and the fear, but now Kennedy was crossing over into an area where she had absolutely no business. Any hint of warmth fled from Frank's eyes. She warned Kennedy to drop it.

"Okay. Sorry," Kennedy said contritely. She pushed the biscuits toward Frank. "You should have one while they're warm."

Frank took a biscuit, but just left it on her plate. She'd spent eight years successfully forgetting Mag until Timothy Johnston's death had suddenly resurrected her. Mag's specter had risen as Frank watched Kennedy bleeding out. It had sat next to her in the ambulance and followed her into the hospital. Noah had given the wraith life and Kennedy fed it. Now it loomed large and powerful, hanging over Frank like a second, much darker shadow.

Kennedy continued making smalltalk, but Frank only answered with nods or monosyllables. After breakfast, she dropped Kennedy off at the house despite the younger woman's protests that she wasn't tired.

"Good. Keep it that way."

"Where are you going?"

"The office for a while."

"Sure you don't want some company?"

"Very."

Kennedy opened her car door but before she got out she turned to face Frank. "I'm sorry I got so nosy back there. I was just curious, that's all."

Frank nodded, staring ahead, deciding what would be the best route to take to Figueroa at this time of day.

Kennedy stuck her hand toward her. "Friends?"

Kennedy's sincerity was genuine, no mocking, no teasing, and Frank thawed a little. She shook. "Sure. What do you want for dinner?"

"Geez, girl, we just had breakfast. Brunch."

"Yeah. And you'll be starving in a couple hours. What do you want?"

"I don't know," Kennedy whined, then brightened. "Surprise me. If everything you make's as good as last night's supper, then I'll be happier'n a dump rat."

Frank squinted at Kennedy. "A dump rat?"

"Yes, ma'am," Kennedy laughed. "You never been to the dump and seen all them big ol' rats runnin' 'round? Fat and happy as can be?"

"Can't say that I have."

"Well, girl, you ain't *lived* ''til you've gone rat shootin' at the dump."

Frank pressed her lips against the smile oozing around the edge of her mouth.

"That's a big thing in Texas, huh?"

"Oh, yeah. Huge. And it being Texas and all, we got rats the size a Rottweilers."

Frank's smile finally spilled over. Kennedy grinned happily and said, "See you later, gator."

She slammed the door and jogged up the walkway. Frank thought about telling her to take it easy, but Kennedy would just flash that damn cocky smile and do exactly what she wanted. Backing into the street, Frank wagged her head. Kennedy had an amazing capacity to bring Frank down then toss her up again, higher than she'd been in a long time. Higher than she was sure she wanted to go.

He worked the late shift. It was okay. He gave his mother most of the money but kept a stash for himself, for the whores. He didn't go home right after work. His mother would still be there. Since his father died she was constantly criticizing and complaining. He could never do anything right. If the weather was nice, he'd buy some junk food and eat his dinner at one of the parks. He liked them. They were free, and big, and it was easy to watch girls without anyone noticing him. He started spending more and more time there.

25

er detectives were used to the click of Frank's Italian loafers, and when she padded into the squad room in sneakers, they were surprised to see her.

"Dude-ess," Noah greeted affectionately, and Johnnie dropped his feet off his desk, grinning a little too broadly. He didn't have time to cover his folded newspaper. Ike lifted a finger on a phone call, and from the typewriter Diego greeted, "*Ess-say.*" She exchanged hand signs with him and slapped Noah's shoulder as she passed to her office.

"You're RODded, babe. Go home," he called.

"You closing everything?" she rejoined, meaning had he handed all the cases to the DA.

"One hundred percent."

"Then I'm outta here," she called back, settling into her old chair, realizing how good it felt. Feeling a sense of purpose in directing other people, guiding them to resolve the final, mysterious destinies of strangers—strangers to the nine-three but vivid memories alive to the survivors of their cases—all of it felt *fine*. Being a homicide cop was the next best thing to being God: telling someone how and why a loved one died was a power trip, and Frank loved that power. A lot of cops shrank from the responsibility involved; those like her fed off it, lived on it. The cost of playing God was high—failed relationships, chemical dependencies, cynicism, emotional petrification. Frank was willing to pay, though. For her it was still worth it.

Sifting through a stack of pink message slips, she prioritized who she needed to get back to and threw away the ones that didn't matter. Along with wads of legal briefs, interdepartmental memos, RHD memos, and department memos, was a pile of evidence reports, 60Ds to be reviewed, copies of prelim, death, and MI reports and personal notes from her detectives. There was also a message from IAD.

Noah leaned in.

"The Fubar finds you in here, he's gonna kick your ass."

"That'd be worth selling tickets to," Frank muttered.

"I'm serious. He says we're to 'report' if we see you around here."

"You're kidding?"

"Uh-uh. Am I gonna have to run you in, Frank?"

"Guess so."

Noah grinned.

"How's Gidget?"

"She's doing well. She's a quick healer."

"Not being too much of a pain in the ass?"

"Not as big as you."

Frank buried her head in the paperwork and didn't see Noah's wide smile. Without looking up she said, "Have a seat. Tell me what's going on. Internal giving you a hard time?"

Noah plucked the knees of his trousers and dropped onto the couch, all gangly joints and limbs.

"Nah, those idiots, they don't have a clue, even though they've been on us like lips on a blow job. They're just blowing smoke." Noah paused, then casually threw in, "They've been askin' a lotta questions about you and Kennedy. Your relationship."

Frank smirked a little, throwing out an old memo.

"That's not surprising. They're just swinging in the wind. It's either grab onto that or grab onto their dicks. They've got nothing legit on this. They know it. We know it. Christ, even the big hats probably know it. But we've got to do it for the commission."

IAD was just doing their usual song and dance, doing CYA, making sure Frank wasn't holding out on them. They'd been just as hard on her detectives, and almost as hard on Kennedy and the uniforms at the bust. There were no holes in any of the stories, but IAD couldn't understand how no one had seen Johnston hiding behind the hall door. They were convinced Frank had overreacted and concocted a story to save her skin.

"Besides," Frank tossed more papers into the garbage, "if they want to bury me they've got years worth of shit."

"Still," Noah cautioned, "you watch your ass."

"Nothing I can do about it," she shrugged. "How's everybody else?"

"Alright. Gettin' back to normal."

The day after the shooting Frank had talked to all her detectives. Jill had requested early leave, but Foubarelle had flatly de-nied it. Frank told her to take it anyway, that she'd hash out the paperwork later. Johnnie was still pretty amped. She'd caught him after work, after he'd already had a few. She let him tell her about standing out on the balcony in the rain and not being able to do anything and how stupid they were for not seeing him and the door slamming behind them and feeling pukey because she and Kennedy were still in there.

"I'm glad you got that motherfucker," Johnnie'd confided earnestly. His voice was huskier than usual, probably from being up all night. She wondered if he'd sobered up at all before going to work. Johnnie needed a tight rein for his own good. With Foubarelle running the ops he wouldn't have that. Their supervi-sor couldn't rein in a hobby horse, and she hoped Johnnie would-n't do something really stupid before she got back.

Noah was a little subdued, but still bopping around with his chronic enthusiasm. He was alright. He had Tracey, and for that Frank was profoundly grateful.

"Has RHD been around?"

"Not a peep."

Frank made a disgusted face. Clearly Agoura/Peterson wasn't high on their list of priorities. Noah filled her in on a slashing Gough had caught, a Belizian who took a razor to his brother's throat over a third brother's wife. Their suspect had fled, probably back to Belize, but the surviving brother and a sister wouldn't cough up anything. Ike got a woman who'd been beat to death with a chair. Her boyfriend denied any involvement, but the neighbors said they'd had an awful fight that night. Her scream-ing had prompted an anonymous call to Figueroa. By the time the responding unit arrived they had to call homicide. Noah beamed maniacally.

"Sa-ame Bat-channel, sa-ame Bat-station."

"Quick, Robin! To the Bat-cave!"

"So what do you think about Robin and Batman...you know?" Noah raised his eyebrows in implication.

"Nope. Purely hetero. They were bringing up porno on those big consoles down in the Bat-cave and slapping the bat together."

"Hmm. You think Alfred was in on that?"

"You bet."

"Damn! Circle jerks in the Bat-cave. But what about Bat-girl?"

"You kidding? Who do you think dressed her up in all that black leather?"

"Damn!"

Frank smiled, relaxed in her old chair.

"Shouldn't you be out playing cops 'n' robbers?"

Johnnie slumped in the doorway just as Noah jumped up, shouting, "Holy Homicide, Bat-woman!"

"You are too fuckin' weird," Johnnie grumbled.

Noah slapped him on the back. "Weren't you one of the Riddler's henchmen?"

Johnnie swiveled to let him by and asked Frank, "What the fuck's he talkin' about?"

"Nothing you need trouble yourself with, good citizen. What's up?"

Now Johnnie took a turn on the couch. Frank felt like an analyst as he griped about his work load, Foubarelle's nitpicking, the absence of witnesses in all his cases, and the absence of anything useful from a witness when he found one. In the middle of this bull session Ike poked his head in. He was resplendent in a three-piece pinstripe, his nails buffed to a high gloss, diamond studs winking like a constellation against his dark hair, which Frank was pretty sure he dyed. What she didn't know was how Ike managed to dress like a Mafia don, supporting his ex-wife and kids on a detective's salary. Maybe she didn't want to know.

Johnnie just stared. Then he said, hopelessly, "On toppa all that, I gotta work in an office fulla faggots."

Examining his cuff links, Ike replied, "You're just jealous 'cause I make you look bad."

"Yeah, that's it. So how much time you gotta give yourself in the morning to look like this?"

"Longer than the two minutes you take."

"Alright," Frank interrupted. "You both look like fuckin' movie stars. Johnnie? Anything else here?"

"Nah. I'll leave you alone with Giorgio."

"*Mille grazie.*"

"*Mille grazie,*" Johnnie imitated in lisping falsetto, and Frank knew how it felt to run a preschool. She looked questioningly at Ike, but he asked how she was doing.

"Good. What's up?"

"IAD must be giving you a hard time."

She nodded, wondering when the social call was going to end.

"Don't let the bastards get you down," he counseled. Then, "Remember the James case?"

Albion James. Twelve years old. Shot in front of the QuikSnak by his friend, one Little Crank, a thirteen-year-old Broadway Crip who was evidently jumping James into the set. A good banger has to work for their set, procuring money, guns, drugs, whatever the gang needs. James' work, his initiation into this particular set, was to jack the convenience store. According to the store clerk, James chickened out at the last minute and Little Crank ragged him on the street corner, telling him to get his ass back in there and do the work or he'd issue a general BOS—beat on sight—for him. James evidently tried to walk away, but Little Crank pulled a piece and ordered him back in. James stood glued to the sidewalk while Little Crank insisted, "Do the work, Little Jim-Jam."

When James still didn't budge Little Crank blew a hole in his chest, then calmly walked into the store and demanded the clerk's money. The clerk and a customer witnessed the entire scene. Neither would testify. The clerk adamantly refused; the customer seemed very reluctant but still open to it.

Ike wanted to work the customer but he had to get an okay from the assistant DA to go with just the one wit. Frank frowned, knowing Ike's chances of persuading McQueen were slim. She became the assistant by winning cases and hoped continuing to do so would land her the DA's job someday. Filing cases wasn't about justice, it was about politics. She took the cases that had the best chance of winning. Those with less than compelling evidence were thrown back to the detectives until they could make them more winnable. Frank could already see this one flying back at them, but she told Ike to keep pressing the wits, especially the customer. She'd take the heat if McQueen didn't like it.

When Ike left, Frank returned calls to the sheriff's office and highway patrol, and responded to homicide-related queries from a number of agencies around the state. Johnnie returned with a question in the middle of one of her conversations. Frank noticed there was mustard on his shirt, and after she answered him she told him to go change. He said he didn't have a clean shirt in his locker.

"Then I guess you better borrow one from somebody."

"Hey. Aren't you ROD?"

"Yeah. What's your point?"

"I don't have to take orders from you," he smirked.

Frank pushed her lips together, considering. Then she stood and wiggled a finger.

"Come here."

She led Johnnie to the bathroom down the hall and positioned him in front of the mirror.

"Look. You want to see a cop show up at your son's homicide investigation looking like you do? Me, personally, I'd call in a complaint on you. Come on. Did you sleep in that shirt too? It's a fucking mess."

Johnnie tried to brush out the wrinkles, saying, "It's not so bad."

"It's trash, man. I've seen cleaner clothes on hope-to-die junkies. Look, I know it's been a rough couple of days, but you've got to go home tonight and do some laundry. Get a six-pack, take it to the laundromat, get your clothes done. I'm not your mother, Briggs. I shouldn't be having to tell you this. I'm running a homicide unit, not a daycare center. Alright?"

"Yeah, yeah."

They walked back to the squad room and Frank added, "Try wearing polo shirts. They got collars and they don't wrinkle so bad."

He nodded. "Maybe I'll try that."

Back at her desk, Frank fiddled with a pen, worrying about Johnnie. He was manifesting all the signs of a crash-and-burn, and she wondered how she could ward that off. Noah was his partner. Maybe she'd ask him to have a few beers with him some night, see if he could get Johnnie to open up.

Before she took his place, Joe Girardi had warned her that ninety percent of the job would be holding her cops' hands. She'd be a sounding board, a mother, a shrink, and a doctor. If she thought getting off the street and getting behind a desk would take her out of the shit pile, she was wrong. It would only get her in deeper. All those interview and interrogation techniques she'd used with cons and perps, now she'd have to use them on her own people just to get them to do their jobs. The trick to being a good supervisor was inspiring your subordinates to do their job. Not to do it for them or order them to do it, but to grease the skids. That meant listening to their marital problems, their economic woes, troubles with their kids, hassles with the bugs that were eating their roses, the dogs pissing on their cars.

If they still weren't performing after all that, then you had to lay down the law. Mandatory counseling, demotion, transfer—whatever needed to be done. Contemplating her role as a glorified babysitter reminded Frank of Kennedy. She glanced at the clock and thought she better be getting back home to start dinner. She wrapped up a few loose ends and returned one more call before leaving.

On the way out she glanced at Johnnie's shirt. He hadn't changed it, but he'd daubed most of the mustard off. He was listening to someone on the phone. He covered the mouthpiece and whispered, "I couldn't find a clean one."

Frank was sure he hadn't tried very hard, but at least he'd gotten rid of the worst of the stain. She pointed a menacing finger at him. "Laundry. Tonight. Else I'll partner you with Giorgio."

Johnnie grimaced, and Frank headed out into the afternoon traffic.

Walking in the front door, Frank was pleased to see Kennedy on the couch watching TV.

"Afternoon, Lieutenant."

"Hey. How's it going?"

"I'm almost outta my gourd. How many talk shows can a person watch in a day without goin' crazy?"

"Don't know. How about all those books in the den?"

Kennedy made a face like she'd smelled something bad.

"Boring."

"You don't read?"

"I got a short attention span. I like *doing* things."

While Frank was thinking about that and pulling groceries out of bags, Kennedy walked barefoot into the kitchen. She had color, like she'd been in the sun. Frank asked her how she'd gotten it.

She indicated the patio and said, "Napping in your lounge chair. Guess who woke me up?"

Frank popped the top off a Corona and squeezed a lime into it.

"No clue," she answered.

"IAD. Made a house call. They want you in their office at 1:00 P.M. tomorrow afternoon."

"Yeah, I know. They left a message for me at work."

"That Stuka's a creepy bastard. I get the feeling he'd fuck a snake if somebody'd hold it's head."

Frank had to smile. "They're big on animals where you come from, huh?"

Over homemade pizza and salad, Kennedy asked how the office was. Frank said, "I managed to get one 60D read and answer some calls. Had to give Johnnie some etiquette manners."

Kennedy waved a hand. "That boy is positively prehistoric."

"Aw, he's not so bad once you get used to him."

"Well, I don't reckon I'll get used to him seeing as we don't have a case anymore."

Kennedy waved at the photos and reports and notes stacked next to their plates. "You gettin' anywhere with all this?"

Xeroxed pages were spread all over the dining room table in loose disarray. Frank could spend hours walking around the table, picking up a report here, a note there, studying one photo and then another. She was patient with the case, convinced that something would break for her if she worried it long enough. Besides, what else did she have to do?

"Not consciously," Frank explained, "but I keep working it anyway, reading protocols for the twentieth time, staring at pictures for the hundredth. Sooner or later, if I'm lucky, a light usually comes on and I'll see something I hadn't noticed the first hundred times."

"Noah said you're a great cop. He said you listen to your bones."

Frank shrugged, uneasy with the compliment.

"Do anything long enough you get good at it," she said indifferently.

"He said you're a first-rate Loouie, too."

"He's prejudiced."

"I don't know. I've seen you in action. He's probably right."

Frank almost retorted, If I'm so good, what are you doing with a hole in your neck? She poked at a tomato and Kennedy said, "It's gonna be a drag going back to Luchowski. That bastard's so uptight he could open a beer bottle with his asshole."

Frank grinned. She'd heard plenty like that about him.

"Goddang, you got some kind of a pretty smile, Lieutenant."

Frank looked up from her salad to see if Kennedy was teasing her, but the younger woman's smile was soft and happy. Frank resumed eating as she felt a flush creeping up her neck.

"So tell me," Kennedy said, pulling at a strand of cheese, "how come you ain't got no girlfriend?"

Frank sucked in a long breath. Kennedy's effrontery never failed to amaze her.

"I thought we went through all that this morning."

"That was who you bought the house with," Kennedy corrected. "This is a completely new subject."

Not really, Frank thought, somehow it always comes back to Mag. "Why wouldn't I have a boyfriend?" Frank stalled, always looking for a way out.

Kennedy laughed in disbelief. "Gimme a break. Have you seen yourself in a mirror lately?"

Pulling her crust apart, Frank said, "I see. Walks like a dyke, talks like a dyke, must be a dyke?"

"Am I wrong?"

Frank leaned her elbows on the table, like she was about to share something particularly juicy. "Kennedy, my personal life is just that. Personal. I'm not about to discuss it with you. What do I have to say to make you understand that?"

Much to Frank's surprise, the young cop appeared hurt by her words.

"Nothing," she said, rising to clear her dishes. Frank sat musing at the table while Kennedy clattered in the kitchen. She could feel the tension behind her, and though she was determined to help Kennedy, she wasn't about to open herself up like a home entertainment system.

From the kitchen, Kennedy said, "Frank, you've been great about taking care of me and I appreciate all the effort, but I'm going home tomorrow. Frankly, I'd rather pop a stitch than sit around here talking to you about the weather all day."

She came around the table and stared down at Frank, brown arms crossed, eyes cool. "You can take me or I'll call a taxi. Just let me know."

Kennedy was really pissed. Frank almost laughed, not sure what the hell she was so fired up about.

"You think that's a good idea?"

"I think it's a *jim-dandy* idea."

"I don't."

Kennedy slapped her palms down onto the table and leveled her face with Frank's. "I don't care what you think. All I want to know is if I need to arrange for a taxi tomorrow morning."

Frank pursed her lips over laced fingers, studying the angry face so close to her own. "I'll take you," she finally said.

"Good. I'll see you in the morning."

Kennedy disappeared into the guest room, leaving Frank to wonder just what the hell had happened.

He liked watching the girls and thought about tackling them with his full body, pounding his head and shoulders into them. He'd get excited and usually wound up masturbating in the car. Sometimes at work he'd start thinking about the girls and whack off right on the forklift.

He'd been doing a whore about a week ago and pretended it was a girl in the park. He'd gotten so carried away he'd almost strangled her with the towel. She was really freaked. When she could finally breathe she threatened to call the cops. That rattled him, and he kicked her out of the car.

"You've got to think about your next play," his father had always said. He hadn't been thinking with the whore. He'd almost gone too far. But if he was careful enough, he could go as far as he wanted.

26

Mornin'," Kennedy yawned, plunking her suitcase by the table. Frank looked up from the paper, surprised that she was already dressed and packed.

"Morning," she replied. "Want some coffee?"

"I'll get it," Kennedy said, but Frank had already walked behind her and taken down a mug. She filled it, putting it next to Kennedy, then got out the milk. Their silence was awkward. Kennedy fixed her coffee. She looked expectantly at Frank.

"Ready?"

Frank felt a tug in her chest, realizing she wasn't. She tried to rationalize that Kennedy had to go sometime, then argued with herself, Yeah, but when she's better, not walking around in stitches. Frank told herself she was still liable for Kennedy. She didn't know what had happened last night, but it was her responsibility to find out. She wasn't ready to send the kid home. Not yet.

"Look. Last night…I'm sorry if I was short. I'm just…I'm not used to…talking much to people. Not about myself. I'm not real good at it."

Kennedy politely kidded, "That's an understatement. But hey, you know, it's no big deal. I'm just always pokin' my nose where it don't belong, makin' a pain of myself. Your hospitality's been wonderful, Frank, and I truly appreciate it, but I should be gettin' on home and outta your hair."

"You're not in my hair," Frank responded quickly. "I mean…I like having you here."

Kennedy searched for something in Frank's face, finally saying, "You're such a paradox. You walk around like some Nazi in jackboots, but then you've got this soft side you flash now and then. You know? Like you're a real human being, like when you talked to me in the hospital. So I start thinking what a neat woman you are, how much I really like you. Then I ask a simple question, and bam! you're Super Nazi again. I don't know what to think and figure I just better leave you alone. I'm never sure who you're gonna be."

"I'm not sure I know who I am lately," Frank said, quietly to her feet. "I mean this stuff with Tunnel, you almost dying, my cops all getting reamed by Internal. I'm not even a fucking cop right now. It's all a little confusing."

Frank met Kennedy's eyes, fumbling for the next words. "I'm sorry I jumped on you. You just...sometimes you bring up stuff that I don't want to get into. It's old stuff. Irrelevant."

"So I'm supposed to tiptoe around like I'm in some sort of verbal minefield? Make sure I don't set you off?"

Frank shook her head emphatically "No. Look, I just...we've been through a lot in the last week, and...a lot of stuff's getting stirred up."

"Like what stuff? Tell me about it."

"I can't," Frank said, talking to the floor again.

"You see? That's what I mean," Kennedy accused. "You're great at talking about my shit, but what about yours?"

"You're better at it than I am," Frank offered lamely. "I'm pretty rusty when it comes to talking about stuff like that."

"Rusty? God*damn,* girl, the Tin Man's got *nothin'* on you."

Frank ducked her head in an embarrassed grin, then looked earnestly at Kennedy.

"Stay," she said.

Kennedy hooked her thumbs defiantly into her waistband and arched an eyebrow. "Gimme one good reason to."

"My cooking."

Kennedy's smile was Machiavellian. "I'll stay," she bargained, "but only if you tell me who you bought this house with."

Frank was too astonished by Kennedy's moxie to be fazed by the question. "Why do you want to know so bad?"

"'Cause I don't really know anything about you that's not related to your job, or this shooting somehow. I do know there's a real person lurking somewhere inside you, someone who's more than just the badge she wears."

"Think so?"

"I know so. I met her in Tunnel's apartment and in the hospital. She was even in your guest room the other night."

Frank was slipping on her hard-ass mask and Kennedy asked seriously, "What are you so afraid of?"

Frank laughed at the ceiling. "I'm not afraid of anything."

"Girl, you lie like a rug," Kennedy said with a heavy accent.

"It's not too late to take you back to your apartment."

Kennedy picked up the suitcase. "Let's go."

Frank had to make a decision, and she didn't want to make the wrong one. She gnawed the inside of her lip, looking at Kennedy but not really seeing her. They waited like that until Frank spoke slowly, measuredly, "I bought the house with my lover. And she's dead now. Okay?"

Kennedy's face softened and Frank looked down at the suitcase. "Why don't you go put that away."

The drive to Parker Center was crowded and slow, but Frank wasn't in a hurry. Now she was just wasting IAD time. The sun felt great pouring in through the window, and even the diesel fumes and oiled asphalt smelled good. Punching the radio's memory buttons and finding only commercials, Frank settled for the freeway's orchestra of random horns and a thousand cars and trucks.

IAD had been grilling her hard over this shooting, and Frank wondered if they had other motives. That wouldn't have surprised her. Honestly, she was amazed she'd made it this far. Her time on the force hadn't earned Frank any loyalty. The department was a machine, consuming people and spitting out statistics, that kept a handful of career politicians in coveted spots. Frank produced good stats so she was useful, but she'd never be one of the boys.

Gough had taunted her about that, telling her she could work for the department for fifty years and still not fit in. He was right. After almost two decades on the job she had yet to develop the proper "us against them" mentality. Frank wasn't a saint—she did her share of bending means to justify ends—but she maintained her belief that her primary allegiance was to the streets, not the department.

The day she'd been sworn in as a police officer she'd taken a fundamental oath to protect and serve the people of the city of Los Angeles. Without that oath, she'd never have made it through her first day. The bitter politics and bloodied back alleys would have forced her out long ago. No matter who was on her now— IAD, Foubarelle, Johnston's mother, hell, maybe even one of her own men—she still owed Nichols' father, Peterson's mother, and Agoura's parents the meager satisfaction of finding their child's murderer. It was that simple. It was all she knew.

Frank pulled up at Parker and ran up the stairs, not because she was in a hurry but for the exercise. She greeted Rothman, who snarled, "You're late."

"Traffic."

Stuka grabbed a folder off his desk and motioned to a conference room down the hall. IAD called their interrogations *interviews*. *Conference room* was a euphemism for hot box. Stuka told her to take a seat, but she said she'd prefer to stand.

She slouched against the wall, casual in pressed jeans and LAPD T-shirt, thumbs hooked into her pockets, Ray Bans on her head. The day was warm enough for Top-siders without socks, and Frank crossed a bare ankle over her shin. She looked like she was waiting to take off on a sailing expedition. Frank knew her posture alone was enough to piss off the IAD men.

"Where's your little chicken?" Stuka clucked.

"Back at the hen house."

"Not worried about a fox getting in while mama's away?"

"I'd feel sorry for the fox," Frank answered calmly.

"Oh, she doesn't like men either, huh?"

"You'd have to ask her that."

"Doesn't she do whatever her sugar mama tells her?"

Frank grinned, but her eyes were as dark and flat as a shark's.

"I wish. She's her own girl, Stuka. If you knew anything about women, you'd have seen that right off."

"Guess I haven't had as much practice as you."

"Nah, guess not. You and the Ratman are too busy being IA moles."

Rothman finally spoke up, telling Frank to cool her jets.

"Don't take it so goddamned personal. This is SOP. We're just doing our job."

"Some job you got. You sleep good at night?"

"Lieutenant, how long have you been with the LAPD?" Rothman asked monotonously, a standard baseline question.

"That's not in your file there?"

"In your own words," Stuka growled.

"Sixteen years."

"You like it here?"

"Love it."

"How come you've never been out of Figueroa?"

"It doesn't get any better."

"Oh really?" said Stuka, feigning surprise. "No better than Rollin' '60s and Pirus going off on each other like rabid dogs, wanting a piece of your ass worse than anybody else's? No better than Salvatruchas and Westsiders sticking each other every night and working leads from strawberries and hookers with running sores and that's the best they got? It doesn't get better than piss and graffiti on your own station house and snipers taking potshots at you and cockroaches in your desk drawers?"

Stuka ran out of steam.

Frank said sheepishly, "Guess I don't get out much."

It was Rothman's turn now.

"Nobody likes IAD, and that's okay. But at least Stukie and I haven't spent sixteen years in Figueroa."

Tapping an unlit cigarette on the table, he asked Frank directly, "Do you know what I think?"

"No clue."

"I think you're afraid to leave Figueroa. You're a big fish in a small, scummy pond, and you know in your heart of hearts that you couldn't make the leap into a better pond. You're a big cheese in Figueroa because nobody else wants to be there. You're a woman in a man's job and you know there's only two ways to rise—EEO appointments or blow jobs. You don't have the guts to leave. If I was a woman, I'd be pretty frustrated."

Frank allowed a glimmer of a smile. She knew they were playing her, shaking her cage. If it were a normal workday she'd be livid wasting her time like this, but on ROD she was actually amused by their tactics.

"That's very insightful," Frank congratulated. "Did you come up with that all by yourself?"

Rothman ignored her, getting to his point.

"Yeah, I'll bet it gets frustrating knowing there's only two ways out for you. So you build a little steam, take it out on felons and colleagues, an occasional hooker now and then."

Rothman was referring to the handful of excessive force and coercion charges she'd accrued over her career.

"That's okay, nobody really cares. Everybody looks the other way. All the claims are unsubstantiated or unfounded. You feel pretty good, but little by little the pressure builds up again. So one day you're out on a routine bust, and some asshole that you know has a record a mile long and has walked on most of those charges, he starts dogging you and he's in your face, and maybe, just maybe, you've heard *bitch* or *cunt* or *dyke* one too many times lately, and you let fly. You give this son of a bitch everything you've got.

"And you know what? There's not a cop in the world who wouldn't sympathize with you. You lose it. And rightly so. There's only so much a man, or a woman, can take. Especially a woman. Nights get lonely, I know, and probably more so for a girl like you. Gotta be secret, gotta be quiet, keep things in the closet. The pressure builds up...it's understandable. You're only human. So this Johnston dude gives you and your team a scare, and you're primed. You blow. It's a normal reaction, nobody's blaming you, Franco. Hell, even your own cops are backing you. It's understandable."

Rothman got quiet. Frank could feel him staring at her. She nodded her head at the floor and scuffed her toe against a black shoe mark.

"You're good," she said softly. "You know what? If you don't make it in IAD you've got a great career in pulp fiction. I'll be first in line to buy your books. Promise."

"Franco, relax. You can level with us. It's okay. We really are on your side. You can tell us how it went down and we'll back you."

"Yeah?"

"Absolutely," Rothman swore, one hand in the air.

"You really want to know?"

Rothman nodded sincerely.

"Alright. I'll tell you."

Frank patiently recounted the exact story she'd already told them half a dozen times. They interjected their own scenarios and events throughout, which Frank carefully refuted before continuing. They played it that way for two and a half hours. When they were done, Frank was wound tighter than a spring and had stains under her armpits. The two IA detectives didn't look much better.

Frank extended her hand to the men, saying, "Gentlemen, I appreciate your resolve in keeping the LAPD the bastion of civil rights that its become."

Stuka reached for her hand before he realized he was being dissed. "Fuck you. You need to get laid proper, Franco. Try a man for once."

Frank ran a hand through her hair, musing, "Maybe you're right, Stukie. Tell you what. I'll try one if you will."

The round little cop moved toward Frank, but his partner grabbed his arm. "Come on, Jer. Don't waste your time."

Frank watched them slip into their office like rats into a hole. She squeezed the back of her neck as she went down the stairs and out into the sunshine. On the way home she picked up a six-pack of Foster's. She slammed two of them before she even pulled into the driveway.

The house was quiet. Frank was slightly alarmed until she saw Kennedy lounging in the back yard. Except for a Walkman and a pair of pink underpants, she was naked. Frank stared through the French doors, then quickly turned away. She made a fuss of slamming the refrigerator door, shaking the utensil drawer, banging the cabinets.

She cracked another beer, grabbed some chips, and carried them around the blue-tiled bar, relieved to see Kennedy had slipped her shirt on. Casually, she stepped outside.

"Hey. How's the tanning business?"

"Good," Kennedy grinned. "How's the bar and grill business?"

Frank shrugged, popping some chips in her mouth.

"Don't know how many times I have to repeat the same story to those idiots. They're so lawsuit-conscious they can't even do their jobs. They wait for the news and civil rights groups to tell them what to investigate, and then they make up shit instead of going out and looking for real problems."

"What'd they say?" Kennedy asked, stretching out on her back, eyes closed against the sun.

Frank told her Rothman's scenario and Kennedy started laughing so hard Frank had to warn her not to pull her stitches.

"Oh geez," she wailed, "that's almost as good as you intimidating me with your awesome rank and power."

In the hospital, they'd pulled the same stunt on Kennedy. Their scenario for her was that Johnston had tried to run past them and accidentally nicked Kennedy, and that Frank had overreacted and blown him away. It was understandable, of course. There was a lot of stress and chaos going down, but Kennedy could tell them the truth. They understood how Frank could "seduce" Kennedy into going along with her story, how Frank's aggressive manner and higher rank would naturally be intimidating to a younger, more impressionable detective.

"Ain't it a comfort knowing your tax dollars are being well-spent by those two yahoos?"

Frank sipped, appreciating the buzz she was getting and the sun's warmth. If Cassandra Nichols' killer wasn't still loose, she might have actually enjoyed this time off. Having Kennedy around gave her a focus, and though the kid didn't need much, she obligingly let Frank fuss over her. But when that was done, Frank's mind inexorably returned to Agoura/Peterson. She was about to get up and start her trancelike circuit around the table when Kennedy said, "When was the last time you saw a movie?'

Frank remembered going to the Plaza last Christmas, but she couldn't remember what she'd seen.

"Been a while."

"Let's go, then. Later on."

Frank felt Kennedy eyeing her expectantly. She pulled on her beer, trying to figure why she suddenly felt uncomfortable. Going to the movies, hanging in the sun, drinking beer—all this was fun. She realized that if Kennedy hadn't been there she'd have been chafing at the bit, gnashing her teeth until she could get back to work. Frank liked being with Kennedy and that made her nervous. But she wouldn't go further with the realization.

"What do you want to see?" she asked cautiously.

"I don't care, anything!" Kennedy threw her hands in the air. "Let's just get out of here. I'm goin' crazy sittin' around all day."

Frank had to admit Kennedy had been awfully good. She was almost hyperactive, and this convalescence must have been excruciating for her. The least Frank could do was take the kid out to a movie. Considering that as an obligation rather than a pleasure allayed Frank's anxiety. She swung her legs off the lounge.

"I'll get the paper."

They picked out a Bond flick and later, as they walked out of the theater, Kennedy gushed, "That was excellent!"

Frank agreed. "Yeah, it was pretty good. I think Brosnan's the best Bond since Sean Connery."

"Since who?"

"Sean Connery."

"Who's he?"

Frank stopped walking and stared at her companion.

"You don't know who Sean Connery is," she stated.

"No," Kennedy said impatiently.

Frank remembered the CDs Kennedy had stacked on her bed-side table. She'd recognized Stone Temple Pilots and Greenday, but most of the other names were foreign to her. As she explained that Connery was the original James Bond she was struck again by the gap in their ages. She also realized that Kennedy had liked the movie more for its nonstop violence and action than its tongue-in-cheek dialogue and Bond's implausible urbanity.

Kennedy wanted coffee, so they stopped at a restaurant a few blocks away. She scarfed a latte and a huge piece of chocolate cake. Frank nursed a brandy, watching the young woman attack her dessert. After she was done, Kennedy smacked her lips and said, "Dang! That was good. Now what do we do?"

"Get you home to bed."

Kennedy's face lit up lasciviously.

"Alone?"

Caught off-guard, Frank almost choked on her drink. She glanced into it, suddenly feeling too hot.

Kennedy leaned forward, adding, "You shore are purty when you ain't bein' so uptight."

Frank tossed back her brandy and stood. "Alright. It's definite-ly time to go home."

She dropped a few bills on the table. Kennedy added some of her own, handing Frank's back. "You gotta learn to take a compli-ment, Lieutenant."

"Whatever. Let's go."

"Have I spoiled a perfectly fine evening?" Kennedy teased, fol-lowing closely behind. Glancing around the small parking lot, al-ways looking for trouble, Frank gallantly opened Kennedy's door. The younger woman slid in and unlocked Frank's side. They drove down Wilshire in silence, both of them unconsciously scanning the street life. At a red light, Kennedy announced, "So tell me something—"

"Christ, now what?"

"Don't get pissed off, it's not about your deep, dark past. I was just curious about somethin'."

"That's news."

Frank stole a look at Kennedy, who'd turned sideways and was leering at her.

"Go ahead. Let's get it over with."

"Why'd you ask me to stay yesterday?"

"Wondering the same thing myself, right now."

Frank shook her head, buying time. It occurred to her that one of the things she liked about the company of men was that they rarely asked personal questions nor divulged their own intimacies. Noah was sometimes an exception to that, but she excused him because he'd grown up with four sisters.

"Kennedy, do you know how I'd feel if I let you go home and you popped a stitch and bled out all over your living room carpet?"

"Grateful?" she laughed. "Just that? You're worried about my health?"

"What are you fishing for, sport?"

"Ulterior motives."

"Well, maybe there aren't any. I almost lost you once. I don't want to lose you again."

"Gee, Frank, that's almost touching. So this is just a huge obligation. Nothing else," Kennedy stated.

Frank spotted a hooker who wasn't really a woman. Transvestites were common prey for pissed-off johns. She hoped his picture wouldn't end up on a homicide desk.

"Not huge at all," she replied evenly, scanning the street. Kennedy appraised her own side, then said, "And no ulterior motives."

"Nope."

"Hm. So tell me somethin' else, why'd you blush back there at the restaurant?"

"I didn't."

"You most certainly did."

"Must have been the brandy," Frank tried.

Kennedy faced Frank and drawled, "Brandy my ass."

Frank had to give the kid high marks for perseverance. "Guess I'm not used to so much flattery."

"Ah, but you like it, don't you?"

They came to another light. Frank leaned against her door to get a full look at the woman next to her. "Isn't it way past your bedtime?"

"You're not answering my question."

"Let's just say it's such a novelty, I don't know one way or another."

The signal turned green as Kennedy settled back into her seat. Turning on the radio, she decided, "I think you like it."

"Maybe," Frank agreed, humoring her.

Kennedy slapped her thighs in time to the music, but suddenly stopped and whirled toward Frank. "Hey! Let's go to the beach real quick and see what the waves are doing."

"Now?"

"Yeah!"

"It's the middle of the night," Frank protested.

"Oh, I *know*," Kennedy exaggerated. "It's *ten o'clock*. Oh my God, that's so late! Come on. Let's go. And besides, you don't have to be anywhere tomorrow."

"Thanks for reminding me."

She looked briefly at Kennedy, hoping she was joking, but the expectation in her eyes was real.

"You can't go swimming," Frank warned.

"I know, I just want to see how the surf is. Maybe poke my baby toe in. *Please*," she begged.

Frank sighed. "Tell me where to go."

The whores didn't satisfy him anymore. He just wanted to look at the girls. It didn't matter if they were Mexican or black or white. He loved how small they were, how unsuspecting. The whores were tough, and certainly not innocent. He never felt bad hurting a whore. They were willing and they got paid for their trouble.

But the girls were different. He thought about fucking them the way he fucked the whores. For a while, his fantasies were enough.

27

The weekend passed amiably. Saturday they fired rounds at the range until Kennedy got tuckered out. She napped in the afternoon while Frank circled the dining room table—restudying, rethinking, trying to be him. She paused once, sensing the sleeping stillness of Kennedy's presence. It was a good feeling, but the sensation bothered Frank nonetheless. She distrusted pleasures inspired by others. They were ephemeral at best, treacherous envoys for disappointment at worst. Squashing the small feeling, Frank resumed her circuit around the table.

The next day Kennedy taught Frank how to play canasta, while Frank shared the finer points of football. The good weather still held on Monday, so they returned to the beach. Frank watched Kennedy wade in the surf. When she jogged back to where Frank hunkered next to a cooler, she was absolutely radiant. Once again, the sleeping desire stirred in Frank. She drowned it with half a beer, wondering how many homicides the Pacific had swallowed.

Kennedy went to bed early that evening, tired from the sun and water. Frank sprawled out on the long couch watching the Eagles beat Dallas. All the Cowboys looked like they were mired in concrete, but if Troy Aikman could get his fat ass out of the pocket they might actually make something happen. Emmitt Smith carried for two miserable yards before succumbing to a flurry of tackles. Frank closed her eyes knowing the next play would either be another hand-off to the overused running back, or a toss to Irvin. The Cowboys' offense was stale and predictable: it was no surprise that Irvin had been busted for blow and Smith ran like an old crab washed up on the beach.

She felt sorry for the running back and didn't envy his Tuesday morning. She thought about the bruises he'd be carrying on his black flesh and remembered the vivid colors on Melissa Agoura's body under the bright autopsy lights. That image was replaced by the outline of the jean rivet on Jane Doe's body. Frank pictured a bear of a man wrapping his arms around the homeless girl and falling on her against the hard street. He'd bruised her with his body, his weight crushing against her. Hitting her hard enough to leave a perfectly readable logo on her skin.

He was ramming his head and his shoulder into me the whole time.

Lisa McKinney's words ricocheted against pictures of Agoura and Peterson's waled corpses. Crocetti's comment fluttered into the mix: *It looks like this poor girl was mistaken for a bowling pin.* And then there was the new ME, whatever her name was, who'd said the bruises were apparently made with something flexible or soft.

Frank whirled her feet squarely onto the floor, concentrating intensely, her head in her hands. She was unaware Dallas had kicked another field goal.

The overall bruising pattern on Agoura and Peterson was consistent with tackle patterns. Above the knees and below the neck. The faces were relatively unblemished. Clean and legal tackles. Many of the hematomas had large, rounded edges, as if they *could* have been made by a bowling ball. Consistent with the size and shape of a football helmet. There were no lacerations because there was padding. Either he wore pads or the girls wore it. Maybe both. Agoura's dislocated shoulder, Peterson's broken collarbone, the contusions—all were classic football injuries. Frank remembered the cuts and gashes and myriad black-and-blue marks from playing with her cousins.

There was no evidence the girls had been slapped or hit with fists. No open hands. Legal tackles from a player on the secondary. A linesman could use his hands, a backfield player couldn't. Ever the skeptic, Frank probed her theory for weak spots. Then she quickly moved to the glass-topped table.

Forensic tests were complete for Agoura, but the lab was still working on Peterson's. Frank reread the DOJ analysis, hoping she'd missed a detail, but the report only frustratingly cited the sample colors and compositions. Upon its receipt, Frank had shipped samples to the FBI's Trace Evidence unit. They wouldn't be back for three or four weeks at the soonest. Still, the DOJ's conclusions didn't exclude the possibility that the fibers could have come from a football jersey.

Frank started pacing around the table, pausing to make notes to call a uniform shop, sports shop, talk to the lab techs, talk to Crocetti. She thought for a moment. Carver and Crenshaw, where the bodies had been dumped, both had football teams. Was it a cheerleader thing? An old girlfriend? She quickly dismissed both notions because the perp had no specific victimology. If he was fixated on a cheerleader or a particular girl, his vics would fit that mold. None did.

Okay. Let's assume you played football, and while I'm assuming, let's say you played in a secondary position, maybe a safety or a tight end. Maybe even a receiver. But you're a big guy, you'd make a good tight end. If you're as much an underachiever as I think you are, you probably never made it to college. So maybe you played in Pop Warner and high school. High school ball. Sure. Something happened to you in school, something around football. And now you're stuck there.

Frank found her notes from the meeting with Richard Clay. She grabbed a legal pad and returned to the couch. Clarifying ideas on paper, she drew lines through the less likely ones and starred her favorites. Thinking of the red-and-white fibers, Frank made a note to check the color of the football uniforms at Crenshaw and Carver. She grinned broadly, her full smile rare and genuine.

First thing next morning, Frank was at Crocetti's office. She startled his replacement when she opened the door without knocking. "Morning. Where's Crocetti?" she demanded brusquely.

Gail Lawless sat back in Crocetti's chair, clearly appalled by Frank's lack of social skills. Frank hadn't bothered to change out of her sweats that morning, and with her yellow hair pulled back in a ponytail, and her hard, intense gaze, she looked like an East Bloc Olympic contender.

"Do you know that most people knock before they enter someone's office?"

"Sorry," Frank said with no attempt at sincerity. "Is he here yet?"

Shaking her head incredulously, the ME replied, "No. He's had the flu all last week and called in again."

The coroner watched as Frank pursed her lips and glanced around the room as if it were empty.

"Are you still Relieved of Duty?" she asked curiously.

"Yeah," Frank answered, and Dr. Lawless offered, "I...we—Crocetti and I—we did your suspect's autopsy."

When Frank didn't reply, the coroner tentatively asked, "Is there anything I can help you with?"

"I don't know. Crocetti did an autopsy for me, about six weeks ago, a sixteen-year-old Caucasian female. Name was Agoura. I've got the case number," Frank said, producing a slip of paper. She'd left the protocol copies in her trunk, not wanting to be seen with anything resembling case work.

"Yeah, I remember," the doctor murmured. "I was there."

She glanced at the number and walked across the large office to a bank of filing cabinets. Lawless found Agoura's folder and scanned it.

"What about it?" she asked, but then her green eyes narrowed suspiciously and she said, "Hey...why are you here if you're ROD? Technically, I shouldn't even be talking to you."

Realizing the new cutter might be able to help her, Frank dipped her head in acquiescence. "You're right. I'm not even on the case anymore. Robbery-Homicide has it. But I had a hunch about something last night and wanted to ask a couple of questions before I go off to the big boys half-cocked and make an even bigger fool of myself."

The doctor weighed Frank's explanation before smiling skeptically, seeming to relent against her better judgment.

"Don't get me fired while I'm still on probation," she warned.

Frank smiled back, her winningest smile, but it didn't ease the tiredness around her eyes.

"What do you want to know?" Lawless asked.

"While you're at it, could you pull this file too? Crocetti did this one, but I'd like your opinion."

Lawless made a reproachful face but pulled Peterson's file as well. "Anything else?" she asked with sarcasm.

Frank offered a quick, placating nod, jutting her head toward the files in the ME's hand. "I'm wondering what you think could have made the bruises."

Lawless returned to Crocetti's ergonomically contoured chair and spread out the autopsy pictures.

"I don't think we came up with anything conclusive," she said as she studied first Agoura, then Peterson.

"Definitely similar bruising, deep, in varying stages, similar placement," she mused. "I remember Agoura looked like she was hit hard but because there wasn't any cutting or abrasion we thought it was with something relatively soft—"

"Or the blows could have been padded."

Frank watched the ME carefully appraise the pictures before nodding her shiny, dark head. She had thick, straight hair in a long bob that bounced whenever she moved. Frank examined her from force of habit. Her eyes were almond-shaped, almost Asian, but she was tall and big-boned, like an Iowa farm girl. She didn't appear to have any make-up on, which was unusual in L.A., but with her dark brows and lashes she didn't need any.

She was wearing hospital fatigues. Frank noted her arms matched her milky complexion. The backs of her hands were red and rashed, a reaction to latex gloves, Frank guessed. No rings, but tiny gold scissors dangled from one ear and a matching gold knife hung from the other. There were two long scratches on her left arm, parallel to each other, almost healed. Frank thought maybe she had a cat.

Gail Lawless looked up apologetically. "There's really no way to tell what did this. There's such contiguous bruising it's hard to find specific patterns."

"You said they were rounded."

"That much I can give you," the coroner agreed, "but as to what the specific instrument was..." She shrugged. "Maybe a bowl, a ball, a bowling ball, who knows. It would be awkward at best to wield something like that, especially as much as your suspect did on these girls."

"How about a football helmet?"

The ME dropped her head over the pictures again. Frank suspected she wore glasses and wondered why she didn't have them on.

"I could see that," she said with enthusiasm. She turned the pictures toward Frank and used a pencil to point to specific bruises.

"That would be consistent with the size and shape and the extent of damage on these leading edges. And it would explain the scale of the bruising, especially if he'd been hitting them with it over a period of time like he apparently did."

"So a definite possibility he was using a helmet on these two?"

"Yes. A definite possibility."

"And if they wore padding, or he was in padding and hit them

226

with pads on, that could explain the deep bruising but no gashes or abrasions?"

"That could explain it, yes."

"Good," Frank said, concisely ending their meeting. She straightened up over the desk.

"Is that all?"

"For now. I appreciate your help," Frank said simply. "And if RHD happens to drop by, keep this under your hat, would you? I want to tell them myself."

The ME couldn't know that Frank would rather chew off her left foot before telling RHD about this.

"No problem," Lawless smiled.

Frank twitched her lips in a brief semblance of civility and moved toward the door. Once there she turned and looked at the ME's hands.

"You should try vinyl gloves."

The doctor followed Frank's gaze and smiled, a slight tinge coloring her cheeks.

Sitting in the Honda with her long legs sprawled out the door, Frank called Carver and Crenshaw High, as well as a sporting goods store, from the parking lot. She got label names and distributors for local and pro football uniforms, and after a few painstaking hours of telephone work, managed to track down over a dozen trade names for the nylon fibers used in football jerseys.

Then Frank went to the SID lab. Here she dared to take the murder book in, because without her badge or ID it was the best piece of evidence she had to show she was a cop. Making a show of opening the binder and extracting the tagged sample along with Agoura's official SID report, Frank apologized to the receptionist for not having her ID, but it was her day off and she'd just had a thought while she was doing errands and wanted to stop and ask about it. The petite and perfectly made-up young woman seemed satisfied with Frank's identity, but informed her that the tech who'd worked on Agoura's fibers was out of town.

After ten minutes of masterful pleading, conniving, and shameless flattery, Frank was able to persuade a tech to look at her samples. Two hours later, Frank had her answer. The fibers matched a multifilament denier yarn called Caprolan, made by Allied Fibers and Plastics.

Back in her car, Frank exhaled deeply, happily. The fiber was by no means conclusively off a football jersey, but it was definitely one of the fibers used in the manufactured high school uniforms. Satisfied that she was still on the right track, Frank again turned her attention to the phone. Punching in a number, she muttered, "Two down, one to go."

Richard Clay was next on her list, and she was apprehensive about talking to him.

His rebuke at their last meeting had embarrassed her, professionally and personally. While her call was being transferred, she wondered if he'd be receptive or refuse to help her. Her curiosity was settled when his secretary informed her that he was at a conference in Seattle and wouldn't be back until Tuesday. Frank was both disappointed and relieved.

She dialed her office and caught Noah on his way out to chase down some witnesses to a drive-by. An eighty-four-year-old grandmother getting out of the backseat of her granddaughter's car had been the unintended victim.

Frank offered to buy Noah lunch and met him twenty minutes later at Zacateca's. Sprawled akimbo in a padded red booth, chewing on an ice cube, he was a helluva sight in his baggy suit and Snoopy tie. She realized as she slid in opposite him how much she missed working. Clay's parting shot gnawed at her.

"Dude-ess," Noah grinned happily, raising his palm in a high-five.

She slapped his hand and responded, "Dude."

"Whaddup, Mac Momma?"

Pulling a plastic-coated menu toward her, she replied, "No thing, J-Daddy."

A pretty waitress said hello to them. Noah glanced up appreciatively. Frank ordered tacos and a beer while Noah went for the wet burrito and more water. He filled Frank in on the last couple of days, bitching about Fubar's micro-management.

"He's got us in that fucking station filling out 60Ds and MIRs and doesn't give a shit about us bein' out in the field actually trying to close some of these things. As long as he's got a pile of papers in front of him he's happy. Man, you should see us in the morning—we can't get outta there fast enough. Even Johnnie."

Noah took another long look as the waitress slid their plates in front of them. "Man," he complained, "that dildo couldn't manage his way out of a paper bag without a guide rope and a seeing eye dog."

The waitress giggled and asked demurely if that was all. Noah grinned goofily and wiggled his empty water glass.

"Damn!" he said, plowing his fork into a huge mound of guacamole, salsa, and sour cream that concealed a burrito somewhere below.

"Jesus, No. Where do you put all that?"

"Gets burned up by all my sexual energy," he replied around a dripping mouthful.

"That's more than I needed to know."

"You asked."

They ate steadily for ten minutes, then pushed their empty plates away. Noah sat back, groaning, and Frank wiped grease and tomato juice off her fingers. The waitress took their plates and Frank motioned for another Negro Modelo.

"So'd you miss me and decide to take me out to lunch?"

Frank smiled slightly, pushing her bottle around the wet rings on the table.

"I had an idea about the Agoura perp. Talked to SID and Crocetti's replacement about it. She agreed with me that the bruises could have been made by a football helmet."

Noah raised his eyebrows, intrigued.

Frank continued with her theory and when she was done, Noah nodded, "Interesting, but what's this have to do with me?"

"I want you to go back to Crenshaw. Interview the coaching staff. Get all—"

"Whoa." Noah held his palms up. "This isn't our case anymore."

"I know."

Noah bent over the table. "Then why am I out there knocking?"

"Because I'm ROD and you're not. I can't get to these people."

Noah laughed incredulously.

"Uh-uh. No way, Frank."

She let him fidget and rationalize all the reasons why he couldn't and wouldn't do it. When he ran out of steam she just kept staring.

"No, if I had my badge this would be an order, but I don't so I'm asking for a favor. Don't play innocent on me. You knew when you copied the murder books for me that I wasn't going to hand it over to RHD and walk away from it. I can't. I'm too into it now. If they close it first, that's great. I hope that prick gets off the street ASAP, but this isn't a high-profile case and you know what they'll do with it. They'll stick it on the burner behind the Carnassian OD and the Woodall capping."

Frank was referring to an influential businessman's suspicious overdose and the shooting of a Hollywood producer outside his favorite Chinese restaurant. "And there are other higher priority cases behind those."

Noah was fiercely shaking his head. Frank slid her bottle out of the way and leaned toward him. "No, when was the last time this guy attacked somebody?"

"Jennifer Peterson. A couple weeks ago."

"Right. And before that?"

"Agoura, in October."

"And before that?"

"What's your point, Frank?"

"My point is he's averaging about a victim per month. Meaning he's due."

Frank sat back and let that sink in, taking a hit off of her beer. "Do we just sit back and say, 'Hey, not my problem anymore. Not my job'?"

Noah stared hopelessly at the traffic out on Slauson. "What about my cases? When in the hell am I supposed to work on those?"

"I'll help you with them, do what I can without a badge. Hell, I'll even write your fucking reports for you. Just go talk to these people for me. I can't do it, No."

"Shit."

"Feel them out, get a roster of kids on the football team for the last twenty years. Get copies of all the old yearbooks. We're looking for a white guy in predominantly black/Hispanic schools. It won't be that bad."

Noah just repeated his prior expletive and rose clumsily from the booth.

"Thanks for lunch," he said with heavy sarcasm, and left her sitting there. She finished her beer, feeling bad about adding to his work load, though encouraged they were taking action. Frank wanted this perp. She saw dead kids all the time, but now and then one got to her, especially when the perp was still out there. She'd known when she was interviewing the rape victims that she wasn't going to be able to drop this case until the guy responsible was dead or behind bars.

She paid the tab and walked out, a cool breeze from the west making her glad she had a sweatshirt on. She trusted Noah would do as much as he could, as quickly as he could. She was just going to wait to hear from him. It was maddening that she couldn't do the work herself, but she was determined to be patient. Meanwhile, she'd distract herself by taking care of Kennedy.

The first time it had been almost like a dream. He could see him-self watching her. She was having a picnic with her mother and another woman and two little boys. He was within earshot of them but was pretending to read a newspaper propped against the steering wheel.

He heard her asking her mother if she could go to the other end of the park. She was bored. The mother reluctantly shooed her off. He watched her, and before he lost sight of her he started the car and drove to the other end of the park. This end was never as busy as the fishing ponds or the picnic areas. There weren't any cars in the lot. He parked near the bathroom and stood next to the men's room. He still didn't really know what he was going to do. He was nervous and sweating, and he felt his heart pumping loudly in his head. Peeking around the corner he saw her walking up the road, swinging a little stick in time to a song she was singing.

He waited. Her song came closer, a soft sound, and he smiled. She was right outside the bathroom. Oh god, he could hear her, she was so close and alone. He looked. She was reading a placard, still singing. He moved from the men's room entrance. What happened next was like he was someone else.

He grabbed her quickly from behind, had her neck in the crook of his elbow before she even had a chance to turn and see him. Somewhere in the calmer depths of his mind he realized that was a good thing. It bolstered his confidence. She tried to cry, but he quietly told her to shut up or he'd kill her. He wondered if he meant that. He didn't know, but it felt good to say it. Holding her against him he dragged her into a thick stand of brush, never letting her see him. And he didn't want to see her. He only wanted one thing.

28

One of the worst things about being ROD was waking up in the middle of the night and not having anywhere to go. Frank picked up the pysch text by her bed, hoping it would distract her from the thoughts that came loose in the night, like boats silently slipping their moorings. After an hour, nowhere closer to sleep, she finally threw off the comforter and headed for the garage, sharply aware how empty the house was.

Kennedy had left a few days ago, promising to call Frank if she needed anything. Her leaving was inevitable, but Frank hadn't expected to miss her. Leaning out the patio door for a moment, Frank noted the thick, damp fog, and thought of the night they'd gone to the beach. Kennedy had pointed out the few stars that managed to outshine the city lights. It had been a long time since Frank had really looked at them. They were beautiful.

Flustered, angry with her own foolishness, Frank retreated inside, slamming the door loudly. She was alone and could make as much noise as she wanted. She flipped on the scanner and turned the volume up, forcing static and chatter into the emptiness.

She started her workout, registering the 12-Adam calls and mostly ignoring the rest. A 7-Adam domestic, woman assaulting a man with a cooler, reminded her of an old partner. Literally up to his ass in women, Petey had a wife at home and a girlfriend in every sector of Figueroa. One night he'd stopped during their break to knock off a quick piece while Frank waited outside in the unit. She was thinking about what she was going to make for dinner when Petey hauled ass out of the complex. His pants were flapping open, he had his gun belt in one hand, his hat in the other. The girlfriend was running after him in a slip, her hair all wild, and a woman Frank had never seen before was right behind them.

The women were hollering in Spanish. Frank couldn't make out what they were saying, but the girlfriend kept slapping Pete with a cast-iron skillet while the other woman jabbed at him with a mop. He'd screamed at Frank, "Drive! Drive!" and she'd scooted into the driver's seat. Pete barely missed her lap as he dove in on the passenger side. Frank gunned away, glancing at her partner. He was bleeding and trying to catch his breath.

"Guess she wasn't in the mood," Frank had noted dryly.

"Christ," he'd sworn. "We're in the kitchen, and I'm puttin' it to Marta, and this woman comes in and starts screaming. I'm trying to figure out what the hell's going on and I look around and it's Luz!" Luz was his girlfriend on 52nd Street.

"How the fuck was I supposed to know they're sisters?" he'd moaned.

Frank had heard the expression, "The clothes make the man," but she'd never seen proof of it until she started patrol. It was true: women were fools for guys in uniform. She was musing whether it was the outfit or the persona attached to it that turned women on, when a dispatcher called a 3-Adam on a possible 187 at Dorsey High School.

Frank slammed the treadmill's emergency stop. Dorsey High was just north of Culver City. The 3-Adam call was being handled by the Southwest Division, bordering Figueroa's north side. A possible homicide at a high school near Culver City. At dawn on a weekday. Frank yanked her towel off the machine and sprinted to the dining room table, grabbing car keys and her old .38. It was one of three revolvers she owned, and the one she carried since she'd been forced to turn over her Beretta. She slipped the holstered weapon on over her wet T-shirt, zipped a sweat jacket over it, and slammed out the front door.

Traffic was minimal, and though she didn't beat the KTLA news van to Dorsey High, she was still there before Southwest homicide. The sky was graying to the east, but there wasn't enough light for the news cameras to get good shots. Headlights from three radio units lit an area behind the school. Frank's heart somersaulted when she saw two patrolmen taping off a section of bleachers on the football field. Half a dozen onlookers, the news crew, and curious cops were trampling the scene. Frank rolled out of her Honda, thankful for the LAPD emblazoned across her back.

Immediately Sally Eisley trotted up to her and Frank held up a warning hand.

"Sally, this is Southwest's call. I just stopped by to see if I could help. I don't know anything, and even if I did I would be in no position to say."

"You just happened to be in the neighborhood at quarter after six?" she asked cynically.

"No, I was on my way home from a jog and picked it up on the scanner. I'm just another curious onlooker."

"Do you think this could be—"

"Excuse me."

Frank strolled away and quickly commandeered the scene, ordering two uniforms who were milling around looking at the ground to clear everybody back a couple hundred feet and stay back.

"Who the hell are you?" the burly black uniform asked.

"Lieutenant Franco, Homicide," Frank answered.

"Do you have your ID, ma'am?" he persisted.

Frank turned on him sharply.

"Hey genius, do I look like I'm dressed for work? It's at home on my dresser, if you want to go get it for me. I picked this up on the scanner after my run. Now can you get your job done or do you want to let a few more people walk around in here?"

Frank's deliberate belligerence was only too familiar to the cop. He retreated sullenly, letting the detective approach the bleachers. When she lifted the white sheet, she felt a jolt of excitement.

Slumped between the first and second rows was a naked female, about 5'4", one hundred pounds. Frank squinted in the poor light. She looked like she was probably Hispanic, but maybe Caucasian. It was hard to tell around all the bruising. She was wedged on the flooring between the first and second tiers, like she'd had too much to drink and had slipped between them. Despite her ungainly position, it was obvious that she'd been posed. Her legs rested demurely side by side on the first row, arms carefully crossed in her lap. A small pool of blood had seeped out from under the girl's buttocks, and Frank quickly noted the absence of bruising below the knees or around the face. Frank stared into her dull eyes, wondering what was the last thing she saw.

The posing was a twist, but Frank knew it was him.

You've really gone all out this time, haven't you? Did you stick around to admire your handiwork?

She scanned the people on the edge of the tape. The news crew was standing around, bored and distracted because they couldn't get a good shot until the body was covered and pulled out. The cops were hanging out by one of the units, talking to each other. Not one of them was talking to the handful of gawkers.

Frank carefully retraced her steps. Addressing two of the cops from their name tags, she told one to start a scene log and the other to check for witnesses. She questioned the responding cop, who said the call came in anonymously. There was no one on or around the scene when they'd arrived.

Inside, Frank grinned wickedly, glad this was going to be RHD's nightmare. She glanced at her watch, wondering how much time she had left before the real detectives arrived. She decided to risk one more glance at the body and peered under the sheet. Just as she picked something off the body a man behind her asked, "Franco! What the hell are you doing here?"

Frank turned with a slight smile and a handshake for the Southwest detectives. The detective who'd greeted her was a small man in rumpled, mismatched trousers and blazer. His name was Mark Cherry, and his partner, who was half his age and twice his size, was Aidan Gerber.

"Hey. You should be thanking me. Before I got here all those shit-for-brains were walking around in here like they were looking for a contact lens."

"Okay, thanks," Cherry said. "Now what the hell are you doing here? And weren't you in that OIS?"

She repeated her jogging story. Cherry looked under the sheet and whistled. Gerber remained mute. Come to think of it, Frank didn't know if she'd ever heard him talk.

"She took a lickin' and stopped tickin'," Cherry mused. Gerber was writing in a notebook. Frank decided she'd better leave while she could.

"Good luck," she said to Cherry. He broke away from his study of the body to look skeptically at Frank. Off-duty detectives didn't just show up at scenes for the hell of it. Frank tried to ease past Sally, but the reporter sidled over to Frank, asking, "Can you at least give me a description of the body?"

"A young female," she answered. "I'm sure Cherry will tell you more. Or Gerber. Hey, does he ever talk?"

"I don't think so," Sally grinned.

Frank was feeling particularly benevolent and she wished Sally luck, too.

"Lieutenant?"

Frank was just about in her car. She turned, guardedly.

"You're still Relieved of Duty, aren't you?"

Frank nodded, wondering if there was anybody in L.A. who didn't know about her suspension.

"Do you think we could arrange an interview to talk about the shooting, I mean, your role in it and how you felt? We'd approach it unofficially, a human drama type of work."

Oh, sure, Frank thought, that's what I want—my human drama broadcast to a couple million people.

"Sally, I'm sure you know whenever there's an officer-involved shooting, there's an investigation. While that investigation is underway I'm not at liberty to discuss the incident one way or another."

"You've suddenly slipped back into cop-talk on me, Lieutenant."

"Maybe we can set something up after this is all cleared up," Frank appeased.

"I'll hold you to it."

With a brief and charming smile, Frank said, "I don't doubt that for an instant."

Having made her successful getaway, Frank stopped at a diner to think and make some notes while the scene was still fresh in her head. A young man, Pakistani she guessed, poured coffee and took her order. While she was jotting notes, four tattooed *cholos* sauntered in and took seats at the counter. Her peripheral vision saw one of them swivel in her direction and say, "Pow, pow. Look at the *placa*."

Frank ignored him. Duly noting the obvious similarities between the cases, what was intriguing her was the body's placement on the football field. She couldn't have asked for a better tie-in to her latest theory. He'd gone to a lot of trouble to get her body onto the bleachers. Frank hadn't seen any drag evidence on or around the body, so he must have carried her.

You wrapped her up and carried her.

Frank stared at the small piece of fuzz she'd taken off the body. They'd been all over. Frank was sure they belonged to a blanket. She squinted at the fiber. It looked blue. That wasn't much help in finding their boy right now, but it might help later.

You wrapped her up in a blue blanket and carried her around a high school on the corner of two main drags.

Remembering the morning's fog, Frank wondered if he'd deliberately used it for concealment. Still, it was a huge risk. The guy must be confident of his physical prowess and his surroundings. He knew exactly what he was doing. There was nothing accidental about this dump. Very calculated, premeditated, and dangerous. It was important for him—a big jump. The others were just practice, like the rapes had been practice before the murders.

Frank's ham and eggs came, but she just picked at them. She stared out the barred window, the *cholos* dimly reflected against the dull dawn.

And why'd you choose Dorsey for this big event?

Did he work there? Had he gone to school there, played football there? Because this last move was so bold, she felt the school was important to him. Frank was helpless without her badge, but she'd do what she could over the phone. Later she could use Noah to get them into Dorsey's records. Hopefully she'd beat RHD there. Even if she didn't, they probably wouldn't check into the athletic records right away, and Frank felt that was the place to start digging. She was sure their boy had gone to school somewhere nearby. Given his affinity for the area, it just made sense. Sooner or later he had to pop up in the system.

The *cholos* had finished eating and were leaving. The one with the big mouth stopped at her booth, saying, "Hey, Blondie."

When Frank looked up, he leaned in and flashed his sign, hissing, "Rifamos."

She nodded unconcernedly, keeping her mouth shut as she thought, Yeah, yeah. You rule this shit heap. Keep walking, *Essay,* or I'll rule your asshole with a .38.

Frank watched them pile into a Chevy and peel out into Vernon's building traffic. Her thoughts went right back to Dorsey. The posing fascinated her. She was sure it was critical.

Did you want her to be seen, like a trophy, or was she there to see you? You posed her like a spectator, but for you or for someone else?

The girl hadn't rigored yet, so she couldn't have been there for long. If he'd wanted her to see him, to watch him, he'd have given himself more time with her. It was more likely that he'd placed her there for someone else. Who?

Frank envisioned herself on the field in uniform, the noise of the crowd, clapping, calls, whistles.

Who's watching me? The coach? Family? Friends? The other players? Who am I trying to impress? Girls? Do they laugh at me? Am I shy, ugly, stupid?

Frank didn't get any feeling that the vic had been posed for a female to see. It was a masculine setting. Players and coaching staff would be the most likely to see her there, and grounds crews, too. The girls were symbols. Props.

I'm just using them...to show somebody something. What? What do I want to show you? And who are you? I'm obviously proving I'm capable, I'm in control. I'm saying, "Look at me! Look what I've done!" Who'd be here that I had to prove something to?

Frank stared at her half-finished plate, wondering if the show was for his peers. Not likely, because that would encompass his whole school experience. He was focusing on or around the gridiron. She narrowed his audience to either teammates or a coach.

I'm a big guy, but maybe the other players gang up on me. Maybe they corner me in the shower, use me like a girl, like how I'd use a girl.

Frank sat with that, feeling his shame and rage and humiliation.

No. I'd lash back sooner if it was kids my own age. Uh-uh. I've been building up to this, been hanging on to it for a while. This is someone I can't fight. Someone special. Someone who has power over me. Someone bigger, older. A coach?

A warm kick in her gut told Frank she was on a good track.

What did he do to me?

Frank stared blindly into her coffee cup.

There were so many things he could have done. So many. And I'd have been helpless to do anything about it. Who would I tell? Who'd believe me? And maybe he was my friend...

Frank hunted the room for a phone. She got up and asked the waiter if they had one, holding her jacket open with her hands on her hips. He glanced nervously at the gun under her arm and nodded her behind the counter.

"Behine da door," he said in a thick accent. Frank cradled the greasy receiver against her shoulder and dialed Noah's number.

His partner picked up.

"Hey, Johnnie. Is No there?"

"Stuffin' a big fat donut in his face."

She heard the phone being passed. Noah mumbled, "Mornin', Frank. Congratulations. You enjoying your last day off?"

"What are you talking about?"

"You haven't talked to Fubar?"

"Uh-uh. What?"

"OIS signed off on you. You're good to go again."

"No shit?"

"Yeah, he told us this morning. He didn't call you?"

"I don't know. I'm not home."

"Where are you?"

"I'm near Dorsey High. Southwest got a call this morning on the scanner. I went to look. Dead female, teenaged, beat to shit. It was him. Look, is Fubar in his office?"

Noah whistled. "You sure?"

"Absolutely. I'll tell you about it later, just transfer me to Fubar."

"'Kay, hang on." She heard a click, then the line went dead. She dialed the captain herself. The son of a bitch wasn't there. After several more tries she eventually managed to track him to a meeting at Parker. She jammed the phone down and paid her bill, leaving the kid a good tip. Frank had worked six weeks as a waitress in college. Next to being a cop, she thought it was the dirtiest service job you could have.

Frank drove home. The blinking light on her answering machine let her know she had two calls. The first was from Foubarelle, telling her to call him. Frank was surprised, and happy, that the second message was from Kennedy, asking if she wanted to have dinner with her.

She did, although her first inclination was to ignore the message, to not call back until it was too late. She hated that she wanted to see Kennedy, was angry at her weakness. If she ignored the feeling long enough, it would fade. With a twinge of guilt she took a quick shower and left without returning Kennedy's call. At Parker Center she paged Foubarelle from a phone right outside the conference room. He came out looking confused, frowning when he saw Frank.

"You wanted to see me?"

"Not now. I'm in a meeting," he hissed.

"Sorry. I got your message so I thought it was important."

She could see he was anxious to get back in, it wouldn't look good to be gone for long. She added, "Is it about my papers?"

He nodded impatiently. "They came through yesterday."

Bastard, she thought, showing no trace of her anger. "When can I get my ID and my gun?"

"Later on," he waved dismissively. "There's paperwork, too."

"When later?" she pressed.

"This afternoon," he whined. "What's your hurry?"

"My hurry is I've been out of work for weeks and I've got a lot of shit to do. The sooner I'm back the sooner I can get stats for your meetings."

"Well, you're going to have to wait until I'm done here."

Which Frank did. The meeting broke for lunch then reconvened until four-thirty. Foubarelle was ready to go home, but in her inimitable style, Frank persuaded him to go by the office and clear her for work. Two hours later she walked into the deserted homicide room with her ID securely clipped to her belt and the Beretta snuggled under her arm.

She felt whole again. The day was gone, though, and she still hadn't gotten back to Dorsey. She wondered how much progress Gerber and Cherry'd made, or whether RHD was on it yet. Dialing the Southwest Division she said in a bored voice, "Yeah, this is 3-Adam-31. I've got an alarm going off at Dorsey High. Who's the EC for this place?"

The desk sergeant gave her the emergency contact number—Milo Davidson, the assistant principal. She dialed his number, introducing herself as a detective involved in the morning's homicide. She apologized for bothering him at home, but it was critical that she review certain records this evening and talk to whoever coached Dorsey's football team.

"You don't think he has anything to do with this, do you?"

"Not at all," Frank lied. "There are just certain logistical situations I need to confirm with him."

"Oh. Well, I was just about to have my dinner," Davidson said glumly.

"Sorry about that. How long will it take you to get to the school?"

"I'm about twenty minutes away."

"Fine. And the coach's name and number?"

"Oh, I don't think I should tell you that over the phone. I mean, how do I even know you're who you say you are?"

Frank rolled her eyes and suppressed a sigh.

"You're right. *You* call him, and have him meet us at the

school at," she glanced at her watch, "eight o'clock."

"Well, alright. But I'm not certain I know his number."

"Mr. Davidson, if you can find his number, call him, and both of you meet me at school at eight o'clock. If you can't find his number, then you meet us at the school at eight o'clock and we'll call him from there."

"Oh. Alright," he said, still pretty glum. "Eight o'clock."

Frank glowered at the huge mound of paperwork on her desk. She had absolutely no justification for continuing with Agoura/Peterson, but then rationalized that Fubar would have let her hang in the wind all weekend anyway.

"I should've known I'd find you here."

Startled, then embarrassed she hadn't heard her creep in, Frank flashed a guilty grin at Kennedy.

"Hey. What are you doing here?"

The younger detective dropped onto the hard couch, throwing an arm behind her head and swinging her feet over the end. Black slacks and blouse made a striking contrast to her inelegant posture. Frank realized she'd never seen her in anything but shorts or baggies and was surprised at how nicely she scrubbed up. Indicating the outfit, she asked, "What's up with the duds?"

"The what?"

"The clothes. Why are you all dressed up?"

Kennedy yawned hugely. "I was in court all day. It sucked."

Kennedy told Frank how the judge had thrown out their search warrant, then asked, "Have you had dinner yet?"

"No. I was going to get some work done. I'm officially back on duty."

"Alright! That's excellent! Let's go celebrate. I'll buy you a beer."

Frank shucked her head down at the desk. This was exactly what she'd been trying to avoid. She bowed out, explaining about the new body and how the perp had posed it this time.

"I've just got this feeling it's there for somebody to see, and I think that somebody might be a coach."

"You don't think he's still in school, do you?" Kennedy asked skeptically.

"Nope. That wouldn't support any of our profile. No, I think he's definitely out of school, at least agewise, but his *head's* still there. I'm going to meet the assistant principal in about an hour, talk to him and get into the files. I want to talk to the coach, too.

See how long he's been there, or who was there before him. I want to find all the kids that played for Dorsey that fit our description. I'll start there."

Kennedy had twisted onto her side and was studying Frank.

"Why are you so involved in this? Why can't you just let RHD finish it?"

Frank sighed and sat back.

"Noah asked me the same thing. You know, usually, people kill each other because they're pissed off, they're angry, they got burned. Usually vics and perps have a relationship, they're linked somehow. Sometimes it's just accident and circumstance, there's no relationship at all, but still you can see what set the perp off. Even if it's totally ridiculous, they've got a reason. But this guy, I don't *know* the reason. I can guess, but until I see him I won't know why."

"You might never know why," Kennedy interjected. "Even if you do find him, he might never cop to any of it."

"True. But I want to track him down. I want the satisfaction of finding him and looking him in the eye, even if he doesn't say a word. Because I know him now. He's part of me. If I know enough to find him, then I already have my answer, but right now he only exists in my head. I need to see him flesh and bone before me. It's the only way I can get rid of him."

Abashed at having said so much, Frank added dismissively, "Besides, he has to be picked up before he kills anyone else. I think I can get to him before RHD does."

Kennedy regarded her curiously, and Frank steeled herself for another question.

"You want help shuffling through these records?"

"No. You don't need to get involved in this."

"I ain't got nothin' else to do. Why don't we grab some sandwiches and I'll go over to Dorsey with you and help you find your boy."

Frank crossed her arms against the by-now familiar jumble of emotions: pleased that Kennedy was willing to help her, wanting her company, then kicking herself for being such a sap and squelching her pleasure.

"Why aren't you out surfing or playing with your friends?"

"The surf's too flat and I don't have any friends."

"Well, go out and make some. You're young and...healthy,"

Frank almost said beautiful, "and I know you can find something better to do than hang with me all night."

Kennedy stood and said, "Well, I can't think what that would be. Come on. Let's go for sandwiches and get to work."

Frank considered the offer, knowing she should tell Kennedy thanks and send her home. She surprised herself, though, saying, "Alright, but I'm buying."

Now he saw girls everywhere. The city was full of them. Hundreds, thousands. If he was careful, maybe he could have them all. He couldn't believe how lucky he'd been. No one had seen him or heard him. The girl never even saw him. No one knew it was him.

The last time he'd felt so good was after his last touchdown, and that was a very long time ago. He felt happy every time he remembered her. It was only his first time, and it had been good, but already he was thinking of ways to make it better the next time. His only regret was that his father couldn't see him. He'd finally be proud of him.

orty-five minutes later, a slender black man, his hair gray at the temples, met them in the high school parking lot. Conscious of how good it felt, Frank let Davidson carefully examine her ID. He blinked forcefully and often. She bet the kids had a field day with that.

Leading them in through a back door to his small, vastly cluttered office, he explained he hadn't been able to find the coach's home number. He turned on the fluorescent overheads and fingered through a Rolodex until he located it. Handing Frank the card, he looked more pleased with himself than was necessary.

Coach Welsh was upset. He'd already talked to detectives this morning. He didn't know what else he had to say. Frank explained she needed to go over some student records with him and that it would be easiest to do that at the school. Welsh grumbled he was busy, that it'd be at least an hour before he could get there.

"Fine. See you then," Frank said, and hung up.

Next, Frank asked Davidson for the school's personnel records, going back fifteen years.

"Oh, boy," he said, blinking faster and harder. "I know where they are for the last four or five years, but I'll have to call Carrie to find out where the older records are kept."

"Set us up with what you've got, then call whoever you need to. And while you're at it, I'd like yearbooks for the last fifteen years as well."

Frank and Kennedy exchanged a grimace as Davidson pawed through metal filing cabinets, mumbling, "Oh boy," and, "That's not it." Frank looked around the office for pictures of the staff or football team, but there weren't any, just inspirational posters and corkboards tacked with sheaves of papers.

The assistant principal handed Frank a stack of manila folders, indicating another cluttered desk she could use. Producing two yearbooks, he explained apologetically that he'd have to ask Carrie where the rest of them were.

Kennedy dragged a chair next to Frank's and said under her breath, "Whoever the hell she is, you should have had Carrie come in instead of this jerk."

Frank slapped some of the folders in front of her.

"We're looking for anyone who's worked in any capacity in the athletic department. Names, dates, SS, driver's license."

"Oh boy," Kennedy mumbled. "Oh boy."

They were working their way through the Cs when John Welsh arrived.

Frank made quick introductions and asked, "How long have you been coaching here, Mr. Welsh?"

He thought a moment. "Since spring of '93."

Frank asked to see all his rosters and followed him to the gym. She questioned Welsh about his players, but the coach was laconic and noncommital. She tried softening him up, saying, "I'll bet when you played you were a back."

"That's right."

"Who'd you play for?"

"USC, then pro for a couple years with the Redskins."

"No kidding? When were you with the Skins?"

"Eighty-one to eighty-three."

He seemed bored until Frank said, "Wow, you must've played with, uh, let's see, John Riggins and Joe Theismann. Art Monk, right?"

Welsh eyed Frank suspiciously.

"You been checking up on me?"

Frank looked sheepish. "Nah. I've been a Giants' fan all my life," and to Kennedy she explained, "They're division rivals."

"That was a long time ago. You've got a good memory."

"Helps in this business. How come you left?"

"Bad neck," he grimaced. "My wife and I decided I'd better get into teaching before I ended up in a wheelchair."

Frank had relaxed Welsh. He told the detectives what he knew about his kids, their abilities and failings on the field, who got scholarships, who wound up where, but he offered nothing personal. They went through the rosters until eleven-thirty, producing a list of thirty-three white males who had played or tried out for football at Dorsey High since 1993. Davidson provided personnel records as far back as 1992. The rest were stored in the district office. Frank made a note to find out who could get her into those files over the weekend.

Davidson protested, but Frank and Kennedy remained behind after they cut the two men loose. The detectives spent the early morning searching through yearbooks for students who matched the perp's physical description. They wrote down vitals and ranked them. Kids with no extracurricular or bio info got highest priority. Moderate bios were second priority, and kids with extensive activities were rated third. Frank felt their guy would be engrossed in football and somewhat of a loner. She wasn't expecting him to be the homecoming king or class valedictorian.

Somewhere around two-thirty, Frank realized it had gotten awfully quiet. She looked up from her legal pad at Kennedy, asleep amid the wreckage of Davidson's desk. Frank watched her for a moment, then returned to her yearbook.

Frank had crashed at Kennedy's. After a three-hour nap and breakfast, Kennedy had insisted on helping Frank with the new leads. Driving to headquarters through a light rain, Frank tuned out Kennedy's chatter.

She felt closer to him. He'd tipped his hand at Dorsey and shown so much more of himself. She wondered where he was right now. Regardless, Frank was certain he was happy. Posing the girl had been huge for him. He'd revel in that for quite a while. It might even slow his spree a bit. Unaware that she was doing it, Frank slipped into a dialogue with him.

Were you a star on the field, or a failure? Were you the coach's golden boy? His whipping boy? Oh, I'll bet you were a star. You'd do anything he asked, wouldn't you? And you're doing this for him now. What happened when you had to leave him? Who was there for you? Was there just a big, empty hole inside you? Does this fill it up for a while?

"Frank?"

Kennedy's hand was on her arm as cars crept past the Honda. Frank gently pressed the accelerator, moving with the flow. Kennedy asked if she was alright.

"Yeah," she answered, but Frank wasn't sure. She felt as if she'd been dreaming and had just woken up. It was hard shaking the sensation. Even as she kept up with the traffic, she sensed herself slipping back toward him.

Where are you? Tell me about you. Help me find you. I know you're close, I can feel you. I know you. Sometimes I think I am you.

"Frank?"

"*What?*" she snapped.

Startled, Kennedy snapped back, "Where the fuck are you?"

"What are you talking about?" Frank said irritably.

"You're like a million miles away and you just about rear-ended that truck!"

Frank sucked in a breath. This wasn't the time or place. She promised herself she'd come back to him later.

When they finally got to Parker, Frank was grateful the homicide room was empty. Kennedy started in with the computers, and Frank took the phone books, preferring their clumsy familiarity to the cold austerity of computer terminals. Frank was tracking down Dorsey's previous coaches, and after a dozen calls she hit pay dirt. She hung up the receiver and slipped into her jacket, telling Kennedy she was going to Fontana.

"I wanna go."

Frank knelt next to her, supplicating, "We'd get a lot more done if you stayed here and worked on these."

Kennedy was running their list of highest-ranked students, searching for priors, and then possibly re-ranking them according to the offense involved. It was tedious work. "I know," she said, reading the monitor. "I still wanna go."

"It'll be boring, probably pan out to nothing. I'd likely get you killed in a car accident."

"Yeah," Kennedy remembered. "You be careful out there. Don't go zonin' like you did this morning."

"Hey." When Frank had Kennedy's full attention, she said, "I really appreciate this."

"Sure. Surf still sucks. I should move up to Oregon, they've got more sun."

"Can I bring you back anything?"

"A Coke."

"Got it. See you in a while."

The phone rang and rang. Eventually Kennedy picked up.

"Where are you?" she whined. "It's almost three and I'm starving. There's nothing around here but empty junk machines."

"Listen. Have you run a kid named Clancey Delamore yet?"

"Hang on."

Kennedy banged the phone down and Frank could hear papers being shuffled.

"Yeah, he's got nothing. So where are you? Christ, you better come back draggin' that sum-bitch, you been gone long enough. I got carpel tunnel settin' in."

"Wha-wha-wha," Frank said. "Hang tight. I'll fill you in when I get there."

Forty-five minutes later she and Kennedy were cruising through the rain to Clancey Delamore's house. Frank talked animatedly behind the wheel.

"So our guy this morning, Miller, he coached Delamore for three years. Said he was a great player, a tight end, but that he was super aggressive. He didn't seem to have any sense that it was just a game. Said a lot of his own teammates didn't want to play with him. Evidently he was pretty rough. Miller would warn him to take it easy during practice, but I guess he was still way too rough. Like his old man, according to Miller.

"Then they're in the middle of a conference game and Delamore goes ballistic on another player. He attacks him from behind after the ball is dead and just keeps ramming into him. Sound familiar? Now get this. As he's beating this poor bastard senseless, he's got a woody the size of a baseball bat. And later, when Miller's dressing him down, he gets a hard-on all over again.

"It totally freaked Miller out. He kicked Delamore off the team."

Frank paused to check Kennedy's reaction. She was taking it all in. Then she asked cautiously, "So why are we going to his place?"

"I called after I got done with the coach. Turns out he lives with his mom. I gave her a big song and dance about burglaries in the area—told her we're with Robbery. Told her we were tracking down a suspect known to habituate her neighborhood. Then I said that the department was offering to do free home security checks and we could come by if she liked. Check her locks, give her some safety tips and a sketch of the suspect, stuff like that."

"And she believed you?"

"Hey. I was very convincing. One of my best roles to date."

Kennedy asked, "Why don't you just question him straight out?"

"One, we've got no real evidence that this is our guy. We're running purely on bones and possibles right now. Two, I don't want him to panic and start cleaning house. If he's got evidence around, I don't want him dumping it. And I don't want him running. I want him confident. I want him to think he's outsmarting us. Sooner or later it'll make him trip. Three, even if I did want to move on him, it's not my case anymore, remember."

"So why are you tipping your hand at all?"

"I want to talk to Mom. Oh yeah, I left out another thing. One of the reasons she's letting us in is because there is no Mr. Delamore and Clancey works nights. I said, 'Oh, is he a cop, too?' and she said, 'No, he works at a bakery.' So sonny should be sleeping even as we speak, but I want to see what we can pull from the old lady, take a look around. With this security gig we can go all over—"

Kennedy interrupted. "Except his bedroom, which is probably the best place to check."

"I thought about that. I figure we can find out his work schedule and make up a reason to come back when he's gone."

"Okay, so here's another question. Seeing as you've got no jurisdiction here, what the hell are you going to do if this kid does look good?"

Frank held up a pontifical finger. "That bridge I will cross, if and when I get there. All I know is this is the best lead we've had yet. You still up for it?"

"You betcha, but I sure hope this goes somewhere soon. You gotta get a life back, Lieutenant."

Frank smiled happily, although her words were chillingly true. "This *is* my life."

After the first couple of girls he'd bought a used camcorder so he could remember them better once they were gone. He watched the tapes in his bedroom, learning and studying, planning how to make it even better the next time. Over and over he watched, remembering, reliving, refueling. The tapes satisfied him for a while, but eventually their appeal faded. When that happened, it was time to make a new one.

30

Well?" Frank asked over her shoulder, backing out of the Delamores' driveway.

"I think you better feed me before I rip your head off and start suckin' on your insides."

"I saw a guy do that once," Frank said, matter-of-factly. "Killed his mother and brother and an aunt. When we came in to arrest him he was sitting as calm as you please at the kitchen table with a big old pan of sautéed brains in front of him. Damned if they didn't smelled good."

"After tonight, I don't know whether to believe you or not."

"I was pretty good, huh?"

Kennedy had to laugh at Frank's unusual lack of modesty.

"*Damn* good," she agreed deferentially.

"Well, Detective, I think it's been a very productive day. How about I buy you some sweetbreads so you don't have to rip my head off?"

"Deal."

They went to Frank's favorite restaurant, where the waiter greeted her by name. Waiting for him to return with her wine, Frank took out her notebook.

"Okay. Tell me what you saw, what you thought, everything."

Frank listened to the young detective, impressed by her observations. Mrs. Delamore had fallen easily for Frank's ingratiating charm and generously shown them her immaculate house. About halfway through the detectives' bogus inspection, Clancey had wandered downstairs, sleepy-eyed and bare-chested. They'd gone into his room, at his mother's insistence, and it was a mess. As if he weren't hulking behind her, she'd talked about what a slob her son was.

Kennedy asked, "You saw the pile of porno mags by the bed and the economy size bottle of lotion? What do you reckon Mrs. D. thinks Junior does with all that hand cream?"

"I'm sure she just thinks her boy's got some mighty soft skin,"

Frank smiled, borrowing Kennedy's twang.

"How 'bout the videos?"

Frank nodded. There had been no books or music in Clancey's room, only a twenty-four inch television with a VCR perched precariously atop it. A shelf of neatly aligned videos above the television contradicted the room's chaos. Frank had noticed that most of the titles on the spines were handwritten, and a brief scan of the commercial titles indicated most of them were skin flicks.

"And all those football trophies on the floor? I'll bet they used to be on that shelf where the videos are. It's the only shelf in the room. Now they're just layin' 'round under his dirty clothes while the videos are carefully stacked up there. Like maybe he's outgrown the trophies and they're just down on the floor with all the rest of his crap."

"Hmm," Frank murmured. "I hadn't thought of that."

"But then it's also kind of odd if football's behind him that he'd have a clean uniform hanging in his closet."

Frank was picking at her antipasto. She froze. "A *what?*"

"A uniform, like for football," Kennedy gloated.

"Are you kidding me?" Frank drilled her young colleague.

"Big as life. Red and white. Number eighty-one."

"No shit?"

"Absolute constipation. I peeked at it when ya'll were admiring his trophies. It was just cleaned, too."

"How do you know that?"

"I smelled it. I think Mrs. D. uses Tide."

"Son of a bitch," Frank muttered incredulously. "What else?"

Kennedy ticked off a few more things, then she sucked noisily on an ice cube. "What about you?"

Frank waggled her eyebrows, pulling a wadded piece of tissue from her jacket. She dangled it before Kennedy.

"When I got the tissue to blow my nose I swiped the bottom of his shower."

Frank carefully unfolded the Kleenex and together the two detectives peered by candlelight.

"There you have it," Frank poked with her nail. "Pubic hairs. We'll see if we can draw a match on them."

She folded the tissue, pocketed it, then reached into her pants pocket. "Did you notice how antsy they got when I asked about that locked door in the garage?"

"And that Junior has the only key."

"Right. And when I spilled that jar of nails on the floor?"

Kennedy chortled, "Yeah, spaz. Like to gave me a heart attack. I was lookin' at the tools on the wall and I thought Junior'd pulled a gat on you or somethin'."

Eyes twinkling, Frank opened the palm of her hand. In it sat a hunk of green/gold carpet fiber.

Kennedy stared at it, then at Frank.

Frank deliberately ripped out a piece of note paper and folded it around the yarn. "This was poking out from under the garage door. I dropped the nails so I could yank some out. Agoura and Peterson both had green carpet fibers on them."

Kennedy's eyes narrowed admiringly. Frank sat back with a short, satisfied chuckle, unable, or unwilling, to hide her pleasure. Studying Frank, the younger detective shrewdly noted, "You love this, don't you?"

Frank shrugged, obviously pleased.

Kennedy asked, "How do you feel now that you've seen him?"

"Absolutely, 100 percent certain."

"But you've got nothing but circumstantials on him. How can you be so sure?"

Frank smiled oddly and took on a thousand-yard stare. "Oh, I'm sure," she whispered. "I *know* it. Seeing him, smelling him, looking at where he sleeps, where he fantasizes..."

Frank's mysterious smile widened, becoming almost cruel. She whispered reverently, "I know him because I am him."

She didn't see the golden hairs rising on Kennedy's arms.

By the time they finished a long dinner it was after ten o'clock. Both women were exhausted. Since the restaurant was closer to Frank's house, she invited Kennedy to spend the night. Once there, the younger woman crashed quickly and easily, but Frank was too wired to sleep.

She was elated at how closely Delamore matched her profile. If this were her case, she'd be slapping a search warrant in front of a sleepy judge right now, but as it was her hands were tied. It didn't matter that she had probable cause and a deep gut instinct. If she told RHD what she had, they'd probably lose or mishandle any solid evidence she found. Plus, once word got out, she'd face disciplinary action for taking on another division's case. That would raise enough jurisprudence questions for the case to get thrown out of court. Clancey would walk after all.

As much as it frustrated her, she had to go slowly. Frank settled in the den with soft music and a pad of paper, starting a list of things to follow through on. Gradually, her own thoughts and Astrud Gilberto's wistful yearnings lulled her to sleep.

When she twisted onto her side the clipboard fell against her chin. Frank woke up and saw Kennedy slumped on the floor beside her. She thought she was dreaming, then decided Kennedy's soft snoring was real. So was the rise and fall of her chest and the slight movement under her eyelids. Frank wondered what the hell she was doing there, then got distracted by the fiery auburn and russet strands gleaming in Kennedy's hair. Frank wanted to smooth the tousled hair, wondering if it would be as silky as she remembered from the hospital. She reached out, then drew her hand back.

Kennedy jerked awake as the clipboard clattered onto the floor. She gaped at Frank, petrified.

"It's okay, sport. You're okay," Frank soothed. "Everything's okay. You're alright."

"What was that noise?" Kennedy blinked.

"Just me. I dropped the clipboard. It's okay."

As Kennedy regained her bearings, Frank whispered, "What are you doing all curled up on the floor?"

Kennedy thought about it for a moment, then mumbled, "I had a dream. I woke up and saw the light on so I came in here. But you were asleep. I didn't wanna wake you up. But I didn't wanna go back to bed either. I just sat down next to you for a sec."

Kennedy's hair was hanging in her face, and again Frank had the urge to smooth it out of the way. She patted the couch and shifted her feet into the corner.

"Come here."

Kennedy cuddled up at the other end, and Frank offered part of the afghan she was under. She frowned as she asked, "Did you put this on me?"

"Yeah. You looked like you were cold. You didn't even move when I covered you."

Frank felt foolish that Kennedy had crept in and covered her with a blanket like she was a baby.

"Tell me about your dream."

Kennedy shook her head adamantly. "Uh-uh."

"Why not?"

"Too scary."

"Tunnel?"

"I don't know. I don't remember. I don't want to remember."

Frank gently tried to persuade her it would help to talk about it, but Kennedy scoffed, "How would *you* of all people know that?"

Frank seriously considered the question. "I used to have someone to talk to," she said finally. "It helped."

"Your lover?"

"Yeah."

"What was her name?" Kennedy asked sincerely. When Frank hesitated, Kennedy bargained. "I'll tell you about my dream if you tell me her name."

Frank bit her inner lip as Gilberto sang about quiet nights and quiet dreams. "Maggie."

"It's a pretty name." Then, "How long were you two together?"

"Eight years," Frank said tightly.

"How'd she die?"

Kennedy asked the question gently, but Frank still felt it was none of her business.

"Look," she snapped coldly, "that's enough with the twenty questions. Just tell me about your goddamn dream. That was the deal, right?"

Kennedy flinched almost imperceptibly, and a guarded hurt dimmed the light in her eyes. Frank immediately regretted her outburst. She tossed off the afghan and started toward the CD player, then turned back. Kennedy was staring at her like Frank was a dog that might bite. She hated the wariness in Kennedy's eyes, hated even more that she'd put it there.

"Christ," she sighed. "You come at me out of left field and get pissed when my first reaction's to protect myself."

Kennedy's armor didn't budge as Frank sat earnestly on the edge of the couch.

"Look. I don't know how to do this. You want me to talk to you, but Jesus, it took me years to learn how to talk to Mag, and even then it was half-assed. It's nothing personal, I just can't do this as easily as you do. I wish I could. I envy you. It's like you've got an emotional flak jacket you put on when you go to work, then just take it off and leave it by the door at night. My jacket doesn't come off like that."

"I'm sorry," Kennedy offered. "I should've stuck to the bargain."

"You always have to go for that extra inch," Frank complained.

"I have to," Kennedy defended. "You'd never give it, and it's the only way I can get anything out of you." She paused, then added, "You want me to tell you all my stuff but then you don't tell me diddly. Is that fair?"

Frank didn't answer, and Kennedy continued, "It's like I'm supposed to trust you, but you can't trust me. How do you think that makes me feel?"

Frank gnashed at her lip, then shook her head at the floor. "You're asking a lot, sport. I don't trust easily. That's no reflection on you, or how trustworthy you are. It's just my own twisted make-up."

Lifting her head and facing Kennedy, Frank said, "And I *do* trust you. To a point. And when I get to that point it's hard to cross over. I feel like my back's to the wall. Hell, you know more about me than almost anyone else. I'd say you're doing pretty good, but I just can't move as fast as you. I watch you go from happy to sad, then mad to laughing, and you're so easy with yourself. I just can't do that."

"*Won't,*" Kennedy insisted. "I've seen you fight with every honest feeling you've ever had."

"Alright then, won't. Whatever. You just need to back off a little. Don't be so damn invasive."

"I don't think I'm being invasive *enough,*" Kennedy challenged. "Somebody's gotta drag you kickin' and screamin' outta that shell you're in."

"And I suppose you've appointed yourself to the task?"

"I seem pretty damn good at it."

Frank stared at the combative young woman. They stalemated until Frank cocked an eyebrow and asked, "Are all the women in Texas as ornery as you?"

"Worse."

Kennedy's lofty smile said she'd concede the battle but not the war. "You wanna hear about my dream or not?"

Frank settled back. "Yeah, I do."

It was a vague, sketchy dream about Tunnel, and when Kennedy finished she asked, "Have you dreamt about him?"

Frank played with a loose yarn in the afghan, admitting, "A

lot," then she stretched and rose stiffly. "Come on, sport. It's late. Let's see if we can get some real sleep."

Frank switched off the lamp and they made their way through the dim house. Kennedy paused at Frank's door, her hand on Frank's arm. Half-teasing, half-serious, she said, "I'm sorry to be such a pain in the ass."

Frank faced her. The streetlight's beam spilled in through the living room window, picking up the shine in Kennedy's eyes. Frank was very aware of the hand still on her arm. She tried to answer, but the thick scent of Kennedy's hair and skin tripped Frank's breath in her throat. After what seemed like decades, she whispered, "You're not."

Kennedy stood on tiptoe and her lips brushed Frank's cheek. "Goodnight," she whispered back.

Long after Kennedy had gone into her room, Frank remained standing in the streetlight's complicit fraternity.

"Let's get going, sport. We've got a shitload of work to do."

Frank put a milky cup of coffee on Kennedy's bedside table and left Kennedy groaning behind her.

They returned to Parker Center and finished running all the names through the computer. Over donuts and more coffee they reprioritized the suspects. It was exasperating work because Frank was sure Delamore was her man. Nevertheless, she was determined to exhaust all her leads before running with Clancey. Even though she had a lot on him, she couldn't afford to overlook anyone. By noon they had a list of nine men ranked number ten. Kennedy was hungry again.

"Oughta get that tapeworm removed," Frank advised, pulling into a Taco Bell. She watched Kennedy devour a burrito, three tacos, and a large Coke like she hadn't eaten in a week. When Frank parked at their first interview, she surveyed Kennedy's face. Skewing the rearview mirror toward her she noted dryly, "They might take us more seriously if you wipe that salsa off."

Kennedy grinned, dabbing at herself with a Coke-moistened napkin. Frank shook her head dubiously.

After questioning their best suspect, Frank and Kennedy decided his work schedule was too tight to make him a viable perp. They'd double-check his story, but if it squared, they'd have to eliminate him. The same thing happened with their next guy; another had just come back to L.A. after a year-long absence. They had to cross off their fourth suspect because he'd lost an arm in a car accident. It turned out that he remembered Delamore from their footfall days.

"Yeah, he was a weird dude. Nobody liked him."

Frank asked why. He scowled. "God, all he could talk about was football. Football this and football that. He was like, obsessed with it or something. And we'd be like changing in the locker room, you know, and Clancey'd take his clothes off and he'd be all like black and blue. It was totally gross."

"What do you think happened to him?"

"I don't know. We figured maybe his old man was beating the shit out of him. He coached us for a while and he was like a total idiot."

"How do you mean?"

"He was always yelling and screaming if we forgot a play or something. He'd get right in our faces and spit would be flying all over. It was totally gross. He never touched us but he shoved Clancey around a lot. I saw him kick him in the ass once."

"He'd hit Clancey?"

"Oh, yeah. He was a bastard. Coach finally told him he couldn't come to practice no more."

It was dark by the time Frank and Kennedy finished. Frank was driving Kennedy back to her car and Kennedy craned her head out the window, looking at the moon. "Are you going to get some surfing in?" Frank asked.

"That sure is a sweet moon. Maybe I'll grab my board and see what the water looks like. Why don't you come with me?"

"Don't think so. I'm going to make some phone calls, see if I can't find some of the other boys on our list."

"You should go home and get a good night's sleep."

"I want to nail these other guys. Then tomorrow, if I can get away for a while, I'm going to check out the bakery, talk to Clancey's supervisor. I want to run the carpet fibers and samples by the lab, too."

"How're you gonna do that without a case?"

"There's a private lab in Claremont that can probably do it for me in a couple of days."

Kennedy whistled. "That'll cost you a fortune," she said.

Frank just shrugged.

"What'll you do if they match?"

"I'm thinking about that."

Frank brought her car alongside Kennedy's and cut the engine. She turned toward her and said, "Hey, I owe you. Big time. I couldn't have done all this without you."

"Yeah, you could've," Kennedy disparaged, "it'd just taken longer."

"No. You were great, sport. Thanks."

Kennedy waved a hand and opened her door. As she was getting out Frank said, "Be careful driving home, okay?"

"Yes, mother."

"And you'll be careful in the water?"

"No, I'm gonna be a reckless idiot so I can wind up back in the hospital again. You gotta learn to relax, Lieutenant."

Kennedy hopped out, then turned and stuck her head back in. "Will you call me?"

Even as she nodded yes, Frank doubted that she would.

He'd seen her at the park a few times. Always alone, never with anyone else. She looked ragged. Maybe she was a stoner, or a runaway. She was a little older than he liked but she was small, and that was important. And she seemed scared. He liked that too.

He watched her. She always had a Walkman and sang quietly to herself, moving her shoulders slightly to the beat. Sometimes she poked furtively through the garbage cans when she thought no one was watching. But he was watching. He liked that she was here a lot. It was reassuring that there was someone he could have. At first he wasn't interested in her, but the more he saw her, the more he thought she'd do just fine. She'd probably be real quiet, not a screamer. He hated it when they screamed. He didn't want to hear them. The idiots didn't realize it only made him angrier, made him want to hit them harder.

And now he figured out she was homeless. She had on the same clothes and was probably in the park because she didn't have anywhere else to go. That her disappearance would go unnoticed added to her attraction. He was smart. He had taken a lot of precautions to not get caught. He didn't think the police were on to him, but he had to pace himself. Sometimes, like with that black girl, he'd acted impulsively. He had to guard against that. Had to take his time, play his plays the way he'd called them, not let the defense rush him.

But he was getting antsy.

31

onday morning Frank was back in the office at 5:00 A.M. A while later she greeted her squad with a grunt and request for updates. Leaning a squeaky chair back as far as it would go, she crossed her natty crimson ankles on the corner of Johnnie's desk. Her socks matched the red turtleneck under her jacket, a small concession to the building Christmas spirit. Nookey had put up a little tree with blinking lights, and Noah had cutouts from the kids pasted all over. Everyone was flecked with their shedding glitter.

Bobby had a tricky suspect in a botched robbery that ended up a double homicide. Frank wanted to ride with him but had to get her sample out to Claremont. Kennedy was right—the cost out of her own pocket would be considerable, but Frank wasn't concerned about that. Single, with no dependents or major expenditures except a locked-in mortgage and tailored suits, Frank could afford to splurge. In addition, a private lab would give her a definitive completion time. Plus privacy. She didn't want her involvement in this case getting leaked.

As it turned out, Frank was swamped and didn't get out of the office until after three. She fought through traffic and delivered her fibers to the lab ten minutes before they closed. Next she headed to the bakery and talked to the plant foreman, who supplied her with Clancey's records and supervisor's name. There were no surprises in Delamore's thin personnel file. He'd started in 1991 as a packer on the swing shift. He'd settled into the night shift in '93 and been promoted to forklift operator two years later. His time cards indicated he worked punctually Wednesday though Sunday, 9:30 P.M. to 6:00 A.M., with a half hour lunch at 1:30. Despite being a seemingly decent employee, Delamore was only making three dollars more than when he started.

Frank wanted to talk to his supervisor but was told he wouldn't be in until later. The foreman had grudgingly given her his address. She was going to try catching him at home. Meanwhile, she was hungry and only about twenty minutes from the Alibi. When she walked in, Johnnie was cheering on the Panthers and close to sloppy drunk. She clapped him on the back and ordered coffee.

"Who's winning?"

"Hey, le Freek!" Johnnie roared, a little too boisterously. "Carolina's kicking Dallas' ass."

Being a Giants fan, Frank found that good news. Mel shoved a nasty cup of coffee at her. She took it to a small table, relieved that Johnnie didn't follow. She watched Kerry Collins throw an incomplete pass, then saw Nancy approach.

"Hey, hon. You must be on call tonight."

Frank nodded and asked how she was doing.

"Alright. Shitty tips, though. And if your buddy grabs my ass one more time I swear I'm gonna break a glass over his head."

"He'd probably like that."

Nancy shook her head disgustedly. "Probably. Have you had dinner yet?"

"Nope. How about a cheeseburger?"

"Rare, no onions, Swiss cheese."

"That's my girl," Frank tiredly encouraged.

"That'll be the day," Nancy smirked. "I'll probably be in Depends before it happens."

Nancy's parting shot made Frank grin. Glancing back over her shoulder, Nancy savored the rare sight. Frank followed the easy sway of her ass across the room, grateful for the diversion from the long day.

Two hours later she was standing in Ruben Benjharad's apartment. She hadn't woken the supervisor, but he still wasn't happy to see her. Frank was used to it; no one was ever glad to see a homicide cop.

Benhjharad had only supervised Clancey for nine months. His employee seemed pretty dependable. If he clearly explained to Clancey what he wanted, it got done. He described Clancey as competent, but never taking the initiative to do anything outside his immediate instruction. Frank asked if he talked to Clancey about things other than work, and Benjharad frowned, scratching his chest. He couldn't think of anything, nor did he think Clancey talked with the other employees, preferring to take his lunch break alone in his car. The supervisor didn't offer anything new, but he at least supported Frank's profile. She thanked Benjharad and reminded him that their conversation was confidential.

At home, finally, she went over the day's notes. They told her nothing new but did nothing to unlodge the certitude in her gut that Clancey was the one. With a pleasure bordering on desire, she pictured Clancey.

You woke up a while ago, all sleepy-eyed and tousle-haired in your bed that smells like old skin and sweat and cum. I bet you slept through the alarm until Mom pounded on the door, ragging your ass like she does. I'll bet you didn't want to wake up, did you? Bet your dreams are better than mine. But you get up anyway. Have to. Mom won't let you be late. What next? Shower?

Frank remembered the damp pile of towels in the bathroom.

Probably. Because Mom's trained you to. You don't really care. Comb your hair for the same reason. Do you look in the mirror? Probably not. Put on whatever clean clothes your mom's washed. Go downstairs. She said she always has a meal ready for you. You'll eat with her but you won't talk much.

There'd been a TV on a plastic cart that faced a small table in the kitchen. Frank bet they watched it during meals.

It's just a matter of time, now, buddy. I am so close to you. I want you. And I'll get you.

Frank felt warm thinking of him, and she marveled that it had been a long time since she'd wanted anything as much as Delamore.

Thursday night, long after the rest of the homicide room was deserted, Kennedy found Frank still bent over her desk.

"I thought you said you'd call," she said by way of a greeting.

Guiltily, Frank answered, "I know. Been busy."

Kennedy took a seat on the couch, hands dangling between her knees. She was in blue jeans and a cracked leather jacket. Frank tried to resist a quick and unbidden surge of affection.

"How's it going with Delamore?"

Gazing absently at the budget in front of her, Frank said, "Still waiting on the lab. Talked to almost everyone on our priority list. One guy actually seemed pretty viable, but his time frame was all bad for Nichols or Agoura. There's one more I still have to talk to. He's in Indiana, be back Monday."

"Dang, you have been busy. And here I thought you were just avoidin' me."

"So what have you been up to?" Frank asked, changing the subject.

"Mostly begging to get reassigned to the street. I think Luchowski's gonna put me back on Monday. But anyway, I came by to ask you a favor."

"Shoot."

"Let me take you out to dinner on Saturday."

"Take me out?"

"Yeah, you always cook, and seeing as I can't cook, it's only fair I buy you dinner. Where do you want to go? Your pick."

Frank considered the offer. "You know," she responded slowly, "I really like to cook and I usually only get around to it on weekends. So if you could choke down another one of my meals, why don't you come over to my place."

Kennedy's tawny mane flew around her face. "Uh-uh. See, the whole point is I'm trying to *re-ci-pro-cate.* Get it? So what's the point in you cooking for me?"

"Oh-h, I see. If it's just paying me back that you want, then forget it, but if you want my company and a good meal, let's do it at my place. Unless you don't like my food."

Exasperated, Kennedy flopped back against the couch. "I love your food, but you *always* treat. I'll only do it if you'll let me pay for the groceries."

"Whatever."

"Cool!" Kennedy bounced to her feet. "How long are you gonna stay here?"

"Little longer."

"Why don't you come surfing with me? It's gonna be a beautiful night."

"Get outta here."

"Come on," Kennedy pleaded. "You'll love it."

"Doubtful."

"Just try."

"Nope. Out you go. I got work to do."

"Come on, Frank, don't be such a wuss."

"Nope."

Their eyes met, sparkling and playful, and Frank was almost tempted to hop in her car and follow Kennedy to the beach. "Go on. See you at five on Saturday."

Kennedy made a disgusted noise and muttered, "Coward."

Frank highlighted an expenditure in red as Kennedy asked from the doorway, "What can I bring?"

"Surprise me," Frank muttered. She didn't see Kennedy's wicked smile.

By the next night, Frank was exhausted. She tried to relax and drank more than she should have, closing the Alibi with Johnnie and Ike. Nancy made a bid to get Frank to come home with her, and tempting as it sounded at the time, Frank was relieved to wake up alone in her own bed on Saturday morning.

Her hangover wasn't bad, just dulling, and it was siphoning her already low energy. A run on the treadmill helped as she thought about what she'd make for Kennedy. Maybe a pork tenderloin napped with a roasted garlic creme sauce and rotelle on the side to hold the sauce, or maybe she'd just barbecue some Porterhouses and bake potatoes. She realized she was looking forward to the evening and checked her anticipation. She spent the morning distracting herself with Agoura/Peterson details, getting so involved that when the phone rang she answered, "Homicide. Franco."

There was a pause before Kennedy said, "I could've sworn I dialed your home number."

"You did. Just forgot where I was."

"Whatcha doin'?"

"One guess."

"You're goin' round that table like a wild dog circlin' a fawn."

"Bingo. What's up?"

"I hate to do this, but I can't make it tonight. We've got this surveillance, and one of the guys on the detail called in sick. Luchowski wants me to take it."

"That's great," Frank said, artfully concealing her disappointment. "You're back on the outside."

"Yeah, *finally*. So you think I can get a raincheck?"

"You bet."

"What were you gonna make? Tell me so I can drool over it while I'm stuck in my car with a bucket of KFC."

"I don't know," Frank lied. "I hadn't really thought about it yet."

"Well, that's good. I was hoping you hadn't gone out and got groceries already."

Frank didn't respond, and Kennedy asked, "You wanna try for next Saturday?"

"Sure."

"Cool. I'll talk to you later, then."

"Right."

Frank pressed her finger down on the receiver button. She replaced the phone slowly. Scanning the suspect list, Frank stonewalled her disappointment and called one of the numbers on the list. A few minutes later she was stalled in traffic. All around her there were families in vans hurrying home, couples in sedans dressed for parties and dinners, truck drivers eager to park their rigs, and single men and women in sports cars fantasizing what their dates would be like. Watching them as dusk blued the skyline, Frank's thoughts kept straying back to her own evening, but she quickly refocused on work.

Studying an elegant couple in the Beamer next to her, Frank pondered her options if the Delamore carpet didn't match the evidence sample. There were a number of ways she could play it. As the Beamer inched forward, she wondered where the couple was going. The man was laughing, the woman smiling, as if she'd just said something clever. They seemed quite happy. Frank looked away.

Later, sitting in the dark, watching shadows against the light—one thin and small, the other tall and wide—Frank was keenly aware of the action around her. A dog trotted down the sidewalk. A car door shut. There was canned laughter from a TV turned too loud. City sounds punctuated the night—a horn, trucks rumbling, a chopper whumping not far off.

"Come on," she whispered, following Delamore's silhouette across the living room window. "Come on, buddy."

And then he was at the front door, light tumbling out around him. She sank lower, slowly, never losing his face as he slid into a shabby Camaro. As his taillights faded, so did Frank's exhilaration. She stared at the house, its allure diminished by his absence. His secrets were in there, though.

By the time Frank pulled away from the curb the couple in the Beamer were in their bed, fast asleep, and Clancey Delamore's house had long been dark.

He was sitting at a picnic table on the edge of the park, anchoring the sports section open with large forearms. The day was cool and blustery, but little kids were running around on the grass and mothers were relieved to have them distracted. At least until one of them fell and hurt himself, or wouldn't share the ball with someone else.

There were two Mexican girls swinging branches at each other, sisters he guessed. He studied them openly, surprised to find he had no feeling for them. He was beyond little girls; they'd been practice for the older and more demanding work he faced now. A quick survey of the park uncovered no suitably aged girls. But that was alright. He didn't want to take them from here anyway. He'd snuck in though a gash of chain-link fence in the thick scrub just to think and relax before going home to his mother and the same dumb questions she always asked: How was his night? What did he want for dinner? Where had he been since he got off work? He thought she'd stop asking because his answers were always the same: Okay. Anything. He'd gone for a walk or to the twenty-four-hour movies.

He knew he couldn't tell her what he was doing, couldn't tell anyone, even though he just wanted to run down the streets screaming, "It's me! I did it!" He was proud of his work, especially the last girl, and thinking about the next one made him feel hot and excited. It was going to be even better. He knew just what he wanted to do.

His chest tightened when he thought about it, and he felt pure pleasure, just like he'd felt before crashing into a defender or bringing the ball home against his chest. In those rare moments of perfect clarity and peace, he'd known the right moves to make and made them flawlessly. Those were the moments when his father had beamed at him from the sidelines. He'd always wished he could stop the clock and stay forever in that smile of acceptance. For those short and shining seconds he felt loved and happy and safe.

That's how it felt when he was with them, right before he made the big play with his father's eyes still somehow on him, bright and smiling, clapping with his hands raised, proud of his son. This was what he felt he'd been groomed for all his life. Football had just been a way to get him here where he truly belonged. His father had known that and tried to show him, but he'd been afraid. Now he wasn't afraid anymore. He knew what he had to do.

32

She was trying to be patient, but ten working days after she'd submitted the carpet samples, Frank broke down and called the lab. A clerk cheerfully told her they'd completed her carpet sample just that morning. Frank grabbed her coat, a handful of stapled papers, and raced past Foubarelle, who had wandered into the squad room.

"Frank, I need to talk to you."

"Gotta go," she said in a flurry. "Be back in an hour."

In the lab's parking lot, Frank opened the sealed report. Skimming past the technicalities she carefully compared the two sample reports. The color, size, shape, and processing of the two fibers were identical. The examiner had traced both of them to a textile manufacturer in Rhode Island and identified each sample as a mutifilament polyester with a distinctly characteristic octalobal cross. In his opinion, it was highly likely that they were from the same source.

Frank closed her eyes, containing her elation. She wondered if RHD had the lab samples back on Peterson yet, and if they would be a match with these. It didn't matter. This was good enough. Though it was impossible to say that the fibers were identical, they were a hard match, and Frank felt an almost sexual pleasure start slowly burning in her belly. She knew she should really be getting back to work. Instead, Frank settled against the headrest. She was perfectly still except for one finger absently rubbing a phantom ring.

She didn't think she'd sleep, but late Friday night Frank forced herself to lie down and was surprised when the alarm went off. She dressed quickly in a navy sweat suit and tucked her hair under an old Dodgers cap. From the dresser she grabbed the holstered Beretta, her badge, ID, wallet, and car keys that dangled from a complicated Swiss knife. Within minutes she was southbound on the 110. It was just past 2:00 A.M. Although Frank had the road to herself, she cruised cautiously at the speed limit. A thin fog dimmed the moon; Frank had hoped the cover would be thicker and lower.

But no matter. She exited easily on Slauson and headed west to Capitol Baking. Parking unobtrusively across the street, she hunkered down and waited. Eventually, a skinny, balding rent-a-cop strolled through the parking lot. Frank sank a little further. He paused at the steps to the front office, joggled the doorknob, and sat down for smoke. Frank had quit years ago, but she envied him now. When he finished, he carefully ground the butt with his heel and retraced his steps through the parking lot.

Frank checked her watch. She knew from Clancey's timecards that breaktime was 3:45. Switching off the dome light, she quietly slipped out of the Honda. She'd driven through the parking lot hours ago, after the swing shift had clocked out, and located Clancey's Camaro. Now she was striding easily toward it on silent running shoes, her red pocketknife hidden in her fist.

Inconspicuously checking the lines of cars, Frank knelt by Clancey's to tie a shoelace. With the awl on her knife she swiftly punctured both his front tires, the air whispering out slowly. For good measure, she stooped and punched the tires on the cars to either side of his. Not nice, but in the long run Frank hoped it would serve a greater humanitarian purpose.

Walking casually back to her car she surveyed the lot again. No one in sight. She started the Honda and eased back onto the side street, then west on Slauson. At a red light she checked the rearview mirror and caught a fraction of her reflection; the satisfied face looking back at her seemed like a stranger's. Frank glanced at the time again and noted she was in good shape, barring any setbacks. She stopped at an AM/PM for coffee. A huge black woman flashed three gold teeth at Frank, saying, "You're lucky. I just made a new pot for myself."

Frank smiled at the towering woman and asked for the bathroom key. It might be a long morning and she wanted to make sure she had lots of room for the coffee. On her way out, the woman told her to have a good day. Frank answered, "I already am."

She still was when she slid against the curb in front of the house next to the Delamores'. Frank pushed her seat back from the steering wheel and assumed her slumped position. Pulling the bill down over her face as if dozing, she listened to her engine tick its heat away. No lights came on, no curtains stirred, no doors shut. Frank sat, motionless, for a few minutes. She took a sip of coffee.

Her watch said Clancey's break was over. Now both of them were waiting for six o'clock. Frank scrunched her neck against her shoulders, easing the knots there. She sighed and stretched her legs, flexed her ass, pumped her arms isometrically, sipped more coffee. As relaxed as it was possible for her to be, Frank reviewed Plans A, B, and C. Then she reviewed them again.

Almost two hours later, a light came on in the Delamores' living room. Frank waited patiently, hoping Plan A was proceeding. It was, because ten minutes later the garage door opened and Clancey's mom backed out in a white Fiesta. As soon as it rounded the corner Frank got out. In the brightening darkness, she crossed the small front lawn and quickly tested the lid on a metal garbage can next to the garage. Using it as a springboard, she pulled herself over the high wooden fence, surveying the back yard even as she landed in it. The fence went all around, but there were two-story houses looking down into it on both sides. Although lights were on upstairs to her left, she didn't see anyone staring back at her. She pressed against a living room window at the rear of the house and it wiggled in its frame. When she and Kennedy had done their fake security check, Frank had jammed the spring latch. Now the window snapped open.

Frank pushed it aside and draped a long leg over the sill. She was in. She stood still for a moment, breathing silently, and listened for sounds in the house. A clock ticked. The refrigerator hummed. Frank padded across the carpet to check the kitchen. Then headed upstairs, making some of the steps creak. She looked in Mrs. Delamore's room first, verifying that Mrs. D. hadn't left a lover curled up in the warm sheets. The bed was empty. So was the bathroom and the sewing room down the hall. Only Clancey's room was left.

What Frank was doing was highly risky, extremely unethical, and completely outside the law. And she was loving every minute of it. Retracing her steps, ears tuned to the subtle sounds of the house and the waking neighborhood, she paused at Clancey's door, noting the keyhole. She tried the knob. It was locked.

Frank yanked the knife from her jacket pocket. Prying out its longest blade, she slid it between the lock and frame, her shoulder to the door. Her father had shown her how to do this with a credit card when they'd locked themselves out of their apartment. These days, house locks were much more sophisticated. But this was just a simple inside lock, and the door swung open.

Frank quickly took in the room, setting the timer on her watch. Twenty minutes max. Clancey's room was a welter of chaos, but Frank headed straight for the VCR. Turning the volume off she ran an unlabeled tape already in the machine. Low budget kiddy porn. Nauseating, but encouraging. She tried another unlabeled one. Fast-forwarded. Same stuff. With an eye on the open door she pulled out a tape in a well-worn box.

Lu-Lu's Love Festival had obviously been replaced by a home-made video. Looking through a windshield, the camera narrowed on in three young Hispanic girls playing at a picnic table in a park. The shot was too narrow to be certain, but the chaparral in the background was similar to that at Leiderman. Frank didn't recognize the girls.

She glanced at her watch. Eleven minutes. She stopped the tape and searched for another frayed box. *Delight of Venus* started the same way as *Lu-Lu's Love Festival,* a far shot of three girls sunbathing taken though a windshield. Frank searched the background, damn sure she was looking at the reservoir near the top of Kenneth Hahn. She fast-forwarded, backing up as the filmer decided on a panoramic shot. Definitely Kenneth Hahn. Frank's heart was thudding in her ears.

Eight minutes. She fast-forwarded until the camera zoomed in on the girls. Barely breathing, Frank rewound the tape. She paused the tape as one of the girls turned her face toward the camera. Frank bent closer to the TV, trying to be certain. Because of the fuzz from the freeze frame and the distance from the camera, she couldn't swear it, but the girl frozen on the screen looked eerily similar to Jessica Orenthaler. Frank swore silently, wishing she could remember all the details about Orenthaler's assault.

A car door slammed loudly and Frank started. She ejected the video, slipped it back into the box, and dropped it inside her T-shirt. Straining to hear, she arranged the videos to hide the gap, switched off the recorder and TV, and turned the volume back up.

Three minutes. She'd blown all her time on the videos and she still wanted to get into the green-carpeted room in the garage.

Frank closed Clancey's door almost all the way and jogged downstairs. She didn't see the Fiesta in the driveway and doubted she'd have missed the sound of the garage door opening, but she peeked carefully into the dark garage. If she was caught here she was fucked. Her timer went off and she muffled the sound against her stomach, feeling the hard video trapped at her waistband.

Opening her knife again Frank dashed across the concrete floor and tried the door. Of course it was locked. Drops of sweat fell onto her ribs as she worked the knife around, hissing, "Come on, baby, come on."

This lock was older than the one upstairs, but sturdier. Frank couldn't press the catch back, and as she pulled her knife out she heard a garage door whir open. She bolted back into the kitchen just as she realized it was the garage next door. Giddy and giggly with adrenaline, she grinned at her mistake.

Minus five minutes.

Frank sprinted up the steps and into Clancey's room. She searched the nasty contents of the drawer in his nightstand but couldn't find a key. He probably kept it with his bedroom key, which he'd probably keep with his car keys.

Minus nine minutes.

Frank waded through the wreckage of Clancey's room across to his closet. The football uniform was where Kennedy had said it was. Number eighty-one. She searched it quickly for blood stains. A number of spots could certainly have been dried blood. Without a test, though, it was impossible to say for sure. Frank turned and froze.

The garage door rumbled again. This time she was sure it was the Delamores'. Frank calmly picked her way out of the room and closed the door behind her. She twisted the knob. It was locked. Frank's senses were firing at full alert. Her brain fielded the messages coldly and clearly.

Down the stairs. The car in the garage. Across the living room. Car doors slamming. Mrs. Delamore's voice. Whiny, angry. The drapes. The window. Still open. Her voice in the kitchen now. Was Clancey behind her or ahead? Probably behind. Drapes aside. No faces in windows. One leg out—Frank peeked through a gap in the drapes just as Mrs. Delamore stepped into the living room—easy. Mrs. D. still talking. Next leg. Go!

Frank hurled herself at the fence, knowing they must have

heard her slam it. She cleared the six-foot planks easily, amazed as always by the potency of adrenaline. Waiting for someone to shout at her, Frank walked quickly toward her car. Off the curb. No one screaming. No one in sight. Door open. Key in ignition. Motor. Clutch. Outta here.

Frank was sure she hadn't drawn a breath since she'd heard the Delamores' garage door open. Two blocks away she breathed down, down, down into her belly, and exhaled with a bellowing roar as she added a fist mark to the Honda's battered ceiling. She was pleased her plan had gone so well, but she would have liked more time inside, specifically in that room off the garage. It was possible Clancey could have transferred fibers from the room to the girls, but it made better sense that the girls had been in there with him. He had to have kept them somewhere. That seemed the most obvious place.

The morning's machinations and two large cups of coffee had left Frank wired. She weaved around the growing lines of cars, anxious to get home and watch Clancey's tape. She felt pretty confident he wouldn't miss it. He'd probably be watching what she believed were the tapes of Agoura and Peterson, not his older, less exciting tapes. Frank stopped at a deli on Huntington. She ordered a double Black Forest ham sandwich with muenster and mustard on dark rye, and picked out a large bottle of English bitter ale.

Once home, she plopped her food on the coffee table and pushed Clancey's tape into the VCR. But first she needed a quick shower to get rid of her stale sweat. Then, wrapped in an old, unraveling bathrobe, she hit the rewind button and pried the cap off her beer bottle. She held a sip of the ale in her mouth, its effervescence tingling sharp and clean.

Frank perched on the couch, hitting the VCR's remote play button. The tape was dark for a moment, then opened with the reservoir scene. She unwrapped the sandwich and tore into it ravenously, never taking her eyes from the tape. Occasionally she paused or rewound it, sure she was watching Jessica Orenthaler sunbathing innocently at the top of the Kenneth Hahn Rec Area. Frank chewed around the thick sandwich as the girl spoke with her companions. When she got off her beach towel and started walking toward the parking lot, the tape went blank. Frank let it roll, wondering if she could get Jessica to confirm the tape for her.

Unexpectedly, the tape came back on. Frank glanced at it and stopped chewing. The scene was dimly lit, taken inside what looked like a small room. The angle indicated that a tall person was holding the camera, pointing it down toward a terrified young woman bound to an easy chair.

Swallowing hard, Frank put the sandwich down. The girl was unmistakably Melissa Agoura. She was wearing a red-and-white football jersey, number eighty-one, over bell-bottom jeans. Her feet were bare and strapped to the legs of the chair with what looked like duct tape. Her hands were taped together in her lap, her torso tied firmly against the chair with repeated lengths of rope. Frank thought it looked like clothesline. Fat strips of tape covered Agoura's mouth. Above it, her eyes were wide and dark and terrified.

Frank assumed Clancey was holding the camera. She could hear his breathing, choppy and heavy. He must have been shaking, because the filming was jiggly. Agoura whimpered faintly against the backdrop of his heavy breath. Frank paused the video, uncertain she wanted to see more. She stood up and paced for a moment, unconsciously rubbing the back of her neck. When she stopped, she stared at the scene frozen on her TV.

"Jesus," she breathed, suddenly overwhelmed. Dropping into a chair next to the TV, she carefully sifted though her ideas. A defense attorney would try to dismiss the tape; there was no proof Clancey was holding the camera, no proof he'd murdered her. Yet. Frank wondered what else was on the tape. Regardless, what there was made a strong link. The defense would have a hard time wiggling out of the connection. For Frank, however, there was no doubt.

"Gotcha," she whispered. She was surprised that the word sounded hollow. She'd expected a sense of triumph but felt deflated instead. She finally had him, just like she wanted, but her victory was empty: the cost of all the lives he'd ruined greatly outweighed her own small success. Frank mashed her eyebrows together for a minute, thinking. At last she sighed. Clearing her half-eaten sandwich off the table and walking into the kitchen, she poured the suddenly nauseating ale down the drain.

She dreaded looking at the rest of the tape but knew she had to. She should make a copy, too. She could do that at HQ tomorrow. The copy would go to RHD along with an anonymous note. But Frank couldn't let them sit on it. She had an idea of how to handle that, too. Tomorrow.

Acutely aware that she was shoving aside her feelings by thinking like a cop, Frank returned woodenly to the living room, where Melissa Agoura was frozen on her television screen.

"Well, well, Lieutenant. I must say I was surprised to get your call. I didn't think you'd keep your end of the bargain without a battle."

Sally Eisley flashed scary white teeth at Frank, who pressed what she hoped was convincing affability through her layers of fatigue. Immaculately made-up and dressed to the tits, Sally blended well with the rest of the clientele. In the background, the Italian boy singers alternated with big band songs. The distinctive clicks of crystal and china filled the restaurant as naturally as the sound of cars humming home on the freeway.

Frank's antipasto sat untouched, and she caught herself twirling her wine glass. She stopped. It had been a long day after a long night. The red wine reminded Frank of her restless sleep, interrupted by glimpses of Mag, then Agoura, wrapped in Clancey's chair. Tunnel was there, too, in the dark room, and then he was Clancey and coming at Frank, who was tied into the chair. Instead of a broom he had a broken wine bottle. Blood kept spilling out of its jagged neck. Frank was amazed how one bottle could hold so much blood.

Sally carefully arranged her skirt. Frank blinked slowly against the dream. She restrained herself from swallowing her wine in one long draft and, instead, held the bottle over Sally's glass. "May I?"

"Certainly." Satisfied with her pose, the reporter casually draped an elbow on the linen tablecloth and inquired, "To what do I owe the honor?"

Frank finished pouring, then admitted, "I've got something for you. Something I think you're going to like a lot more than my pitiful little bio."

"Don't be so modest, Lieutenant. It doesn't play well on you."

"I'm serious. It's about the Culver City Slayer."

Sally momentarily lost her meticulous composure, and Frank saw a hungry little girl who'd never gotten enough of something. A waiter glided to their table and bowed slightly at Sally. She didn't show it, but Frank knew Sally was charmed by the obsequious service. The waiter spoke only after Frank had acknowledged him, patiently detailing the evening's specials. At Frank's suggestion, Sally opted for the porcini ravioli, while Frank ordered the osso bucco. The waiter departed, their order in his memory, and Sally turned on the detective with undisguised glee.

"So what do you have for me?"

Frank lingered over a sip of the dark wine. On the surface she was aware of teasing Sally, but underneath the artful police work, Frank was reluctant to begin. Sighing deeply but inconspicuously, Frank highlighted the Agoura and Peterson cases.

When the waiter presented their plates, Sally impatiently asked, "Why are you telling me all this?"

Frank assured the waiter they were satisfied, then carefully explained how the cases were connected. Without offering Clancey's name or specific details, she laid out the evidence against him.

"You know these cases are being handled by Robbery-Homicide now. They have all this evidence and they're just sitting on it. These girls are not a high priority for them, what with Woodall still not closed and then Marker getting bumped yesterday."

A sitcom personality had been found in an alley, whacked in the head and robbed. All the people in their gated communities and alarmed cars were in high panic about it because it had happened to one of them. Frank ignored her meal, leaning in close to Sally as if to confide in her.

"Honestly, I don't expect you to give a damn about these kids either. But what is news, and what'll get you ratings, is exposing the fact that a two-bit comedian's accidental death is more important to the police that your viewers pay taxes to than the planned and deliberate deaths of at least four young girls. RHD could move on this right now, but the death of a celebrity cokehead is a greater priority than multiple deaths of the average citizen's child."

Frank watched the story playing in Sally's eyes, knew she had her. Even though she wasn't hungry, Frank forced the tender veal down, letting Sally think. Finally the reporter's eyes narrowed and she said, "So you want me to cover this to force Robbery-Homicide into action?"

Bluntly Frank answered, "That's my angle, yeah."

"Why? It's not your problem anymore. Are you using me to settle a score? I want to know."

Frank shook her head and dabbed at her mouth with the heavy napkin.

"You know, Sally, I've been a cop for almost seventeen years. I've seen the worst that you can imagine and then some. But there's a man out there, with no remorse and no compunction, who is stealing girls off the streets. He hurts them. He rapes them. And then painfully...knowingly...savagely," Frank paused a beat, "he kills them. And he loves this. More than anything. And because he loves it, he'll never stop. He'll go on raping and hurting and killing, and he'll only get better at it. I talked to some of the girls that lived through his assaults. They're never going to be the same. Their worlds are shattered."

Frank searched the reporter's face. When she continued, she spoke so softly that Sally had to lean closer.

"When I questioned them, when I had to ask them about the man who'd done this to them, they trusted me. They looked at me like somehow *I* could help them be whole again. Which of course I can't. But I told them, I *promised* them, that we'd catch him, that they'd never have to be afraid of him again. I intend to keep that promise. It's the least I can do for them."

Frank sat back, spent from the veracity of what had started as a line for Sally.

"So yeah, it's not my problem anymore. But I can't walk away from those girls, and whoever he's got his sights on next. Because I can guarantee you, he *will* kill again. As sure as you're taking your next breath."

Sally coolly tapped a lacquered nail against her wine glass.

"Very touching. But if I break this, then every mike jockey in town will be hounding them."

Frank needed Sally, she had to play this last hand as well as she could. Smiling patiently, and she hoped winningly, Frank coaxed the reporter.

"Come on, Sally. You're light years ahead of most the crew out there. Do your homework. You can get an exclusive, and however you do that is fine with me. As long as we've never had this dinner, and as long as RHD moves."

"If I call them on it I'll need more ammunition."

"Trust me. All you have to do is tell them you know they have a suspect in Culver City, and that they have solid evidence connecting him at least to Agoura. That'll get them sweating. The commission won't be pleased that they're just squatting on a quadruple homicide. And besides," Frank hinted, pulling out the last drop of charm in her arsenal, "this could be just the beginning of a useful relationship between us. Don't you think?"

The hungry young reporter stabbed her ravioli and bared her teeth in answer.

33

Kennedy hoisted a six-pack and said, "Congratulations."

Frank opened the door wider, letting her inside.

"What am I being congratulated for?"

"You got your man."

Frank shrugged. "RHD's man."

"Oh-h-h," Kennedy feigned, "and they didn't have any help from you?"

The older cop returned the feint with a brief, enigmatic smile. "What's up?" she asked, examining the three Cokes and three beers in the six-pack carton.

"Did you see the news tonight?"

"Nope."

"It's the lead story. Sally Eisley, KTLA? She had a total exclusive. She was marching in there behind these RHD dicks, filmed the whole thing."

"Yeah?"

"I suppose you don't know anything about that, either."

When Frank didn't answer, Kennedy checked her watch and grabbed Frank's arm, pulling her into the living room.

"Come on. Let's catch the late news."

Frank followed, accepting the beer Kennedy handed her. The younger detective bounded over to the TV, threw herself excitedly onto the couch, and pried a Coke open. Frank admired Kennedy's energy, wondering if she'd ever had as much. Yeah, she thought, but that was light years ago.

Kennedy brandished the remote, picking through the channels until she found KTLA.

"Here we go," she said, sucking noisily from her can. "This is rich, you're gonna love it."

As the last few minutes of a police drama unfolded, Kennedy jokingly wished everyone she worked with was as good-looking.

"So, did you drop a dime to Eisley?" she asked casually.

"What's Eisley got to do with anything?"

"Kinda interesting how she scooped the story, that's all. Like RHD personally invited her."

"Guess she caught a lucky break."

Frank's profile was creased and sallow, but it gave away nothing.

"I'm not keeping you up am I?"

Staring at the TV, Frank shook her head. Kennedy was in fact a useful diversion from the long night. Frank had heard about Delamore's arrest on the radio, driving home through the Christmas-colored traffic lights. She'd switched off the radio, not wanting to know any more. It was out of her hands now. Still, the sense of something unfinished had nagged at her. She'd rolled down her window, even though the air rushing in was sharp. She'd hoped without enthusiasm that RHD wouldn't blow this. The wind had cut through her as if she were hollow, the night seemed to roll out in front of her endlessly. All she could see ahead were glasses of Scotch and sheets damp and twisted from nightmares.

"There it is," Kennedy shouted, pressing the volume higher. The KTLA anchor started his spiel, and Frank watched, without interest.

"Good evening, ladies and gentleman," the anchor smoothly greeted. "We begin tonight's newscast with the discovery and arrest of the Culver City Slayer, the man believed to be responsible for the deaths of four young women in the Culver City area. As detectives from the Los Angeles Police Department apprehended the suspect, KTLA's Sally Eisley"—he paused dramatically—"was there."

"Pretty coincidental, huh?"

Frank just pulled on her beer, focusing on Sally's glossy visage. The cameraman segued into the highlight footage of Clancey in jeans and sweatshirt, appearing sleepy and confused as he was led to the police car. Sally did a brief voice-over bio on Delamore, adding that police were responding to a lead made by an anonymous caller.

Kennedy's eyes were all over Frank, who watched the police gingerly help Clancey into a squad car. The footage changed to Clancey's bedroom and an RHD captain holding a videotape. He was saying that Delamore had actually taped himself with at least two of the victims.

Kennedy whistled at that. "Betcha there's one happy DA out there tonight."

Indicating the line of videos on Clancey's shelf, he added that they didn't know what was in the rest of the footage, but what they had seen already was pretty gruesome. The next shot showed the captain in a room they didn't recognize. Kennedy muttered, "Look at that carpet. That must be the room in the garage."

The camera panned the bare room, focusing on a small pile of clothing and a ragged easy chair with a stack of porn magazines next to it. Sally said detectives presumed the clothing found in "the chamber of deadly terror" belonged to one or more of the victims. Interviewing the captain directly, Sally asked why the delay in catching the Culver City Slayer.

"Well, the basic problem all along was a lack of witnesses, but if you're diligent and keep working a case, investigating all the leads—and sometimes it can take a lot of time—hopefully, eventually, you'll hit on the right combination of events and wind up with your perpetrator. That's what happened here. We just kept working the case, following the leads we had. Of course, I wish none of this had happened, but I'm glad we apprehended our suspect as quickly as we did."

"And, of course, the tip from the unknown caller helped," Sally added without the slightest trace of sarcasm.

"Yes, that was advantageous, too," the captain agreed. "We'd already had Mr. Delamore under surveillance. The tip confirmed what we already suspected."

"What a crock of shit!" Kennedy exploded through Eisley's wrap-up. "Did you hear that son of a bitch?"

As the newscaster went into a segment about insurance rebates, Kennedy muted the sound. Frank kept watching anyway.

"Damn! What a prick."

"Who's the wiser?" Frank said without heat.

"Well, you are. Doesn't it piss you off that those greasy RHD fuckers are gonna get all the credit?"

"It's their case. Why shouldn't they get the credit?"

"But you did all the work! They didn't know shit about Delamore until you told 'em."

Frank just shrugged.

"That doesn't bug you at all?" Kennedy asked unbelievingly.

"It's not my case. I'm just glad they're on to him, and it sounds like they found good stuff against him. Case closed."

Frank reached for another beer.

"Well, I think it sucks that you did all the work and then they get all the glory."

Without conviction, Frank said, "It's not about glory, Kennedy. The bottom line is that Delamore's out of action."

"That's very noble, but it's still not fair."

"If you're looking for fair, you're in the wrong line of work, sport."

"So you're not at all disappointed?"

Kennedy had her arms folded across her chest and Frank was familiar with the interrogating tone.

"I wish I could have seen this through, but I'd rather see RHD slam him than have him loose."

"I don't believe you!" Kennedy moaned. "Two weeks ago you were so hot for this guy I thought I was gonna have to hose you down, and now it's just no big deal?"

"Kennedy, what do you want me to do? Fall to the floor wailing and pulling my hair? It's over!"

Kennedy had briefly pierced Frank's apathy.

"No, I'm just saying you must be disappointed. You keep doing that goddamn stone-faced thing that you do. Why can't you just be disappointed?"

"Maybe it's not as big a deal as you think it is."

"Then what are you so fucking glum about?"

Frank sighed. "Look. I'm tired, okay? It's been a long day. I need some sleep."

"Alright then," Kennedy said, rising. "I'll go. I just wanted to tell you I thought you did a great job."

"We did a great job," Frank corrected.

"There you go again. Just say thank you and accept the compliment."

"Thank you and accept the compliment."

At the door Kennedy turned. "Hey, you know, it's almost Christmas."

Frank nodded, asking, "You going to see your old man?"

"Nah. It'd be too weird for both of us. How 'bout you?"

"Hadn't even thought about it."

"You wanna do something together? I could come over Christmas Eve and beat your ass at gin."

"Sure," Frank said without enthusiasm.

"Does that sound good?"

"Yeah. That'd be great."

Kennedy scrutinized Frank. "Are you sure you're alright? You look shitty."

"Thanks. I'm fine," Frank answered quietly.

"You don't look fine."

"Just tired."

"Alright. I'll get out of your hair. I'll talk to you later, okay?"

Frank nodded, opening the door. She mustered the strength to call after Kennedy, "Be careful."

Kennedy flashed a grin, answering, "Yes, mother!"

In-line skates surrounded Frank, in every color known to man and then some. She looked for a salesclerk, frowning that they were all busy. She was tired and ready to go home, even if it was only to coax sleep and battle nightmares. But it was December 23rd and last-minute shoppers like herself were swirling around like piranhas. She finally clamped a firm hand on a kid who'd just left a customer and asked what was the best brand of skates.

"Well, that depends on a lot of things," he said sulkily, trying to turn away.

"Like what," Frank said, stepping in his way.

"Like who's using them, how they use them. Lots of things."

"A young woman who goes up and down the street in them, jumps curbs," Frank shrugged.

"She's using them for recreation?" the kid said patronizingly.

"Yeah. She's not jumping off rooftops or gliding down banisters on them. I guess that's recreational use instead of homicidal use."

"K-2," the kid spat, with an evil glare.

"You carry them?"

"Over there," he pointed.

Picking up one of the pairs the punk had indicated, she stopped another clerk passing her.

"Hey. Are these good skates?"

"Yeah, they are," he said eagerly.

"They'd be a good present for a recreational skater?"

"Wa-ay."

"Can you ring these up for me?"

"Sure. I just gotta help that lady over there, then I'll be with you."

"Great."

Frank leaned against the counter by the cash register, waiting patiently. She hoped Kennedy would like the skates. Frank had overheard her talking to Noah about the pair she had, how they were falling apart. These were pricey, but Frank wanted the best. And besides, if Kennedy didn't like them she could always bring them back.

The kid bounced up to her and took the skates.

"For your kid?" he asked.

Frank smiled faintly, amused that she could really be mistaken for someone's mother.

"No. Just a friend."

"Must be a pretty good friend."

Frank hadn't thought about that, but decided she was.

After the clerk wrapped the skates, Frank headed home. She made herself go through her exercise routine thinking it might perk her up. It exhausted her, though, and she was tempted to quit. She drove herself on anyway. When it was over she opened a beer, but it didn't taste good, so she let it sit while she took a shower. Then she decided she should eat something, but nothing appealed to her. Contemplating the refrigerator's holdings, she wondered what was the matter with her. She decided she just needed some sleep, that things must be catching up to her.

Over the last week or so—actually, since Delamore's bust—Frank had noticed she wasn't very hungry. Nor was she sleeping. The exercise she usually looked forward to had become a trial, and that puzzled her. She'd blamed the lack of energy on the lack of sleep. Always sparse at best, it had become even more sporadic, caught in snatches between dreams and alarm clocks. She longed for it at the same time she was afraid of the terrors it brought: bloody, mangled visions of Tunnel exploding, or Maggie and sometimes Kennedy bleeding and staggering toward her, or them or herself or Cassie Nichols tied against Clancey's lounge chair. She'd wake herself with her own sounds and turn the lights on, then pace and drink until the adrenaline subsided.

Letting the beer drain into the sink, Frank grabbed a handful of cashews and poured a small tumbler of Scotch. *Dinner of Champions,* she noted humorlessly, sitting on the couch with the remote. She'd found waking up in front of the TV wasn't as frightening as waking up in the den or in her bedroom. Resigned to the long night, she munched the nuts for nutrition's sake, finding no joy in them nor the hot liquid that chased them.

She was surprised when the alarm went off. The last thing she remembered was Jay Leno interviewing a leggy young actress Frank didn't recognize. She showered, grateful for the four hours of sleep she'd had. Rolling down the quiet highway, she thought about all the cases the ninety-third had outstanding. There was so much work to do and not enough hours in a day. A homicide cop in South Central was like Sisyphus in Tartarus: always rolling the rock to the top of the hill just to have it come crashing down again. Frank sighed, turning on some trashy talk radio to distract her from the weight in her chest. Sliding into a parking space she remembered Kennedy was coming over tonight. The thought brought no spark of pleasure, merely a feeling of obligation.

Upstairs, Gough was making coffee. As she passed him she grunted, "Morning."

He grunted in reply, going back to the newspaper spread out on his desk. Frank neatly hung up her jacket, then stared at the pile of papers on her desk. She'd probably not get to any of it today, either. She had a meeting with Foubarelle at 7:30 followed by a ride to the sheriff's office where she and Nookey had to talk two guys from OSS about a couple of bangers suspected in a double homicide Nookey had caught last week. After that there was a lieutenants' meeting at noon. Her own people would weave in and out of much of the remaining time.

And she was right. At 1:00 P.M. she was still in the lieutenants' meeting. Rubbing a hand across her forehead she thought, God, I wish I were home. She thought about Clancey Delamore, how she'd circled around the dining room table before she knew who he was, trying to uncover him and become him, to flush him out. She realized she missed him, missed losing herself in the challenge of finding him.

She wondered grimly if maybe Clay was right. Maybe all she had in her life were dead people. And Kennedy, who was very much alive. Frank thought about calling her and telling her she was sick. The idea of spending an evening with Kennedy suddenly seemed draining. Frank didn't know where she could find the energy for it. But she knew Kennedy would be disappointed, and somehow that penetrated Frank's funk.

While Keating in Vice went off about needing more detectives, Frank tried to convince herself that the night would be fun, or at least different. After all, when Kennedy wasn't pissing her off, she had a way of making Frank laugh. Determined to have a good time for Kennedy's sake, she concentrated stoically on the meeting.

Frank shared some leads that had been generated from the meeting when she got back to the office. Her phone rang and she waved her detectives out when she heard Kennedy's hello. "Hey," she greeted quietly.

"Hey, yourself," responded the chipper voice on the other end. "Do you know you have never called me? Not once."

"Why don't you hang up. I'll call you back."

"Why do you suppose that is?"

"I'm sure I couldn't tell you."

"So how late are you working?"

Frank glanced at the clock. "I'm done."

"*What?* It's not even two yet. Since when have you ever left the office before quitting time?"

Frank heard the excitement in Kennedy's voice and regretted she wasn't deserving of it. But she'd try. She'd put in the effort to give Kennedy a nice Christmas.

"Since it's Christmas Eve and I have a delicious dinner to cook. I've got to stop and get groceries, then I'll be home."

"Excellent! I'm still at work, then I'm going home and change. See ya around six?"

"Good," Frank said, about to hang up, but Kennedy asked, "Can I bring anything?"

"I got it covered."

Replacing the receiver, she heard a phone ringing in the squad room. Ike and Diego were catching tonight, but they were out. Frank knew no one else would answer it at 1:45 on Christmas Eve. As she was mulling that over, Noah stepped into the room and threw a little box at her.

"Tracey saw that the other day. It reminded her of you."

As she unwrapped the present, Noah asked when she was leaving.

"Soon as I open this."

"Good. You look like shit. Go home and get some rest."

"Easier said than done. How you been sleeping lately?"

"Like a baby."

Inside the box was a plastic figurine of a hula dancer. Frank pressed under the base and the dancer's knees and waist buckled and her arms waved about.

"Reminded you guys of me, huh?"

Noah laughed. "Hey, that's an antique, man. They don't make those anymore."

"I see," Frank said, slipping into her coat. "That's what reminded you of me?" Noah laughed again.

"We just thought you'd have fun playing with her. Next time Fubar traps you in here, just take that Honolulu honey out and start flapping her around."

Frank forced a sparse smile as she walked out with her detective. "You going down to Tracey's folks?"

"Yep, for rubber turkey and more neckties. How 'bout you? Whatcha gonna do?"

"Just hang at home."

"Why don't you come over tonight, have dinner, read Christmas stories with us."

"Nah."

"Come on! Come over, Trace'll love it. So will the kids."

"I can't."

Frank shook her head, and Noah stepped in front of her.

"Why not?"

"I can't."

"Why?"

Frank said dismissively, "I'm making dinner for Kennedy."

Noah lifted both eyebrows. "Now that's *chummy.*"

"Whatever."

Frank moved around him and he followed her down the stairs.

"Are you two spending a lot of time together?"

"Christ, you are such an old auntie."

He laughed and pressed, "Well? Are you?"

"No, we're not. She doesn't have any family and invited herself over for dinner. And I let her. It's that simple."

"Okay. If you say so."

Frank loved Noah, but he really was an old nanny.

"Give Trace and the kids a hug for me. Have fun in San Diego."

Noah wiggled his eyes and gently punched Frank's shoulder. "You have fun with Gidget."

34

Frank looked at the fireplace. She hadn't used it in years. Mag had loved fires, and whenever the temperature dropped below seventy she'd build a raging one. Frank would curse and open all the windows, but after she'd realized the fat rug in front of it was one of Mag's favorite places to make love, she hadn't objected anymore.

"Probably start a chimney fire," Frank muttered, stuffing in wadded paper and pseudo-logs from the grocery store. In the low-forties and damp, it was cold by L.A. standards. Frank cranked the heat up. When Kennedy knocked and let herself in, Frank was standing at the sink dressing a standing rib roast.

"Hey, girl, this is a dangerous city. Pretty lil' thang like you oughta keep her doors locked. Good God on a mountain! What are you cookin', a whole calf?"

"Heard you Texans like things big."

"Dang! What army's coming over for dinner?"

"The way you eat we'll be lucky to have the bones left. You like your meat medium, right?"

"That's right. Damn, that's some impressive sum-bitch. You gonna put those curly little white hats on the ends?"

"Nope, no hats. Only Yorkshire pudding and peas with pearl onions in a green peppercorn sauce."

"Jesus...what's Yorkshire pudding?"

"You never had that?" Frank asked, poking garlic slices into the fat.

"Uh-uh."

"It's kinda of like a popover. You ever had them?"

"Uh-uh."

"Well, it's kind of a greasy bread. You make a dough and bake it with the drippings. It's good."

"I've never had anything from your kitchen that wasn't. I didn't know what you were making so I got you a bottle of red and one of white."

Frank glanced up at the bottles Kennedy put on the bar and hefted them appreciatively.

"This is some primo wine, sport."

"The guy at the wine store said they were topnotch."

"Must have set you back a pretty penny."

"What the hell, it's Christmas."

"Let's check this red out," Frank said, cutting a circle in the protective foil. "Thanks."

"You're welcome. 'Sides, it's the least I can do seeing as you're doing all the cookin' again."

"My pleasure," Frank lied. All she wanted to do was sink down on the couch with the TV blasting some inane show and sleep for twenty-four hours, a deep and solid amnesiac sleep. She poured a glass of the wine, then pushed it aside and drank from the glass she already had going.

"Aren't you gonna try it?"

"Have to let it sit, let some of the alcohol burn off so you get a truer taste. Smells great, though."

Frank shoved the roast into the oven and mixed the pudding batter while Kennedy told her a story about the narc surveillance she was on. Frank listened diligently, tweaking out a smile at the funny parts, but she didn't get past Kennedy's watchful eye.

"Somethin' on your mind, Lieutenant?"

"No, ma'am." Frank said, drying her hands on a dishtowel.

"You wouldn't tell me if there was, would you?"

"Just tired," Frank said to the towel. "Lots of work to catch up on. Delamore got me all behind, there's the usual end-of-the-year panic meetings, just a bunch of stuff. So, I hear you're going to whip my ass at gin."

Frank's attempt at levity sounded hollow even to her, and a blind person couldn't miss the flatness in her eyes. They were pinched and tight, like she had a bad headache, and the slump in her carriage was completely out of character with her typical square-shouldered stance.

"Why don't you take a nap?" Kennedy said. "Just tell me when to put the batter in and I'll take care of it. 'A little nipper,' as my dad used to say. I won't let you sleep more than twenty minutes."

It was tempting, but Frank shook her head. "I'd rather kick your ass at gin."

She was relieved when Kennedy went along with the con, answering, "Oh, so you're going to kick *my* ass? A month ago you didn't even know how to *spell gin* and now you're talking about kickin' my ass, you ingrate."

"Wha-wha. You going to whine or play?"

They played while the roast burbled and steamed out smells that made Kennedy sigh and drool. Frank actually managed to win a couple of hands, more through luck than skill. As she finished the kitchen details, Kennedy set the table. Then she surprised Frank by going to her truck and producing a bouquet for the centerpiece.

Dinner was outstanding. The beef was tender, the outer pieces pink for Kennedy, the inner ones deep red for Frank. The pudding had a golden crust with a soft, buttery underbelly, and the peas popped sweetly between Frank's teeth in a creamy, peppery sauce. Kennedy raved, but Frank didn't taste much. She took little bites and spent a lot of time rearranging what was on her plate. Frank knew it was good. She was pleased that Kennedy thought so, too.

Drinking the excellent wine, watching it glow like liquid ruby against the fire, Frank knew that Kennedy was carrying the evening. She was lively and animated, chatting about Christmas in Texas, telling stories about being a female cop in Corpus Christi. Frank responded with vague smiles and tried to ask questions that would keep Kennedy talking, but half the time she wasn't hearing what Kennedy said.

At length, Kennedy groaned and stretched away from the table. She started clearing their plates while Frank stared into her jeweled wine. A cello suite played softly in the background. The fire popped and flickered warmly. It was a lovely Christmas Eve, and Frank was intensely detached from all of it. She felt like she was living the night from inside a plastic bubble. She could see and hear everything around her, and seemed to respond to it appropriately, but she couldn't feel any of it. It was like watching herself in a dream. She started to wonder if maybe she was asleep. Maybe she'd taken that nap after all and was just dreaming all this. When she woke up she'd taste the food and laugh at Kennedy's stories and be grateful for all that she had tonight.

Frank realized Kennedy had said something to her, had knelt next to her chair.

"I'm sorry. What'd did you say?"

"I said, 'Where are you?' You're a million miles away."

"Sorry."

"It's okay. Just tell me where you are."

Kennedy's face was compassionate and concerned. Frank wanted to ease her worry but didn't know how. It was an effort just breathing around the cold heaviness in her chest, no less speaking.

"Sorry I've been such a drag tonight."

"You haven't been a drag. It's just obvious you're not all here."

Frank reassured Kennedy it wasn't anything to do with her.

"You sure? 'Cause I can go home. It's no big deal, it's still early."

"No. Stay."

"You sure? I feel like I've been in your hair all night."

"No."

Frank looked at the shiny hair, remembered how she'd wanted to touch it that night. The feeling seemed distant.

"I'm glad you're here, sport. I've just got to...I don't know...get some sleep."

"Tell you what. I'm gonna go for a walk. Why don't you head on to bed? Get a good night's sleep."

Facing the night alone and so early was the last thing Frank wanted to do.

"I might go read in the den for a while."

"'Kay," Kennedy said, rising, "I'll try to work some of this food off."

"Hey." Frank took Kennedy's hand. She wanted to explain where she was but she didn't know. She studied the young face as if a clue might be there. Finding no answer and no words she finally said, "Be careful, huh?"

Kennedy chuckled. "As always, mother."

Emptying the wine bottle, Frank paced slowly in front of the fireplace. She was restless but exhausted, tired but not sleepy. Pausing in front of an old marble-topped desk that had belonged to Maggie's grandmother, she wondered about her folks, how they were doing, how old they were now. She shook her head, definitely not wanting to go down that road. Frank moved in front of the fire. She wondered what pressed logs were made of that made them flicker blue and green. She hoped Kennedy was safe. A sigh did nothing to ease the weight in her chest. Frank meandered into the den. The Bach had grown wearisome, and she flipped it off.

The fire crackled in the living room. Frank closed her eyes and saw Maggie on the floor, glistening and sated, her breath slowing to normal. Frank remembered feeling sure her heart had to burst because it couldn't possibly hold that much love.

She held the wine up in front of her. Red. Like the blood in all her dreams. Frank's life story was written in blood. Suddenly, the house was too quiet. Frank searched through her CDs. Plopping Donizetti into the CD tray, she cued it to "Una Furtiva Lagrima." She listened to the music sitting on the couch, and when it ended she played it again.

Frank had laughed when Maggie'd lovingly unpacked all her opera tapes, but before long she found herself walking to class whistling a love song from *Turandot* or *Tosca*. After she'd died, Frank had put all her tapes into a box and stored them in the hall closet, planning to get rid of them eventually. Then, almost two years to the date of Mag's funeral, Frank heard the "Flower Song" on the radio. She'd been driving home from work on Manchester and had to stop in a U-Auto-Do-It parking lot to listen to the music. Cranking the Honda's creaky stereo up as high as it would go, she'd let the music wash over her, cleansing her. She'd been glad it was dark and that no one had seen her wiping her face.

Yet here she was, years later, hoping that another opera could force the tears. Frank was even willing to cry to rid herself of the hollowness inside her. At least then Frank had had a good reason to cry. Now she had none, and that was even more maddening. Her life was good—she was a lieutenant with the LAPD; she'd found a serial killer, the largest coup of her career, even if she hadn't gotten any credit; she was healthy, physically at her peak; she was financially secure. She didn't have Mag but she'd learned to live with that. It was okay.

So what's your problem? Frank asked herself. She promptly assured herself with another sip of wine that there was no problem, she was probably just getting her period. Relax, she told herself, don't worry about this. Listen to the music.

She'd self-medicated for so long she really believed that arias and alcohol could cure anything. So she drank and let the music cry for her. Picking out each tremulous note and haunting chord, Frank gave herself up to the opera. She regretfully turned it off when she heard Kennedy close the front door. The silence flooded back into her like cold, gray river water. When Kennedy popped into the den, Frank stared at her. In the handsome young face, brown again from sun, Frank saw happiness and confidence, optimism and courage—all the things that Frank had lost. She felt broken, and wanted to push Kennedy away.

"Why don't you go home?" she asked quietly.

"Do you want me to?"

"You should be out having a good time, dancing and laughing with someone your own age instead of nursemaiding a broken-down old cop."

"I am having a good time. I had an incredible dinner with a wonderful woman and I'm gonna go to bed and sleep without an alarm clock and have wonderful dreams."

"I hope you do."

"Are you sure nothing's wrong?"

"Very. You get to bed, sport. Have those sweet dreams you're talking about."

"You too. Go to bed soon."

Frank nodded, aware of the soft breeze Kennedy left behind. Now there was nothing left to do but stare down the night.

Kennedy wasn't surprised when she woke up thirsty; Frank was a great cook, but heavy on the salt. Throwing the covers back she heard music playing in the den and saw the lights on. Frank had probably fallen asleep in there. Kennedy popped a Coke and downed half the can. She put the rest back in the fridge and tiptoed quickly to the den, the tile like ice against her feet. Peering around the doorway, she was surprised to see Frank awake and sitting on the edge of the couch.

"Hey, girl, you're supposed to be asleep."

When Frank didn't respond, Kennedy walked into the room. She stood right in front of her, but Frank wouldn't look up. Kennedy bent over, her face just above Frank's, and said her name. She still didn't respond. Kennedy felt the first cold fingers of alarm. Kneeling, so she could see into Frank's face, she said her name, sharply and loudly.

Frank's eyes flickered toward hers, and Kennedy reflexively checked their reaction time. The pupils were normal and bright, but Frank stared at her like she was a stranger.

"Frank, what's the matter? Are you sick?"

Frank didn't answer. Kennedy was beginning to wonder if

she'd had a stroke, maybe some sort of seizure. She grabbed Frank's shoulders and shook her.

"Frank, say something or I'm calling a fuckin' ambulance!"

Slack-jawed, Frank struggled to focus on the face in front of her. She saw Kennedy's fear and heard it, but she felt too far away to respond. She'd found a place inside her that was deep and dark and quiet, and she didn't know if she wanted to leave it. When Kennedy rattled her, snapping her head back, Frank tentatively reached for her. Her fingers found Kenndy's face. They landed lightly, but Frank was too far away to feel the soft skin beneath them.

She heard someone asking, "Did you have a bad dream? Is that it?"

Frank struggled to understand the question. She whispered, "I dream all the time. I can't stop dreaming."

Kennedy opened her palm against Frank's face, and Frank felt like she was falling, falling, falling. Kennedy pulled Frank against her. Frank gave in easily, without resistance. She felt an arm around her back and another on her head. Then she was rocking back and forth, back and forth, and someone just kept saying, "Shhh, shhh," even though Frank hadn't made a sound. Frank pressed her face tighter into Kennedy's neck.

"I can't sleep," she whispered, the words warm and damp and secret. "I'm so tired and I can't sleep. There's so much blood. Every time I close my eyes there's so much blood."

"Shhh, you're okay. There's no blood here. It's all gone. It's all gone."

And then the arms were tighter around her, and Frank felt her own arms come up, grabbing at Kennedy, clutching her shirt in her fingers, kneading it in hard bunches, and the still rational part of Frank's brain wondered if she could burrow any deeper into Kennedy's shoulder without breaking bone. But Kennedy just rocked and shushed, rocked and shushed.

Frank held on while Pavarotti cried for her, while she tried breathing around the chasm in her lungs where the nightman stalked with all his demons and henchmen. She squeezed Kennedy to her, wondering how she couldn't be crushing her, but not caring, knowing this was her last hope. That this tender young woman was all there was to keep her from falling into the hole where death and dying swirled redly, hungrily.

She gulped air jaggedly and unevenly, praying, Please God, don't let me fall in there, please don't let me fall in. There was no light in that hole. In it whirled sucking chest wounds and spattered brain matter. Dead green babies with gonorrhea sores in their gaping mouths clawed at her, and twelve-year olds giving high-fives over the bodies of friends they'd just shot. And always blood flowing, dripping down the walls of the chasm, pooling on the floor, streaking hands and faces. Lucifer's own blood.

When she stopped breathing, her body forced her to open and swallow, and she concentrated on the ridge of bone mashing against her cheek and the nuzzle of Kennedy's hair on her nose, the soft skin against her lips, the arms hard and secure around her, the sweet smell of woman filling her brain. She just held on, and Kennedy whispered assurances until finally Frank's fingers unclenched and her breathing evened out. When her arms relaxed, Kennedy let go and pulled back slowly.

"Come on," she said gently, helping Frank stand. She led her into the master bedroom, asking where her pajamas were. Frank was confused but managed to mumble they were on the back of the bathroom door. Kennedy got them and gently tugged Frank's turtleneck over her head. She slipped Frank into the pajama top, then helped her take off her shoes and socks and slacks. Frank held onto Kennedy's shoulder while she silently stepped into the pj's. Then Kennedy led Frank into the guest bed.

"Come here," she whispered, and guided Frank back into the haven of her arms. "I want you to sleep, okay? Just sleep, and if any dreams come we'll chase them away together, okay? You're safe right now. Nothing's gonna get you. I won't let anything happen to you."

Somewhere in the back of her brain Frank knew that couldn't possibly be true, but she wanted to believe Kennedy's soft words, wanted the warm arms to wrap around her, and, gradually, she slept.

When her lips found Kennedy's, Frank was still asleep, dreaming that she was making love to Maggie. It felt so good to have her back again. Frank didn't know how that could be possible after all this time, but she didn't question it, just kept responding to the mouth against hers, and the heat starting between her legs and rising through her. She pressed Maggie's body against her, and they started slowly moving against each other in a dance as old and as sweet as air.

As the kisses became hungrier and the dance more urgent, Frank realized she wasn't dreaming anymore. She thought, I'm sorry, Mag. The radiant image she always had of Maggie laughing and turning to say something flashed in her mind, the sky blue behind her, the wind curling her hair around her face. Maggie laughing and Frank knowing it was okay to let go, seeing Maggie speak but not hearing the words the wind carried away.

She said good-bye and tasted the lips heavy on hers, pulling the slight body tighter against her own, rocking together for a different reason now, the breathing labored for a better reason, arms clenched in pleasure and not panic. They moved rhythmically together, like one body, and when Kennedy's breathing faltered, Frank's did too, until neither one of them was breathing anymore, and when Kennedy gasped and cried out, Frank breathed again and fell with her, and the dance slowed as gently as it had begun.

They lay entwined in silence, learning to breathe again, gently finding each other's lips. This time they searched and explored, palming hollows and ridges, tracing bumps and scars, seeking and finding, and after, they slept deeply and unafraid.

35

rank woke gently and saw gray light out the window. She didn't know if it was still early morning, or if the day was overcast. She pressed the length of herself against the back of Kennedy and wrapped an arm around her waist. Her reward was Kennedy pushing even more firmly into her and caressing her arm before they both fell asleep again.

The next time Frank woke up, Kennedy was gone and sunlight poured into the room. Frank groped at the clock and thought it must be wrong when she saw 12:11. She located her pajamas and stretched, sore in places she'd forgotten existed.

Following the faint clunk of metal against metal, she found Kennedy on the Soloflex.

"Hey."

"Hey, yourself, sleepyhead," she grunted.

Frank left her, wondering if there was coffee and what was in the house for breakfast. She was starving. She sniffed the coffee Kennedy had made and poured a cup. Kennedy appeared behind her, and Frank raised the pot.

"Want some?"

"Girl, I've been up for hours already. I done coffee'd myself out."

"Is it really noon?"

"Noon and then some," she teased. "How ya doin'?" Kennedy asked gingerly.

Frank looked at the woman she'd made love to last night, the woman who'd held her while she whispered her terrors and then lulled her to sleep. Unsure where to start answering, she set the pot down slowly and deliberately.

Placing her hands lightly on Kennedy's waist, she said simply, "I'm good. How are you?"

"*Very* good."

Frank kissed Kennedy's forehead and they held on to each other, neither knowing what to say, wondering if anything needed to be said. Frank felt only relief and gratitude, like the night had brought a deadly storm, yet here in the bright light of the next day she knew she had miraculously survived it.

She pushed away enough so that she could see Kennedy's face and said, quietly, "We should talk."

"Oh, now you want to talk. Uh-uh."

Kennedy's hand flew up and landed on Frank's mouth. She kissed Frank into silence while her coffee grew cold. In Kennedy's bed, after the sweat had dried and their hearts had slowed, Kennedy generously offered, "Now you can talk."

"Thanks."

"I bet I know what you're going to say."

"What?"

"That this was a mistake and you didn't mean it to happen and we can't see each other anymore."

To her own amazement, Frank laughed. She kissed Kennedy, pulling her closer.

"You know me too well, sport."

"That's what you were going to say, wasn't it?"

"Well, it was an accident, I didn't mean it to happen. But, as for a mistake," and here Frank breathed deeply, "it wasn't a mistake. I think it was the best thing that's happened to me in a very long time. Absolutely not a mistake."

Frank touched the silky head against her shoulder, remembering that old feeling of wanting to stop time, to have it stay as perfect and peaceful as it was this second. Instead, she continued. "As for seeing each other...I know I don't want to let you go. Not just yet. But I don't want to hurt you or use you, either. That's the—"

Kennedy twisted out of Frank's arms and leaned over her.

"Frank. One thing—you're not using me and you're not hurting me. What happened last night, and just now...," she bent closer to Frank's face, as if she were about to whisper a secret, "...Frank, I've had sex with a lot of people but I've never made love to anyone. I wanted to cry last night I hurt so bad for you, and then when you started kissing me in the middle of the night..."

Kennedy shook her head, her hair brushing against Frank.

"...that was something...*awesome*...and I don't want to let you go yet either, not today, not tomorrow, or the day after that. Let's just take what we have for as long as it lasts, and when it's over we'll both know it."

"Sounds very noble," Frank murmured, "like something out of *Casablanca*."

"Out of what?"

"Never mind."

Frank rolled Kennedy off and stared hard at her. "I just don't want to hurt you or lead you on. I've got places to go—to go back to—there are things that I've walked away from that I just can't ignore anymore. I've tried for years to bury things without a proper funeral. More and more they're coming back to haunt me. I can't do this anymore—I need to revisit places. And I need to do it alone."

"That's fine. I don't want to settle down with you happily ever after, I just want to be with you for a while. The *real* you."

Kennedy searched Frank's face, then demanded, "Let me."

Frank studied Kennedy's eagerness, her ardor, and goddamn if it didn't feel good to be a part of that. "There'll be a price for it."

"You're such an idiot, Frank. There's a price already. You don't think if I walk out that door right now you're not going to pay? I know I will."

"Might not be as bad."

Kennedy stopped arguing. "Hey," she said, "Merry Christmas."

Frank grinned, "Oh, yeah. I forgot."

They kissed deeply, and that seemed to settle the discussion.

"You hungry?"

"Does a Crip wear blue?"

"Come on, I'll make break—"

"Lunch."

"Lunch, while you open your Christmas present."

"Frank," Kennedy protested, "I didn't get you anything."

Realizing Kennedy's dismay was genuine, she cupped the woman's face in her hands and kissed her ever so softly.

"Oh yeah, you did."

36

The next day, Frank was at Parker Center. Most of the employees had taken the day off, making a long weekend that stretched into New Year's, and the parking lot was almost empty. She studied the building in front of her, absently stroking the bare spot on her ring finger. Sunshine warmed the car; a light wind ruffled her hair. She sat for a while, feeling the easy weather on her and thinking about what she had to do next. She'd have almost been content to sit there for the rest of the day, just watching the light change across the face of the building.

Frank climbed took the steps up to the homicide bureau, suddenly chilled inside the cool, dark building. She ran some checks on the computer. When she'd finished, she gathered her courage and walked the few blocks to the BS unit. She thought that Clay's secretary might be in but was surprised to find Clay himself sitting at her desk.

"Lieutenant," he greeted, extending his hand. "Good to see you."

"You too. Thought you'd be taking advantage of the holiday."

He waved a hand. "All the children are off doing their own thing this year, so it's just me and my wife puttering around the house by ourselves, getting in each other's way. I figured I'd try to do some catching up. What brings *you* here?"

"I actually wanted to make an appointment with your secretary."

"Ah-hah. Have you got another interesting case for me?"

Frank hesitated, then answered, "Yeah. Mine."

Richard Clay cocked an eyebrow. "Well, it just so happens I have some time. Come on in."

He sat against the linked fence, apart from the men shooting hoops. He liked being outside. It reminded him of the parks. He'd close his eyes and feel the sun burning around him. He'd pretend he was there, watching the girls. He'd close his eyes and dream he was flying. He'd close his eyes and plan.